CISTERCIAN FATHERS SERIES: NUMBER SEVENTY-NINE

JOHN OF FORDE

The Life of Wulfric of Haselbury, Anchorite

CISTERCIAN FATHERS SERIES: NUMBER SEVENTY-NINE

JOHN OF FORDE

THE LIFE OF WULFRIC OF HASELBURY, ANCHORITE

Introduction, Translation, and Notes

by

Pauline Matarasso

Cistercian Publications
www.cistercianpublications.org

LITURGICAL PRESS
Collegeville, Minnesota
www.litpress.org

A Cistercian Publications title published by Liturgical Press

Cistercian Publications
Editorial Offices
Abbey of Gethsemani
3642 Monks Road
Trappist, Kentucky 40051
www.cistercianpublications.org

2 3 4 5 6 7 8 9

Library of Congress Cataloging-in-Publication Data
John, Abbot of Ford.
[Vita Wulfrici. English]
The life of Wulfric of Haselbury, anchorite / John of Forde ; introduction, translation, and notes by Pauline Matarasso.
p. cm. — (Cistercian fathers series ; no. 79)
Includes bibliographical references (p.) and index.
ISBN 978-0-87907-579-8 — ISBN 978-0-87907-799-0 (e-book)
1. Wulfric, Saint, d. 1154. I. Matarasso, Pauline Maud. II. Title. III. Series.
BX4700.W85J6413 2011
271'.1202—dc22
[B]
2010036914

CONTENTS

ACKNOWLEDGMENTS

I owe much to the support of family, friends, and strangers in the preparation of this book. Particular thanks are due to Professors Christopher Holdsworth, Michael Clanchy, and Christopher N. L. Brooke for pointing me to sources of information which might have escaped me; to Hilary Costello, OCSO, who has been for years my first port of call in all that concerns Wulfric and to whom I owe most of the scriptural references, and to Denis Geoghegan, OCSO, both of Mount Saint Bernard Abbey, for help with textual difficulties; to Alexander Murray, University College, Oxford, whose comments have amended and enriched the introduction; to Dr. Keith Day, who generously placed his transcript of the Cambridge ms. at my disposition prior to the publication of his forthcoming edition; to Catherine Wybourne, OSB, for drawing my attention to the relevance of Saint Benedict's chapter on the cellarer; to Dr. Philip McCosker, who, with unflagging kindness, facilitated access to research materials; and last but far from least, to John Trappes-Lomax, who unravelled with expertise and patience the many linguistic knots I sent his way—to him goes my gratitude, and any mistakes remaining are mine alone.

INTRODUCTION

1. John of Forde
2. Wulfric of Haselbury
3. Dating the *Life*
4. John's Principal Sources
5. The Language of Transmission
6. The Social Context
7. Biography or Hagiography?
8. Wulfric as Wonder-worker
9. Holy Man or Saint?
10. The Writing of the *Life*
11. The Song of Songs: Thematic Unity

1. John of Forde

There are difficulties in presenting to a readership potentially drawn from a wide spectrum of interests and persuasions a text of which almost every assumption, including the declared intentions of the author, is now subject to question. John of Forde's stated wish was to write something which would glorify God and strengthen and build up (*aedificare*) the faithful. Over the centuries, through a semantic shift corresponding to an evolution in religious sensibility, the *Vita Wulfrici* became a work of edification, which is, and is not, somewhat different. The Enlightenment judged it irrational, the Victorians found it unedifying, the modern age categorized it as hagiography, a genre to be approached with caution and a sack of salt. Theologians prefer straight theology, and this has the appearance of a hybrid work, made up of fact worked on by memory and further embroidered with meaning; the theology is there but must be sought. Social historians, dismissing the theology, hunt around in the text like truffle hounds for evidence to lay alongside that of charters, acts, and chronicles. Yet the Cistercian order which John of Forde joined a generation after its foundation acknowledges him today as one of its Fathers and this translation is being published under its aegis. The monks of this age stand by their founders, and I have tried to do the same, standing beside John wherever I could, while maintaining the historical perspective.

It might be thought strange to begin an introduction to a Life with the author rather than the subject, the more so as the author held himself of no importance or interest compared to the subject, and the rest of the world shared that view until quite recently. It is, however, the *Life*, as a work of biography, hagiography, social history, or art, that is under study, rather than the author or the subject per se. Moreover, almost everything we know about Wulfric of Haselbury comes from John; were it not for the *Life*, the written record would hold only the name and a miracle story.[1] It is also

[1] Henry of Huntingdon, *Historia Anglorum, The history of the English people*, ed. and trans. Diana Greenway (Oxford: Clarendon Press, 1996) 696–97; see note to 1.9.

true that for centuries little was known about John save that he wrote the *Life*. His *Sermons on the Song of Songs* have since come to light, yet the earlier work, with its wider context, is perhaps for a post-modern readership the more revealing of the man.

The verifiable facts of John's life are too few to allow the drawing of a continuous outline; more space is covered by sketching in the unknown and shading energetically with conjecture. When John came to write a *Life*, the first thing he put down was where and of what class of people his hero was born. We do not know even that much about him. He was almost certainly a Devon man and stayed rooted in Wessex all his life. The demographic balance makes it likely he was English, though he may have been of mixed parentage; his level of learning suggests that he attended the Exeter cathedral school. So much for probabilities. To come at an approximate date for his birth, one must work backwards: John died in 1214, an old man surely, an abbot since the late 1180s, a monk of Forde perhaps as early as 1165. This would see him born around 1140.

Devon was no bad place in those days for a bright boy to be born: in the mid-twelfth century there was more learning in Exeter than Oxford.[2] Learning was fostered by, among others, a notable Norman named Bartholomew. Appointed archdeacon of Exeter in 1155, six years later he succeeded to the see. He would remain in place until his death in 1184, in the top flight of English bishops of his day, active as papal judge-delegate, alternately counselor and opponent of Henry II, effective in his diocese, gathering men of intellectual caliber around him, a friend of John of Salisbury and a supporter of Thomas Becket. Among his first appointments was that of a certain Baldwin, learned, brilliant and austere, to the archdeaconry of Totnes. This Baldwin, himself a *magister*, had come back to Exeter from Italy a few years earlier and John may well, at some stage, have been taught by him. What is certain is that these

[2] See Reginald Lane Poole, "Robert Pullen and Nicholas Breakspear," *Essays in Mediaeval History presented to Thomas Frederick Tout*, ed. A. G. Little and F. M. Powicke (Manchester, 1925), who places the future Cardinal Pullen in the Schools of Exeter rather than Oxford, describing Exeter as "a place of studious activity," 62–63.

two men, themselves close friends, became significant figures in John's life, to the point of standing as godfathers twenty years later to his first and best-known work, the *Vita Wulfrici*.

John's boyhood spanned the period of Stephen's reign, known, with good reason, as the Anarchy, and Wessex was particularly harried. Civil order was reestablished under Henry II, but king and Church came into conflict as soon as Henry appointed his chancellor, Becket, to the See of Canterbury. In November 1164 the archbishop fled to France and the next few years were at times uncomfortable for his supporters, among them the Cistercians, who gave him refuge at Pontigny. In 1169 the bishop of Exeter found it expedient to spend some months with the community at Forde abbey, forty miles east of Exeter,[3] and appears to have taken his archdeacon with him.[4] If John, as seems likely, had made his profession there a few years earlier, he will have had the opportunity to meet Bartholomew, or perhaps remind him of a fleeting acquaintance. The bishop returned to his diocesan duties, but the archdeacon became a monk and soon the community's third abbot, perhaps as early as 1171, certainly before 1175. The years of his abbacy saw Baldwin, now "of Forde," write most of his theological works. These were also the formative years of John's intellectual life and he was lucky to be brought into daily contact with one of the best minds in the order.

[3] Forde was founded from Waverley in 1136 on land given by Richard de Brionniis at Brightley in Devon. The site proving unsuitable, in 1141 the monks were on their way back to Waverley, when they met their late patron's sister and heir, who resettled them by a ford on the river Axe, then in Devon, now, since 1842, in Dorset. John will have entered under the second abbot, Robert of Penington.

[4] "The bishop of Exeter . . . retired into a religious house until the storm should have passed over. This must have been after 29 September 1169, on which date Bartholomew held a diocesan synod at Exeter. It was probably soon after this that archdeacon Baldwin decided to resign his archdeaconry and become a Cistercian. It must also have been about this time that Peter of Celle wrote to Bartholomew offering him an asylum in his monastery at Rheims, with all the conveniences of a good library and leisure for study." A. Morey, *Bartholomew of Exeter, Bishop and Canonist* (Cambridge: CUP, 1937) 29. There is no indication that Bartholomew went overseas. A brief period of respite close at hand seems much more likely, especially given the continuing close connection between Bartholomew, Baldwin, and Forde. On such a journey a box of books apiece will hardly have posed a problem.

In 1180 Baldwin was elected bishop of Worcester, to be succeeded at Forde by Robert II, an abbot about whom almost nothing more is known except that he died in 1190. For John the decade was one of activity and change. In the course of it he wrote, or at least finished writing, the *Vita Wulfrici*, where he figures on the title page as prior of Forde. In 1187 he was elected abbot of Forde's daughter house at Bindon, only to be recalled in 1191 to serve as abbot of the mother house, an office he held until his death in 1214. The years of John's rule at Forde have been covered in this series in the introduction to his *Sermons on the Song of Songs*[5] and are not relevant here. It is time to turn to the *Life of Wulfric* in search of its subject and of answers to the when and wherefore of its composition.

2. Wulfric of Haselbury

Blessed Wulfric, as John calls him on page one of the *Vita*, lived as an anchorite or resident holy man in a village some eight miles from Forde, where he died and was buried in 1154. A number of the monks had known him well and stories about him circulated freely among the community during John's early years. Good storytellers are first good listeners, and the more John listened, the greater his interest grew. At some point during Baldwin's abbacy, John found himself travelling to Cîteaux as companion to the abbot; they were joined on the road by Wulfric's greatest advocate, Henry, abbot of Waverley, who, blessed with a captive audience, recounted in rich detail the tale of his own conversion, foretold by the recluse, and left John fired with an enthusiasm for Wulfric which would come in time to rival Abbot Henry's.

The knowledge of Wulfric's "being and doing" contained in the *Life* is limited to what John thought important and what had burnt itself onto the minds of the generation before him—for example, the day and year of Wulfric's death, which in a holy man might have liturgical significance, but not that of his birth. Places

[5] John of Ford, *Sermons on the Song of Songs I*, intro. Hilary Costello, CF29 (Kalamazoo: Cistercian Publications, 1977) 3–10.

were more significant than dates and John knew that Wulfric had been born near Bristol in the village of Compton—now Compton Martin—of what he calls modest (*mediocris*) English stock. He was ordained unusually young, driven probably by an ambition to better himself socially: John speaks of his "shallow immaturity" (*iuvenili levitate*) and the passion for hunting and hawking that he exercised alongside his priestly ministry in his first parish. A conversion experience and a change of life led to his being recalled to Compton by the lord of that manor, William fitzWalter. There a desire for greater austerity and solitude grew on him and eventually the same lord offered him an anchorhold abutting on the church in another of his manors, and in that restricted space he spent the last twenty-nine years of his life. With the date of his enclosure established at 1124–25, we may assume him born around 1090; this would have made him contemporary with Saint Bernard and Christina of Markyate.

As anchorholds went, the one at Haselbury was of a reasonable size and consisted of an inner cell where the holy man lived and an outer room for the use of his servant and his visitors. This *domus*, as John terms it, is not described but can be roughly reconstructed from the stories. It stood to the north of the chancel—the colder side and the furthest removed from the normal comings and goings of parishioners—on a site now incorporated in the extended and largely rebuilt church. Close to the sanctuary on the one side, it jutted out into the graveyard on the other, its occupant entombed between life and death.

John says that the cell had been empty for some time prior to Wulfric's enclosure. The fact that it abutted on the chancel, not, as was more usual, the nave,[6] suggests that the former inhabitant was, like Wulfric, a priest, requiring access to the church and whose proximity to the sanctuary would not be seen as unfitting. The cell proper had a raised altar against the east wall with a step in front, and to the left of that a chest containing whatever the holy man

[6] E. A. Jones, "Hermits and Anchorites in Historical Context," *Approaching Medieval English Anchoritic and Mystical Texts*, ed. Dee Dyas, Valerie Edden, and Roger Ellis (Cambridge: D.S. Brewer, 2005) 10.

possessed of value. In the north wall was a window (2. 5). The cell will have been furnished with a table and a couple of stools: Wulfric needed to eat his meals, which he occasionally shared with a chosen friend; he also read and copied books, though possibly at a lectern. The bed, consisting of a wattle hurdle, took up little space and could be propped against the wall.

Elsewhere, probably in the north wall, was a door to an earth closet[7] and between the inner and outer cells a shuttered window which he opened when a visitor knocked. In the outer cell, referred to by John as *vestibulum cellule sue* and which may have extended the *domus* westwards along the nave,[8] his servant prepared his food, was probably expected to sleep,[9] and served any visitors who might be offered hospitality. Here also his scribe, when he employed one, worked (1. 28). Here, above all, his visitors sat and communed with him, made their confession, confided their troubles, and listened to his pithy words of wisdom. The outer cell must have been large enough to allow for a trestle table and benches, since the holy man insisted one day on feeding a noblewoman and all her retinue (2. 11), unless of course it was summer and these ate outside, but guests were not infrequent. This room had a door to the outside to which his servant held the key and which he locked behind him whenever he went out (1. 20; 2. 10). Beyond that, a stone's throw away, was the lord's outer court with its imposing gate (3. 10), and, closer in perhaps, other outbuildings: until it was stolen, Wulfric had a packhorse, and mounted visitors would want to tie theirs up.

From the inner cell a door led into the parish church of Haselbury, dedicated to Saint Michael and All Angels. Wulfric passed freely in and out, often spending the night in prayer before the altar of Saint Michael; he also celebrated mass there publicly at least on

[7] *cellula necessariorum*, 1. 21.

[8] The nave of an early Norman village church was not necessarily wider than the chancel.

[9] Medieval servants were expected to sleep "on the job," often literally: inventories list beds for upper servants in their "offices"; scullions bedded down where they could. Wulfric shouted one night repeatedly for his lad but got no answer because the lad was "fast asleep in a house some way away," 2. 2. Clearly, he was expected to be within earshot.

Saint Michael's feast day,[10] and John says that anyone asking how a penitent might gain access to that inner room heard about the door between cell and church (1. 18). As well as his close friends, the sick were admitted for the laying on of hands.

Three chapters of the *Life* are given over to Wulfric's austerities: his fasting, his vigils, the extreme discomfort of his bed, his hair shirt and cold baths, and these were only the physical exercises to which he subjected himself.[11] John admires these exploits, which were part of the recluse's stock-in-trade, but with moderation; formed by the Rule, he shares Saint Benedict's suspicion of excess of zeal and comments approvingly when the bishop of Bath—another Benedictine—insists on a bolster of twisted hay being added to the bedding (1. 4). "Intemperate physical training" might help on the ascent to godliness, but the all-availing grace of God was better, and he is relieved when Wulfric too comes to that conclusion (1. 6).

John gives less space to his intellectual pursuits: hermits and anchorites were first and foremost athletes of God. Wulfric must have been a promising boy to have been put forward, coming as he did from a modest background, to train for the priesthood, but those who paid for his schooling, whether parents or patron, were not overly ambitious for him. His formal education, such as it was, would have ended with his early ordination; John says of him that "his knowledge of divine letters was not great" (1. 7). On the other hand, not only did he employ a scribe to copy books for him, he set time aside for study—*sacris studiis*—and he also copied and bound books both for his own use and for that of the church (1. 27; 2. 10), so work and study each formed a part of his routine.

John devotes the second chapter of the *Life* to Wulfric's solitude. Solitude was what the recluse left the world to seek; finding it was another matter. It was possible to enclose the body, said John, while leaving the soul outside. Wulfric he describes as a true solitary, achieving inner solitude while all the world was knocking at his window. And all the world did, men and women, commoners

[10] 2. 8. For a detailed examination of where Wulfric celebrated, see notes to 1. 12 and 2. 20.

[11] 1. 3; 1. 4; 1. 5.

and kings. This semi-public life was John's material, the interface through which the effects of the anchorite's enclosure spread far beyond the confines of the cell. Wulfric's mystical life, which remained necessarily hidden, is explored in certain chapters[12] and often adverted to as John directs his readers' attention to the primacy of the inner life, bringing them back from the portrayal of events to their significance.

This said, it is doubtful if Wulfric's mystical—even spiritual—life can furnish much real matter for discussion. He was a man who wrote nothing and spoke little. He had one confidant in Br. William, the hospitaller of Forde, to whom John owes many of the stories, the majority originating with Wulfric himself, but no recognizable element of their intimate conversations, so tantalizingly alluded to, has passed into the *Life.* John describes the anchorite's mystical life in terms equally—perhaps more—applicable to Saint Bernard and largely inspired by the Song of Songs, the book of choice for both Bernard and himself. The chapter titled "On Keeping Vigil," purporting to describe Wulfric's night watches and a finely wrought piece in its own right, is a seamless weave of scriptural quotations which begins and ends with verses from the Canticle. Elsewhere John envisages a meeting between "blessed Bernard" and "blessed Wulfric" in terms of wisdom and simplicity exchanging the kiss of peace (2. 26). That Saint Bernard humbled himself so far as to seek Wulfric's intercession for a sin (2. 25) was for John a more eloquent encomium than any miracle.

John brings us closer to the historical Wulfric when describing his psalm-singing, his frequent genuflections, his cold baths, his hair shirt and hauberk: forms of private devotion general, with the exception of the expensive hauberk, among recluses.[13] Wulfric found his role models not so much around him as behind, not in the ranks of the new monastic orders (his enclosure predated the foundation even of Waverley), but, as these themselves did, in a tradition stretching back through the Rule of Saint Benedict to

[12] Particularly 1. 2; 1. 7; 1. 8; 1. 13; 1. 18; 1. 19; 1. 20; 2. 1; 2. 4; 2. 5; 2. 17; 2. 19.

[13] Henrietta Leyser, *Hermits and the New Monasticism* (London: Macmillan, 1984) 63–64; *Life,* 1. 5; 1. 9.

the Desert Fathers. His struggles with demons, rendered with nice particularity by John,[14] have long roots, as do the metaphors of warfare and armor summed up in the mail shirt which the anchorite tellingly dons at the outset of his new life, and which falls of itself from his shoulders a year before his death.[15]

Wulfric's distinguishing quality in John's eyes is his *simplicitas*. He adverts to it, sometimes at length, in seven of the chapters in Book 1, where the focus is on the anchorite's inner life. It is a quality rather than a virtue insofar as John sees it as innate, yet "by the sanctification of the Holy Spirit this gift of nature was made a gift of grace."[16] Simplicity was at the root of his candor (1. 7) and a childlike artlessness preserved him from all trace of self-conceit (1. 10; 1. 13; 1. 29). The over-subtle and cynical made the mistake of underestimating him and got their due deserts (1. 19; 3. 30). Simplicity is the essential determinant of all his relationships, be it with his visitors or with his God.

The work closes with a fine and full account of Wulfric's death and burial, the last involving an armed struggle for his body between the villagers of Haselbury and the neighboring monks of Montacute, to which is finally appended an angelic revelation and two miracle stories—a saint's necessary afterlife.

3. Dating the *Life*

The dating of the *Life* depends essentially on information included by John in the two Letters, or Prologues,[17] which precede the body of the text. These give us, along with much rhetoric, a brief history of the genesis of the project, but as is often the case with documents which are as clear as air to those they are directed to,

[14] 1. 21; 1. 22; 1. 23.

[15] 1. 3; 1. 5; 3. 41.

[16] "This purity of faith was refined, and one might say overlaid with gold, by a certain holy and sincere simplicity which had been his from his mother's womb" (1. 2).

[17] The manuscripts differ—three, including C, having *epistola*, while E gives *prologus*, the reading reproduced by Maurice Bell, ed., *Wulfric of Haselbury, by John, Abbot of Ford* (London: Somerset Record Society 47, 1933).

time has rendered these cloudy. A case can certainly be made for reading the *Life* as written evidence put forward in a cause of canonization, and this will be explored in due course. For now it would seem best to look at the work in the widest terms consonant with John's own presentation of it. The first Letter is addressed to Bartholomew of Exeter, John's diocesan, reminding him that it is at his intention and good pleasure that a *Life of Wulfric* has been written "for the glory of God and the profit of the faithful" and more specifically to repay the Church's debt to a holy man who by his life and works did good to many, and thus make amends for the silence into which his name and deeds have so quickly fallen: for "although he was with us only yesterday, today it is as though he had never been." Bartholomew, perhaps diplomatically, is presented as the moving force, and certainly, having approved the project, he intended to take a leading role; he even promised, according to John, to put the finishing touches to the work himself before finally referring it to two other prelates for their opinion. These are designated—but not named—as the bishops of Worcester and Bath. Towards the end of this letter Bartholomew's part is further emphasized: "the work is yours, undertaken at your wish, finished under pressure from you, embellished by your title and sealed with your authority." The whole tone suggests a piece freshly composed to accompany a work completed and ready to be presented.

The second Letter, if anything more formal, is addressed to Baldwin, archbishop of Canterbury. This is Baldwin of Forde, John's former abbot, elevated to the see of Worcester in 1180, enthroned at Canterbury in 1185. Bartholomew, says John, has been released from human concerns, so he presents his work to the lord Baldwin, already identified as one of the triumvirate of judges. Bartholomew died in December 1184, knowing that his friend Baldwin was appointed to Canterbury. The first Letter was therefore written after August 10, 1180, the date of Baldwin's consecration at Worcester, and almost certainly in the latter months of 1184, since Bartholomew, assuming he received the *Life*, did not have time to send it on. Bartholomew's death was a blow to John's hopes. Before proceeding further, he doubtless waited for Baldwin's enthronement at Canterbury on May 19, 1185, which leads to the assumption that Baldwin's fair and definitive copy was made during the course of 1185.

This gives us a *terminus ad quem.* The *terminus a quo*, and indeed the whole question of the prime mover in the writing of the *Life*, is rendered problematic by an ambivalent phrase in the second Letter. Who made the original approach to Bartholomew about the project? Not John in person, it would seem. Here is what he writes to Baldwin after Bartholomew's death: *Consultus ergo a domino abbate scilicet pie memorie Exonie episcopus voluntatem non solum probavit sed et accendit et instruxit.* The bishop of Exeter was consulted by the lord abbot, but which lord abbot? And which of the two, abbot or bishop, was dead? Dom Maurice Bell, who edited the *Vita* in 1933, placed the words *scilicet piae memoriae* between commas, which connects them syntactically with the preceding abbot; the manuscripts, however, have no such punctuation. The expression *pie memorie* (lit. "of pious memory") might seem more appropriately placed after the noun it qualifies rather than before, but John, who uses it several times in the *Life*, positions it before or after, apparently at whim.[18] The sentence can therefore be read in one of two ways: either "the late revered bishop of Exeter, consulted by the lord abbot, not only approved my wish, but gave encouragement and guidance," or "the bishop of Exeter, consulted by the late revered abbot, not only approved etc." One argument in favor of version 1 is that we know the bishop to be dead; indeed John himself confirms it more rhetorically two lines further on. Bell, however, took the words to refer to the abbot (version 2) and others have followed his lead.[19] But in 1180 the community at Forde had only lost two abbots to death. The second of these, Robert I of Penington, was abbot when John entered, dying around 1170, but he could not have nominated as judges

[18] *viro pie memorie Brictrico*, 3. 16; *de pie memorie viro Henrico*, 2. 20; *Roberti pie memorie Bathoniensis episcopi*, 1. 4 and 3. 41.

[19] Bell, *Wulfric*, xvii and 137; Christopher Holdsworth, "John of Forde 1191–1991," *A Gathering of Friends*, ed. Hilary Costello and Christopher Holdsworth, CS161 (Kalamazoo: Cistercian Publications, 1996) 27–28; Keith Day, "John of Forde's Life of Wulfric of Haselbury and the Identity of 'the lord abbot *pie memorie*,'" *Cîteaux*, 49 (1998): 221–32.

the bishops of Worcester and Bath, since Baldwin, incontrovertibly the bishop of Worcester in question, was not elected until 1180. As for Robert of Lewes, bishop of Bath and Wulfric's diocesan,[20] his death in 1166 was followed by an *interregum* extending until 1174. Before 1166 John would have been, if at Forde at all, in the noviciate. It is true that he speaks in the Letter of his *iuvenili levitate*—and in 1180 he must have been approaching forty—but this smacks of the inadequacy *topos*: the literary novice prostrating himself before his intellectual and hierarchical superior.[21] It is hard, too, to see how this work could have been a labor of twenty years. Baldwin wrote half a dozen treatises during his eight-year abbacy, and John's own literary output as abbot was not inconsiderable, given his varied responsibilities and frequent absences on business connected with the order or the king.

An alternative candidate has since been put forward, and Keith Day has made a strong case for Abbot Henry of Waverley.[22] If there must be a dead abbot, then Henry of Waverley alone fits the criteria: he died in 1182, he was a Wulfric-enthusiast, as abbot of Forde's mother house he was visitor of Forde, he was also in a good position to seek permission for the writing of a Life from General Chapter.[23] There is one objection only, but it is serious. A reference

[20] Put forward by Christopher Holdsworth, *Learning and Literature of English Cistercians 1167–1214, with special reference to John of Ford* (Cambridge University, PhD thesis, 1959) 100–101.

[21] Interestingly, he uses the same expression for Wulfric's reason for seeking ordination.

[22] Day, "John of Forde's Life," 220–32. Without a doubt Wulfric had no greater admirer than Henry of Waverley, with the possible exception of John himself. The story of his conversion—a lengthy journey from robber baron to Cistercian monk—whiled away the hours which Henry once spent with "the abbot of Forde" (undoubtedly Baldwin) and John travelling down the long road to Cîteaux. Attempts have been made to date this journey, but as abbots had to attend General Chapter annually and did so more often than not, the fact that Baldwin is known to have consulted Abbot Alexander at Cîteaux on a private matter before the latter's death in 1178 (Baldwin of Forde, *The Commendation of Faith*, trans. Jane Patricia Freeland, ed. David Bell, CF59 [Kalamazoo: Cistercian Publications, 2000] 40, and n. 12) is not really material; the three English monks could have made this particular journey at any time between Baldwin's election and his resignation—certainly between 1173 and 1179.

[23] On the question of such permission, see below, note 31.

to an unnamed abbot by a monk of a given community can only, in logic, be to the abbot of that community. If John does not name in his Letters the bishops of Worcester and Bath, it is because they are the current incumbents: thus it is understood. It is necessary to identify either the man or the place in which he exercises his office; here neither is named, therefore the conclusion must be that John is referring to his own abbot. A trawl through the *Life* shows that this is indeed John's practice. Twice Henry of Waverley is given his full name and title, prefaced by *venerabilis*; these chapters (1. 21; 2. 11), in which he figures only as witness, precede in the book the story of his conversion (2. 20), and may have been written earlier, during his lifetime, as the words *pie memorie* are absent. This third entry (2. 20) presents him as dead and gives, as well as name and title, his place in the abbatial line, while in the course of the story he is more familiarly *vir venerabilis Henricus, idem abbas, pater Henricus.* Wulfric's diocesan, Robert of Lewes, is also given name and title, separated by the words *pie memorie*, to distinguish him from the bishop of Bath in office when John was writing.[24] There is throughout a striving for that clear identification of witnesses demanded in Lives written with a view to the canonization of their subjects. The rendering of *consultus a domino abbate* as "consulted by *a* lord abbot"[25] is unconvincing. *Dominus* is a title, not a description, and therefore appropriately applied only to a specific individual. Also, one would expect *a quodam* (*venerabile*) *abbate* if there was to be no name; *quidam* qualifies all unnamed and unspecified persons in the *Vita*.

That John was partially inspired by Henry of Waverley and strongly encouraged by him to embark on the *Life* is not in question. The latter may even have used his influence and authority to lean on the abbot of Forde. These things are not dependent on reading him into the second Letter. The most likely person, on the evidence, to have approached the bishop of Exeter must be Baldwin's successor, Robert II. That he slipped through his decade

[24] A nameless abbot of Malmesbury must, on this argument, be the current one, and indeed we find John using the present tense: "he says," "he testifies" (3. 15).

[25] Day, "John of Forde's Life," 224.

as abbot leaving barely a trace in history in no way diminishes his potential for influence in his day: given the paucity of records, it is unexceptional. In fact, as a prominent member of the community at Forde, he would have been familiar to Bartholomew; he was also well acquainted with Jocelin de Bohun, bishop of Salisbury,[26] and sufficiently esteemed by Baldwin to have been invited to accompany him on crusade to the Holy Land in March 1190. Baldwin died there on November 19; Robert, presumably, around the same time.[27] He was therefore perfectly placed to approach Bartholomew between 1180 and 1182 on behalf of John, his prior, with the encouragement of the abbot visitor, and seek the bishop's authority for a Life of a local holy man well known by reputation to them all.

The Letter addressed to Baldwin contains another significant admission on the part of John: that the wish to write a Life of Wulfric originated with himself long before the first approach to Bartholomew. *Res ista diu me multumque moveret,* he writes, but he has "subdued these pricks of zeal till wish and piety should be confirmed by authority and rule." It is reasonable to see John, initially attracted to the figure of Wulfric by tales circulating at Forde and fired by Abbot Henry's story told on a journey to Cîteaux in the 1170s, being gradually led to make his own enquiries and, like a collector, adding to his store. It was during Baldwin's abbacy that John was at once stifling and feeding this covert desire, yet the abbot seems to have shown no interest nor taken any steps to encourage him. It is only when Baldwin leaves that John steps out of the shadows, first as prior and then, under Barthlomew's wing, as author. Varying views of Baldwin were taken by his contemporaries. Generally admired for his learning, recognized as upright and austere, he was not universally

[26] After his election in 1180, he first surfaces as a witness to an undated charter of Jocelin de Bohun, bishop of Salisbury, in which a co-witness, Baldwin, chancellor of Salisbury, does not appear in diocesan charters before 1182, *English Episcopal Acta,* ed. B. R. Kemp (London: British Academy, 1999) 18, no. 130, and 44. See also below, 16..

[27] Christopher Holdsworth, "Baldwin of Forde," *Dictionary of National Biography,* updated 2004 and online. David Knowles, C. N. L. Brooke, Vera C. M. London, *The Heads of Religious Houses,* 2nd ed. (Cambridge: CUP, 2001) 132: "1190; ? at Acre".

loved.[28] He lacked the wide human sympathies of John and it may well be that the two men were not close. Baldwin was very focused in those years on his own writing and busy too with his duties as papal judge-delegate. John certainly gives no hint that the abbot associated himself with the project at an early stage.

If one looks with attention at the years 1180–85, there are other straws blowing in the wind that are worth snatching at. Henry of Waverley, an old man now, two years from his own death, was at Forde in 1180[29]—perhaps for the installation of Robert II. He could have taken the opportunity to move John's matter forward. The other adjudicator appointed by Bartholomew, namely, the bishop of Bath, gets no mention in the second Letter; he has apparently disappeared from the scene. It is likely that at this stage John considered the authority of the primate to be quite sufficient; however, there is another possible explanation for the bishop's absence. Reginald fitzJocelin had been appointed to the see in 1174, no doubt with the weight of his father, Jocelin de Bohun, bishop of Salisbury, behind him. The latter, a man of no little power and influence, came into conflict with Becket and was excommunicated by the archbishop in exile. This would have left him at odds with both Bartholomew and Baldwin, but time heals many divisions and in 1184, feeling perhaps that death was not far distant, this very political cleric resigned his see and entered Forde, where he died on November 18. Reginald fitz Jocelin, whose name appears frequently on his father's charters at Salisbury, once together with that of Robert II of Forde, surely visited the monastery during his father's last months, opening up the possibility of conversations with John about the *Life*. What is apparent is that all these men knew one another well and were regular visitors at each other's houses during the years when John was collating and composing.

[28] Described as gloomy and nervous by Gerald of Wales, by Stubbs as harsh and wanting in tact (see Morey, 106); latterly by David N. Bell as "learned, ascetic, godly and gullible," *Baldwin of Ford, Spiritual Tractates I*, trans. and intro. David N. Bell, CF38 (Kalamazoo: Cistercian Publications, 1986) 9.

[29] Knowles et al., *The Heads*, 147.

In a culture with a strong oral tradition, memory plays a predominant role, and the training given in the medieval Schools honed its effectiveness as a tool. Nonetheless, the store of tales, gleaned by John over several years, need not have all been lodged in his head. He was also a man of the written word, and it is reasonable to assume that he made notes, probably on wax tablets, from which to write up the considered and polished version.[30] If he began the serious collation of this material and then composed the *Life* between the resignation of Baldwin in 1180 and the death of Bartholomew in December 1184, when, if at all, did he get that permission from the General Chapter incumbent on all Cistercian monks proposing to write a book? The situation with regard to the restrictions on writing was unclear at the time and is likely to remain so.[31] What is certain is that John began with the authority of his abbot and of a respected bishop and in 1185 was confidently requesting a blessing on his work from his former abbot and present primate. Permission could have been sought on his behalf by Henry of Waverley or by Baldwin at their last attendance at the Chapter, before any formal approach to Bartholomew. Abbot Robert could equally have sorted the matter out during the 1180s. And John, by the last quarter of the century, had plenty of examples to invoke. One of the English saints he places beside Wulfric in the second Letter is Godric of Finchale, whose Life, written by Reginald of Durham at the behest of Ælred of Rievaulx, he surely knew. Ælred's own *Life* had been written by Walter Daniel. John's deeply venerated Bernard had written the *Life of Malachy*, and of course several Cistercians had contributed to that of Bernard. John must have felt fairly relaxed on the subject. Even Guerric of Igny, whose example is cited as evidence that the rule was taken seriously, waited until his deathbed to order the destruction of his sermons (and was not

[30] Eadmer mentions transcribing the first draft of his *Life of Anselm* from wax onto parchment, *The Life of Saint Anselm by Eadmer*, ed. and trans. R. W. Southern (London: Nelson, 1962) 150.

[31] The position in general and with regard to John has been well set out by Christopher Holdsworth in *A Gathering of Friends*, 18–19, including note 3, with particular emphasis on Baldwin of Forde's reference to the apparent relaxing of the prohibition, now in Freeland and Bell, *The Commendation of Faith*, 41.

obeyed). Other monks of Forde were writing in those years; either the General Chapter was liberal with permissions, or a blind eye was sometimes turned by individual abbots. In any event, there were enough well-disposed abbots around at the requisite time to seek permission on John's behalf.

The *Life* provides internally some precious scraps of information in regard to dating. When William fitzWalter sought Wulfric's advice on installing Augustinian canons at Haselbury, Wulfric told him that the foundation would not prosper, and so it turned out. According to Bell the canons were still there in 1174 and perhaps as late as 1180, but John describes them as having been driven out (*expulsos*),[32] though the fine buildings stood, awaiting some other use. The last chapter of the *Life* is an account of a healing miracle which took place, according to John, "fifteen years ago and at least fifteen years after the holy man's death." This makes the earliest date for the miracle 1169 and has John writing his final chapter in 1184. Interestingly, he gets his information on both the canons and the miracle from people still alive when he was writing, and not, in the case of the miracle, from the witnesses known to have been present in 1170. There is one story, on the other hand, where John's informant, the recluse Odolina of Crewkerne, is apparently dead when he commits her tale to parchment (3. 2). There is nothing in the *Life* to suggest he was collating evidence before 1180, but it is more than likely that he was noting down stories as he heard them.

4. John's Principal Sources

The *Life of Wulfric of Haselbury*, written in the language of the Church, the Schools, the law, and generally of written record, yet spoken as a conscious choice only by an elite, was itself a product of the oral tradition. Only one of over a hundred stories came to John in written form; the rest he heard from a variety of people and in at least two languages. It is necessary to present the most important of these witnesses (to use John's term, though many are repeating what they have heard from others), because their background and

[32] Bell, *Wulfric*, xviii and 3. 22.

personalities are an integral part of the matter of the book and various themes can only be discussed with reference to them.

William fitzWalter, who appears in the first chapter, was one of "those local lords, ranging from great lords to country knights" on whom "the hermits of twelfth century England relied primarily for support."[33] Hermits were rural almost by definition, but anchorites too were initially more commonly located in villages than cities,[34] established and maintained there by lay patrons. William fitzWalter is described by John as *vir potentissimus*,[35] but his sway may never have been more than local as he remains unknown to the chroniclers who supply the narrative and much of the gossip of history; he was, however, undoubtedly well-connected,[36] and rather grander relations seem to have imposed themselves frequently on his hospitality. His powers of patronage within his different manors were considerable, extending to the appointment of priests, the installation of an anchorite without recourse to the bishop, and the establishment of a priory of Canons Regular.[37]

Indications of his political allegiance emerge both directly and indirectly in the course of the *Life*. The West country baronage, starting at the summit with Robert, earl of Gloucester, the half-brother

[33] Brian Golding, "The Hermit and the Hunter," *The Cloister and the World. Essays in Medieval History in Honour of Barbara Harvey*, eds. John Blair and Brian Golding (Oxford: Clarendon Press, 1996) 104.

[34] Ann Warren, *Anchorites and their Patrons in Medieval England* (Berkeley: University of California, 1985) 37. The empty cell at Haselbury had certainly already had at least one earlier occupant.

[35] 3. 22. He adds "in those days," suggesting that the family's power and influence had waned since, which seems to be true.

[36] For the fitzWalter holdings and genealogy, and the history and topography of Haselbury, see Bell, *Wulfric*, xlii–xlv and 139–42.

[37] A lord could commend a clerk for ordination. He could also commend a priest to a church. The bishop did not always have a free hand. See Susan Wood, *The Proprietary Church in the Medieval West* (Oxford: OUP, 2008) 519–30. The church at Haselbury predated Wulfric and probably William fitzWalter, but may well have been built by his predecessor, as it was common practice between the Conquest and the mid-twelfth century for manorial lords to build new churches and appoint their own priests. See John Blair, *Minsters and Parish Churches, 950–1200* (Oxford: OU Committee for Archaeology, 1988) 11.

of the empress Matilda, were strong supporters of the latter's claim to the throne, and all those whose names surface in the text[38] were of this group. Lady fitzWalter is publicly snubbed by the queen because her husband is known to be not a king's man (3. 23), but within a short time Wulfric speaks to William fitzWalter of King Stephen as "our friend" (3. 33), indicating a shift in allegiance.

William fitzWalter was a good lord to Wulfric. It is possible that he paid for Wulfric's education; an intelligent boy could render useful clerking services. If he recommended him for ordination, the pious man he was may well have been disappointed with the way the youth turned out, but as soon as he got word of Wulfric's change of life, he brought him back to Compton, taking him into his own household as a kind of personal chaplain,[39] and then meeting the priest's growing wish for solitude with the offer of the anchorhold at Haselbury. From that time on he was a constant visitor, helper, and benefactor. The first "sign" worked by Wulfric—the cutting of the hauberk (1. 9)—is presented in the *Life* as a joint operation by holy man and knight. It is the lord who provides the mail shirt, ceding his own armor "as to a mightier knight than he" (1. 5), and he who obediently shortens it, cutting the steel with a pair of shears while Wulfric prays behind his closed shutter. When the saint breaks off to go and see how the task is progressing, the shears refuse to respond any longer to the knight's pressure. Wulfric has to return to prayer, telling his friend to finish the job he had started "in the same power of faith you had before." The knight is presented as an essential coworker, perfectly illustrating the contention that medieval recluse and patron "were joined together and shared virtue."[40]

William fitzWalter does not reappear in person until the last quarter of the book, but he is rarely far away: his wife, daughter, steward, and visitors all pass through the pages, while his son Walter is one of John's principal and most trusted sources. William was not

[38] Redvers, Mandeville, Mohun, Lincoln, Nonant. Some were connected by marriage with the fitzWalters. See notes via index.

[39] "When a priest ate in his lord's hall, like Wulfric of Haselbury . . . , this must have marked his dignity as well as his dependence." Susan Wood, *The Proprietary Church*, 529.

[40] Warren, 281.

himself a direct source—his death before 1166 rules that out—but information about the early years at Haselbury, before the coming of the monks to Forde in 1133, came to John through the fitzWalter family, and principally through this Walter who, under Wulfric's guidance, entered the religious life.

A resident holy man and one attached to one's person, family, and interests is of course a precious commodity. He can be counted on in illness, for powerful prayer, and for a constant supply of advice and wisdom.[41] The members of the fitzWalter family benefit in all these ways, and the shifting balance finds at the end the lord of the manor addressing his erstwhile protégé as *domine mi*—"sir," or "master," even "my lord" (3. 20). The daughter, Beatrice, was known to John, who writes that she is still alive to witness to her mother's healing (2. 9), creating the presumption that by 1184 Lady fitzWalter, the subject of the story in question, was dead. She was present, however, at a miracle worked at Wulfric's grave "at least fifteen years after the holy man's death," thus around 1170, but there is no indication that John ever spoke to her himself.

Brihtric, the parish priest of Haselbury in Wulfric's day, who was almost certainly dead by the time John came to Forde,[42] occupied, like the lord of the manor, a pivotal position in the anchorite's life. There might have been a feud between two priests with interests in the same church and sharing the same sacred space; in fact they appear to have come to a perfect accommodation. Brihtric spent his days in the church, Wulfric his nights before the altar. The priest had no responsibility for the recluse's upkeep, and where there was an overlap of duties, it was clearly by arrangement.[43] John describes

[41] Or there is the more hardheaded view: "as wills and testaments throughout the period attest, supporting an anchorite was a sure-fire way of guaranteeing a secure place in the hereafter, whilst also establishing one's place and status in the here-and-now." *Anchoritic Traditions of Medieval Europe*, ed. Liz Herbert McAvoy (Woodbridge: The Boydell Press, 2010) 14.

[42] He was present at Henry of Waverley's first visit, probably in the early 1140s (2. 20). It is clear, however, that his son Osbern was in sole charge during the later years of Wulfric's life.

[43] For the delineation of their responsiblities and roles, see Henry Mayr-Harting, "Functions of a Twelfth Century Recluse," *History* 60 (1975): 346–47.

them as mirror images of one another: "So close was the spiritual twinning between these blessed men, this pair of pigeons, that they were always seeking in a friendly way to outdo each other in reciprocal subservience and humility. Brihtric assisted the other as he might a superior, humbly giving him 'sir,' while blessed Wulfric, for ever belittling himself in comparison, would say that Brihtric was the true anchorite of that place, whereas he, constantly exposed to conversation, could more properly be called the parish priest (1. 16)". So mutual is their charity that a passing fit of pique on Brihtric's part evokes astonishment in Brother William: "Whatever could have provoked so mild a man to anger, above all with you" (1. 14)?" The priest played on occasion a significant role in Wulfric's healing ministry; in one long and dramatic story of possession his help is indispensable.[44] John held him in high esteem, referring to him as *venerabilis*, and *dominus Brictricus*, and employing on one occasion the phrase *pie memorie* otherwise reserved for bishops and abbots.

Brihtric, quite possibly the son of a priest himself, and the father of another who would step into his shoes, was one of a breed facing extinction, but showing in England at least a certain stubborn resistance. John, in whose pages father and son are major players and where even Godida, Brihtric's wife, peeps round the door, passes no comment on the situation. Another priest named Segar, whom Wulfric once sent for to hear his confession, had four sons who all entered the monastic life, three as choir monks at Forde, the fourth as a lay-brother (1. 20). Brihtric's seems to have been the last generation where marriage was still tolerated, albeit discouraged.[45]

[44] 1. 17; see also 3. 15.

[45] John's silent witness conforms to that of the historians: see C. N. L. Brooke, "Gregorian reform in action: Clerical marriage in England, 1050–1200," *Cambridge Historical Journal* 12 (1956): "Between the Conquest and the Anarchy clerical marriage was sufficiently common to be safe and even respectable," 19; also Marjorie Chibnall, *The World of Orderic Vitalis, Norman Monks and Norman Knights* (Woodbridge: Boydell, 1984) 8–9. On hereditary tenure, see Susan Wood, *The Proprietary Church*, 552. Osbern was perhaps fortunate to have as diocesan the bishop of Bath; Bartholomew of Exeter refused to induct a clerk who had been presented to the parish of Salesby by the patron of the living, on the ground that he was the son of a priest. The clerk appealed to Rome and Pope Alexander overturned the decision. Morey, *Bartholomew*, 90.

The once widely held view of an ignorant parish clergy with little Latin and less learning is not borne out by its representatives in the *Life*. It is true that Brihtric felt acutely his lack of French (1. 29), but there is no suggestion that either he or his son Osbern was unworthy of his calling. Rather the reverse. They seem to have been punctilious in their ministry, they received and carefully conserved books copied by Wulfric for the use of the church, and their relationship with him was one of close friendship and, in some senses, equality.[46] Indeed John speaks of all the rural clergy mentioned in the *Life* with marked respect.[47]

Walter of Glastonbury. The weight that John laid on the shoulders of this son of William fitzWalter led him to devote a whole chapter to his witness in chief. "Since I," he writes, "have often called on Walter of Glastonbury to bear witness to the truth, it is time that I myself bore summary testimony to my witness so that you may judge and measure his fitness for the part" (3. 38). What follows is the story of a boyhood, of a time spent in semi-captivity in a London house as surety for his father's debt, of Wulfric's prayerful and prophetic support, of the youth's return home, his growing friendship with the holy man and gradual conversion to the religious life. By the time John met him, he had been a monk at Glastonbury for many years and was only too happy to tell stories stretching back half a century or more. He spoke for a lineage. He had known two parish priests of Haselbury. He had friends and acquaintances in different walks of life and, most important of all for John, he was a man of many years and unblemished moral character. Age, with the expectation of eternity on the horizon, conveys in John's eyes a strong assurance of truthfulness in a witness.[48]

[46] For a positive view of the level of learning among rural clergy in England and Normandy, see Michael Clanchy, *From Memory to Written Record: England 1066–1307* (Oxford: Basil Blackwell, 1993) 241–43; and Chibnall, *The World of Orderic Vitalis*, 99.

[47] Ralph of Wareham, 2. 29; Richard of Corscombe, 3. 3.

[48] Respect for age was general and Reginald of Durham makes similar claims on behalf of witnesses to events in the life of Godric: *Libellus de vita et miraculis s. Godrici, Heremitae de Finchale*, ed. J. Stevenson (London: Surtees Society, 1847).

Walter of Glastonbury is cited as the source in ten of the stories, and other anecdotes in which his father figures—for example, the prophecies concerning Henry I and Stephen—can safely be attributed to him. He was not always an eyewitness: he passes on what he himself has heard from the man of God. Given that he was an old man in 1180–84, we may imagine him born around 1110–15 and thus only a boy when Wulfric was first enclosed. He would have heard much on his return from exile in London and learned more in the hours spent with Wulfric discussing his vocation. John clearly knew him well and had talked with him of Wulfric on many occasions.

Brother William and the monks of Forde. The entire community was an ever-flowing source of information on Wulfric's life and doings, and almost a quarter of the material is said to have been vouched for by one or more monks of Forde, but apart from Brother William only two are named: a certain Joseph of whom no more is heard, and Richard the scribe. This Richard, one of the sons of Segar the priest, worked as scribe both for Wulfric and for the abbey and seems at that time to have been a married layman. We find him later at Forde, where his son, also a monk, suffered from insomnia. Richard himself became a cantor at the abbey. He is a patently reliable witness to three stories.[49] Brother William, the abbey's lay-brother hospitaller, was by far the most valuable of John's sources within the abbey. An old man in the 1180s, he had, says John, "spurned in the very flower of his youth the pomp of the king's court." A man of noble birth, then, which would make him French by culture and language, and yet he was a lay-brother at Forde, rather than the choir monk we might expect. This is how John describes him: "Once Wulfric had clasped Brother William closely to his heart and was loved as greatly in return, the man of God held absolutely nothing back from him, clearly deeming him worthy to be let into his chambers and made privy to his hidden

The assurance was strongly backed by Scripture, since "wisdom is found in the old, and discretion comes with great age" (Job 12:12).

[49] 1. 28; 1. 29; 3. 19.

treasures. He would discuss with him such matters as the mysteries of God's kingdom and the blessed hope of the saints, how graciously God's mercy had gone before him and how favorably followed after—spiritual things to the spiritual, matching the subject to the man (1. 14)." This is not the stereotype of the illiterate noble, too bovine to acquire in the noviciate the elements he never learned in boyhood. It is much more likely that Brother William spurned not only the pomp of the king's court but the higher status of the choir monk, choosing to live out his monastic life among the humble whose mother tongue was English.[50] He must have been a godsend to Forde: as a bilingual aide to the guest-master, he could be all things to all men who knocked at the abbey gate.

John gives him as source for a number of stories, but the word source is itself ambiguous. Brother William was an eyewitness on at least two occasions when Wulfric winkled links off the chain mail of his lorica and handed them to his visitors. Indeed the monk himself provoked the second occasion because he took such delight in the feat. We know he was present when Wulfric made his last dispositions and also at his deathbed. More often he is simply the intermediary, passing on to John what he has heard from Wulfric, repeating stories for which he has no actual evidence. As a witness at the bar he would not last a minute, yet our debt to him is great, for he alone was in a position to pass on the "hidden treasures" of the anchorite's mystical life, and the fact that John "wrote up" these conversations in a mode hallowed by tradition, which robs them of the immediacy we now look for, in no way invalidates the underlying experience. Brother William served too almost certainly as a bridge leading from Brihtric and Osbern to John.

Henry of Waverley (ca. 1110–82). Exceptionally, John has him introduce himself in the *Life*, on the grounds that his story will prove more lively if told in the first person, and so indeed it does. The

[50] For the context and motivation of young nobles entering the cloister, see Alexander Murray, *Reason and Society in the Middle Ages* (Oxford: Clarendon Press, 1978) 350–82; and C. Harper-Bill, "Piety of the Anglo-Norman Knightly Class," *Proceedings of the Battle Conference*, ed. R. Allen Brown, II (1979) (Woodbridge: Boydell, 1980) 63–77.

few points of reference the story offers enable us to tease out some approximate dates. Henry of Waverley visited Wulfric five times over a space of some ten or twelve years. Civil disorder on the first occasion is portrayed as general, with armed cohorts roaming the countryside, a fair description of conditions prevailing in the west of England from 1139 through the early 1140s. "I myself," admits Henry, "was one of that band who hated peace. I strove to ply my soldier's trade as circumstance allowed and succeeded better than many of my kind" (2. 20). Born into the ruling class, he was not, it seems, a Wessex man, since it was business that took him to those parts, where an unquiet conscience diverted him to Haselbury. Wulfric's words and personality worked powerfully on him and he called in a second time on his return from farther west. But this was no Pauline conversion: things had to get worse before they could get better and the robber baron finally sought refuge from himself in a Cistercian house. His stay there was brief: he had not long made his profession when he was called to be abbot of Tintern. This both confirms his class and caliber and acts as a pointer to where he entered the order. He was not, we may be sure, elected to Tintern at that stage of his life for his holiness. To be a candidate for this particular abbacy, he must have been not only adequately grounded in Latin as a boy (when attending Wulfric's mass he picks out at once a "special" collect) but known as a man who "got things done": his successful career as a freebooter probably helped. Tintern had been founded from L'Aumône in 1131, three years after Waverley, and struggled from the start. Some fifteen years on the new abbot found a monastery that had "gone to rack and ruin" (2. 21). Undeterred, Henry invented a pretext for going to Haselbury to show himself off to Wulfric as the fulfillment of his prophecies, only to have his pride deflated by the sage's medicinal word: "Right, my son, keep your rule and you will be able to save your soul" (2. 20).

Putting the monastery back on its feet got Henry into serious debt, and he set off a fourth time to seek advice from his prophet and mentor. Wulfric, after questioning him closely, told him that whatever he had disbursed for the glory of God would come back to him, and so indeed it did, through a chance meeting on his way home (2. 22). It was during the next three or four years, certainly before the deaths of the Cistercian pope Eugenius III and Saint Bernard of Clairvaux, both in 1153, that abbot Henry of Tintern went to Cîteaux and then to Rome, singing the praises of Wulfric as he went, and stopping at Clairvaux on the way back (2. 23). Saint Bernard, who had probably never heard of the sage of Haselbury, was so impressed that he confided to Henry a sin of presumption, dating back to the schism in the 1130s, and asked him to seek Wulfric's intercession on his behalf (2. 25). So Henry made his last visit to Haselbury perhaps two or three years before Wulfric's death. Around 1160 he was elected abbot of Waverley[51] and as such became visitor of Forde; he would therefore have been a familiar figure to John, even if they had not spent so many happy hours discussing Wulfric on the road to Cîteaux. John repays his debt by consecrating a chapter to his praises (2. 21). The effort was unnecessary: if Henry of Waverley were in a novel, he would be hailed as a splendid creation. As it is he springs off the page as a gift; it is hard not to think of him as a friend.

It has been assumed that Henry entered the order at Tintern; this seems unlikely as there is no evidence that he was native to the west of England, let alone Wales. The phrase *in abbatis ministerium ad Tinterniam vocatus sum* implies he was going there from somewhere else. I believe he entered at Waverley and was called to Tintern by a community in disarray who could not elect from among themselves. Flourishing Waverley, ten years later, would have had no reason to look to Tintern for their third abbot unless they had been recalling one of their own. It is the pattern of Ælred returning from Revesby to Rievaulx and, closer to home, John going to the daughter house of Bindon, only to be called back to Forde. The move confirms John's statement that Henry reestablished Tintern on a sound footing, leaving behind a memory crowned with praise (2. 21).

Unlike Walter of Glastonbury and Brother William, much of whose testimony is secondhand in the sense that it comes from Wulfric and

[51] Knowles et al., *The Heads*, 1, 147.

not from their own observation, Henry of Waverley speaks entirely from experience. The relationship of the two last must have extended over some ten years, and before the end Wulfric trusted Henry enough to confess or confide to him private temptations (1. 21), proving that as the younger man matured, so too did the friendship.

Osbern is one of the most interesting figures in the *Life* and surely the most mysterious. We see him as a boy: serving as acolyte but keener on playing, anxious not to annoy his father, running messages, pert on occasion. Then as a grown man: parish priest, devout, celibate (he slept in the church), the chosen friend and intimate of the holy man, entrusted with all the arrangements for his death and burial; a man who could assume authority and keep his head in a volatile and dangerous situation; a man who handed over his most precious relics of the saint to a stranger and yet was so protective of him that he moved the body twice and died without revealing its whereabouts; a man who was moved to tears by a woman's account of her dream and Wulfric's continuing life-giving presence, yet put obstacles in the way of a public cult.

Osbern was *in puerilibus annis* ca. 1140 when a kinsman of the fitzWalters named Durand de Mohun died and Wulfric sent the lad to carry a message to his father (3. 21): sixteen perhaps, since he served for some time as parish priest during Wulfric's lifetime. He was still in that position "at least fifteen years" after Wulfric's death (3. 47), which takes us to 1169–70. The next few years saw crucial changes at Haselbury: between October 1174 and the end of 1175 William, son of William fitzWalter, gave Saint Michael's church as a prebend to the church of Saint Andrew at Wells.[52] Bell assumes that Osbern was dead before this alienation took place.[53] Shortly after 1174 the Canons Regular installed by William fitzWalter also left Haselbury. John says they were expelled, but refrains from further comment.[54] There is no way of knowing whether these

[52] Bell, *Wulfric*, 139–40.

[53] Bell, *Wulfric*, xxxiii.

[54] 3. 22. They had been gone several years when he wrote, for he remarks that the buildings were "still standing."

events were connected, but major upheavals were plainly under way and Osbern disappears from the scene, or at any rate from the *Life*, again without comment from John.

Osbern ought by rights to have been John's best and most quoted witness, yet the latter never states unambiguously that they spoke together, nor, on the other hand, does he deny it. He prefaces a section near the beginning of Book 2 with the words, "lest someone should accuse me of giving more space to my own opinions than to facts, let me set down two stories in which the one who saw and heard testifies in person" (2. 5). The witness in question is Osbern, and the stories relate, one to his boyhood, the other to his years as parish priest. The use of the present tense implies, I think, that Osbern was alive at the time when John wrote down these particular stories. If it could be proved that Osbern was dead by 1174–75, when the church of Haselbury passed to Wells, it might give an indication of when John began inscribing his stories on wax tablets.[55] But the lack of evidence either way leaves open the possibility that Osbern entered a religious house or remained in Haselbury under a new dispensation: it was not unknown for a lord to give a church to a monastery while securing the present priest's life tenure.[56] Moreover, other reasons can be found for John's silence.

Osbern figures in thirteen of the stories, once as a simple witness but usually playing a significant part. He is an actor in three of the "light" stories at the beginning of Book 2, in one as a child still, in two as parish priest. Dialogue features notably in all of them. We then jump to Book 3, where Osbern appears to be introduced for the first time: "What follows was related by Osbern, the priest of Haselbury, who succeded the late revered Brihtric in the charge of that church. While he was still a lad, he said, he used to go into the holy man's cell to serve when he celebrated mass [3. 16]." The implication is surely that the story was related to John, though he writes merely *retulit*, omitting *mihi*, and this time uses the past tense.

[55] That he relied a lot on memory is clear from the throwaway comment, "if my memory serves me right," when naming Corfe castle as the site of a court held by Queen Matilda (3. 23).

[56] Susan Wood, *The Proprietary Church*, 564.

There follows the boyhood tale mentioned earlier (3. 21), which ends *Hec idem Osbernus*, again an indication that John had it direct. Yet another story ends *Hec venerabilis mulier Muriel dicta et Osbernus et Segarus presbiteri* (3. 25), and though Muriel was still alive when John wrote the bulk of the *Life*, Segar died before Wulfric (3. 19), and John certainly heard his version through his son Richard. Of the last seven chapters of the *Life*, three are given over to the saint's last months, his death and burial, one to the translation of his body, and three to what may be termed his afterlife. One of these ends with the words: "Walter of Glastonbury declares that he had this from Osbern himself [3. 45]." Exceptionally, none of the others carries any attribution, although Osbern plays an important role in all but one of them and was the sole confidant of Wulfric's last wishes. Since much turns on these, it is important to look at the narrative in some detail.

About a year before his death Wulfric became aware that his end was approaching and sent for "his closest and most trusted friends, namely Brother William the hospitaller, Henry of Corscombe, Osbern the priest and others high in his regard, and when he had told them these happenings one by one, he consulted them as to what should be done. The matter should be referred to the bishop was their advice, so Osbern the priest was sent, and brought back these instructions: he was to take off the hauberk and not wear it any longer, but keep it by him wrapped in a cloth." Wulfric in turn sent his instructions to the bishop: "When you hear that I have departed this life, see that you lose no time in coming to officiate at the commending of my soul and the committal of my body [3. 41]." Then, five days before his death, he sent for Osbern to come and speak with him "one to one," and told him that his body would be a great nuisance to him. Men would come to take it, backing their claims with armed force, but the holy man trusted that right would prevail: "I was called to this place by God, here have I labored, and here he wills that I should take my rest [3. 42]."

When the time came, Osbern found himself in a dilemma, wanting to obey the holy man's wishes and yet respect due form. He sent at once to the bishop, but predictably the news reached Montacute first. The body snatchers arrived in force and Osbern was hard put to win both the tussle and the truce that followed. He showed himself at once quick-thinking, hardheaded, and conciliatory. The bishop came not long after and Wulfric was laid to rest in the cell according to his wishes (3. 43).

Osbern now became the interpreter of these wishes. Fearful, John says, lest a thief should steal his treasure, he removed it secretly from its resting place and reburied it on the north side of the altar (3. 44). And there it laid under the pavement gathering dust for, I think, a number of years. Presumably, anyone coming to seek the saint's intercession went or was shown to the cell. Then the dreams and revelations started, and in one a woman was directed to "go to the north end of the altar and collect some dust from the man of God's grave" (3. 47). A healing took place and the gossip began. It was at this point, I believe ca. 1170, that Osbern "looked around for a still safer cache, and finally hid his secret in the western end of the church in a spot known only to God and himself" (3. 44). The short chapter titled "How the Holy Body Was Twice Translated" is a rare example of pure reporting by John. The only words that are not strictly factual are in the brief concluding comment: "using, without a doubt, the lowliness of this inferior position as a sign."

Osbern's behavior is highly unusual. One could say that it showed an obsessive fear of going against the saint's wishes and the will of God were it not for the freedom with which he interpreted them. He might well have been reported to the bishop and called to account; indeed, perhaps he was. In a sense John can be seen as reporting him: in both Prologues his chief complaint is that Wulfric lies in an unmarked grave. This would have come to his notice early on, when he first became interested in the saint, and it is something he must have discussed with Brother William, who had clearly not been taken into Osbern's confidence, giving rise to hurt and withdrawal of trust. It seems very likely that this caused a rift between Osbern and Forde. It would have become obvious to everyone as John pursued his enquiries that his hope was for some kind of public cult—recognition and reverence at the least—fostered by a marked grave, preferably a tomb. If not a quarrel, even a prevailing coolness would go far towards explaining the paucity of open reference to Osbern, the unattributed stories that nonetheless ring so true. Osbern is present in the *Life*, a three-dimensional figure whose boyhood is a delight and whose adult behavior intrigues as it puzzles, as behavior often does. He stands beside Wulfric and Henry of Waverley, fully fleshed out, while Walter of Glastonbury, despite John's enthusiastic advocacy, remains insubstantial.

That John passes no comment on Osbern's attitudes and actions is characteristic of the man. Again and again he pointedly avoids passing judgment, thereby of course implying that he could: he is past master at drawing veils. Osbern was someone he clearly respected. How well he knew him and how often they spoke hangs on Osbern's continued presence in Haselbury, which cannot be affirmed or refuted beyond 1170.

5. The Language of Transmission

John's *Life of Wulfric*, now presented in translation, is itself the end product of a series of translations or renderings. Behind it stretches a fluid process from a vernacular, usually but not always that of the lowest class, to a written, literary language used only by the learned. Parts have passed on the way through a second vernacular socially superior to the first. And this, ironically, to reawaken popular devotion to a holy man, whose very holiness had rendered him classless but whose birth set him squarely among the *mediocres*, the ordinary. So that all these anecdotes, so carefully harvested and preserved in studied Latin prose, had in some way, perhaps in homilies, to percolate down again, through the same layers of vernacular, in order that common people might forgather at an unmarked grave.

In southwest Britain in the twelfth century, English, Cornish, Welsh, Anglo-Norman, and Latin might be heard, all in the mouths of the native-born, and Wessex English was itself a dialect barely comprehensible to northerners. It has been said that the number of these languages rubbing shoulders, as it were, actually facilitated the dissemination and transmission of collective memories from group to group.[57] On rare occasions we are made aware of the different lan-

[57] Ian Short, "Language and Literature," *Companion to the Anglo-Norman World*, ed. C. Harper-Bill & E. Van Houts (Woodbridge: Boydell & Brewer, 2003) 193;

guages underlying John's Latin as they compete for attention; more often they lie dormant. The simplified view is that, in the twelfth century, Latin was the language of the Church, Norman French that of the ruling classes which included the higher clergy, while pre-Chaucerian English was spoken by everyone else. The reality was of course more complex and more fluid. There was also a whole generation between Wulfric and John: Wulfric's Wessex would have been more divided, less bilingual, than John's, and bilingualism tended, in any case, to be the preserve of the educated, "the English-speaking majority . . . from vicar to villein, [remaining] stoutly monoglot."[58] Bearing all this in mind, we can but feel our way through the text.

The first thing John finds it necessary to tell us about Wulfric was that he was "of modest English stock," one of those apparently destined to remain "stoutly monoglot": a parish priest like Brihtric, a solitary like Godric of Finchale, with little Latin and less French unless the Holy Spirit intervened. Yet there is evidence to show that Wulfric was competent in two languages beside his own. A clever boy and socially ambitious, he was probably educated above his station. He had enough personal graces to commend himself to the ruling class before any signs of sanctity became evident: John says that he was uncommonly good-looking (1. 3), which always helps, and a quick ear for languages is certainly no hindrance. When William fitzWalter recalled him to Compton, he ate in the hall with that lord's retainers, dining off beef, mutton, pork and venison—as opposed to steer's, sheep's and swine's flesh—and hearing, in the 1120s, the language of the Conqueror reverberating round him. Whatever he lacked, he learned or polished in that ambience. Henry Mayr-Harting sees this bilingualism as enabling Wulfric to be "the principal link between his village and the outside authorities, both secular and ecclesiastical."[59]

A parish priest's Latin did not always extend beyond the strictly necessary (the same was sometimes true much higher up the scale:

---

and "On Bilingualism in Anglo-Norman England," *Romance Philology* 33 (1979–80): 478.

[58] Short, "Language and Literature," 205.

[59] H. Mayr-Harting, "Functions," 344.

jokes abounded among the clever about the poor latinity of clerical colleagues[60]), but Wulfric, if not learned in John's view, was certainly *litteratus*: he instructed his scribe one day to omit a passage "because he had it elsewhere" (1. 28). Besides, one cannot recite the whole Psalter daily, as he did, without the language sinking in; even the self-taught Godric surprised three monks of Durham by following their—Latin—conversation.[61] Wulfric's fluency in spoken Latin is a matter of conjecture. What is known is that, in private prayer, "with a special tenderness and intimacy of love, he called the Lord God his lord in his native tongue" (1. 2). John presumably didn't, since he finds it necessary to comment, and yet there was precedent, namely, the highly literate Ælred on his deathbed repeating: "Festinate [make haste], *for Crist luve*," because, wrote Walter Daniel, it sounded in English sweeter to the ear.[62]

If Wulfric was trilingual to some degree, this was by no means true of his visitors. With one or two exceptions, they had at best two languages, and most of these would have favored one vernacular over the other. Who determined the language two bilingual people chose to speak together? Presumably the one who held the social or psychological advantage. A bishop and an archdeacon could choose to exclude a parish priest from their conversation. An abbot could insist on Latin rather than a vernacular, on French rather than English, Anglo-Norman being admitted to the cloister as a second best, while English was firmly shown the door.[63] The day he entered his cell, Wulfric stepped outside the boundaries of class and category and took possession, as a recognized holy man, of an unassailable high ground. Could he then choose the language he conversed in? Perhaps more easily. But his courtesy is constantly emphasized. I think he would have met his interlocutors on their own ground. Certainly he would not have greeted Stephen or his queen in English: they would have heard their home truths in their native tongue.

[60] Short, "Language and Literature," 199; Morey, *Bartholomew*, 19.

[61] Reginald of Durham, *Libellus*, 79, 179–80.

[62] Walter Daniel, *Vita Ælredi* 54; *The Life of Ailred of Rievaulx*, ed. F. M. Powicke (London: Nelson, 1950) 60.

[63] Short, "Language and Literature," 198 and 205.

In John's case doubt barely arises: if, as seems probable, he was of English extraction, he would have been proficient in three languages. The very fact that he gleaned much of his material from lay-brothers, recluses and rural clergy tends to confirm his origins: he had English from childhood. Among clerics of his standing and learning, the use of Latin as an acquired spoken language was then widespread.[64] Bartholomew's *familia* at Exeter, as doubtless that of his predecessor Robert Warelwast, seems to have been largely Norman, by bloodline if not importation, and these were the men who taught in the cathedral Schools what they had themselves acquired there. They were John's contemporaries and classmates. Had his Anglo-Norman not been fluent, he could not have acted later as confessor to King John, any more than Wulfric, without French, could have heard Stephen's confession and challenged him with a hidden sin. John's fluency across the board was of great benefit to him in gathering material for the *Life*, enabling him to speak with witnesses of varying backgrounds. Interestingly, he shared this advantage with Henry of Huntingdon, William of Malmesbury, and Orderic Vitalis, all of mixed parentage.

It has been doubted whether many of Henry I's bishops could speak the language of the lowest classes,[65] but was it "could" or "would"? The *Life* trains a brief but searching beam on Robert of Lewes, bishop of Bath, and the social gulf dug and marked out by language. Wulfric heals a dumb man who reveals himself suddenly fluent not only in English but in French.[66] This is too much for Brihtric; years of humiliation come spilling out: "You have never given *me* the use of French," he explodes, "and when I come before the bishop and the archdeacon I have to stand as mum as any mute" (1. 14). That particular bishop of Bath was born in Lewes of Flemish parents and entered the Cluniac priory there. He was a protégé of Henry of Blois, brother to King Stephen, also

[64] Short, "Language and Literature," 198.

[65] Morey, *Bartholomew*, 80.

[66] 1. 14. Ian Short offers an excellent overview of three incidents, including this one, where an ability to speak French is seen as illustrating supernatural powers. "On Bilingualism," 474–79.

incomers. A man born in England could hardly have been less English than Robert of Lewes. Did he in fact need an interpreter to communicate effectively with his parish clergy, or was Brihtric just galled by being the rustic left standing dumbly by while his superiors chose to chat in their superior language? Bishop Robert sent instructions to Wulfric on more than one occasion. John does not say how often he visited him during their overlap of eighteen years, but he certainly came before he died (3. 41) and again to bury him, when he spoke some salutary and calming words to the villagers (3. 43). Again, we do not know whether he addressed them in their own vernacular or brought an interpreter. Gerald of Wales describes Baldwin, a few years later, preaching the crusade in Latin as he travelled through the principality, but he could not have been expected to know Welsh, and as he was targeting the nobility, some at least would have got the gist of his message.[67]

There is a story (2. 16) that perfectly reflects the way competing languages muddied, or enriched, the oral tradition in twelfth-century England. It has its beginning at the court of Henry I, where a Norman baron named Drogo de Munci, who stood high in the king's favor, broke into a conversation extolling the holy man of Haselbury to say: "The king would do well to send to the cell of this charlatan and confiscate his money, for it cannot be that a man so many flock to has not got plenty stowed away." As he spoke, he was felled with a fit and ended up with his mouth twisted round to his ear. The courtiers, crying, in John's Latin, *Ve! domine*, and *Ve! inclite*, went to the queen, who in turn approached the king. So when affairs took Henry to Wessex, he and all his company, including the sick man, rode into Haselbury, where the king spent a longish time in converse with the saint before pleading the cause of his friend. Wulfric agreed, without much enthusiasm, to do what he could, whereupon one of the bystanders took his hand and placed it on the knight's face. Healing followed; the king and his retainers went away strengthened by Wulfric's blessing and, apparently, highly delighted with his appearance. Here is a story, originating

[67] See "The Question of the Literacy of the Laity" in Clanchy, *From Memory*, 231–52.

in a French-speaking milieu. The events which had taken place at court were related in French, and probably by the king, to an English anchorite, who added his own part before recounting the whole story successively to Brother William and a woman called Muriel de Beauchamp, both, as far as we know, of Norman extraction. They in turn told it to John. That the story took form in French seems clear. Was there an intermediate English version? It is conceivable that John heard it in French from one source and in English from the other. The final rendering is quite sophisticated, and it is tempting to see this as John's part: the man of letters giving literary form to an inchoate tale. But this is to devalue the art of storytelling, so integral a part of the oral tradition. In an age when the *trouvère* and the *jongleur* were received in court and castle, when all information came by word of mouth and every village had its teller of tales, it is probable that even the anchorite's servants, a not infrequent source of Wulfric-lore, knew how to present a good story for maximum effect.

6. The Social Context

Anchorites and hermits find themselves frequently grouped under the umbrella word "recluse," which defines them in terms of what they have in common: withdrawal from society, either between walls or to unfrequented places, and the abdication of all creature comforts for a life of prayer, with which went usually some form of service, practical or spiritual. Post-Conquest England saw a proliferation of recluses of both kinds, and attention has been focused latterly, and rewardingly, on the social dimension of this phenomenon, its value for the communities which fostered it. Recluses have been seen as representing a familiar and yet still effective power in a world where discontinuities, political, religious and social, had suddenly opened up.[68] What has tended to recede from view is the recluses' understanding of themselves, their reasons for withdrawing from society,

[68] H. Mayr-Harting, "Functions," 337–52; Christopher Holdsworth, "Hermits and the Powers of the Frontier," *Saints and Saints' Lives. Essays in Honour of D. H. Farmer* (Reading: University of Reading Library, 1990) 70–72.

and whether or not the social consequences now seen as following had meaning for them. Since their own style leaned toward the terse and the oracular, we depend largely on the writers of their *Lives* and of works, now commonly termed guidance texts, to interpret them to us.

Recluses, by renouncing everything that society valued—power, honor, wealth, and bodily ease—placed themselves beyond the reach of its judgment. At the same time, by incarnating other values which the world made a pretence of honoring, they stood as judges over against it. They are rightly seen as hinge figures, able to look Janus-like in different directions, moving easily between social groupings with mutually conflicting interests. Recluses saw themselves, however, as hinge figures on the vertical plane between human and divine, time and eternity, and were similarly perceived by others. "The symbolic elements of the immurement—the cell as holy vessel, the door as a closed threshold, the windows which no longer signify as a conduit of sunlight and air and vision—all combine to transform the occupant into an other-worldly figure who is both absent and present simultaneously. The anchorite lives, in effect, 'between two deaths,' offering the faithful of the community an example of both how to live—and how to die."[69] Thus poised between two realities, they served alternately as channels and lightning-rods for the power of God: either beneficent in graces of healing or terrible in warning and chastisement.[70]

Wulfric enters another reality at the moment of his enclosure. Here is John, trying to express what the new recluse experienced and falling back on Scripture:

> And so the man of God, having entered into the rock to hide from the face of the Lord and the glory of his majesty,[71] began to build for himself an inner solitude, straining to penetrate to the hiddenness of that face[72] as to a still farther solitude, and,

[69] Liz Herbert McAvoy, Introduction, *Anchoritic Traditions*, 19.

[70] On the nature and power of liminality in the life of the recluse, see Holdsworth, "Hermits and the Powers," 64–69.

[71] Isa 2:10; Exod 33:22.

[72] Ps 30:21.

> panting with open mouth, to draw the Holy Spirit[73] into the very depths of his being. Otherwise, to condemn the body to such close confinement leaving the soul outside, as is the way of some, is a deplorable folly. . . . That was not blessed Wulfric's way, indeed not;[74] on the contrary he began to feel he had found a vast space within these narrow bounds, allowing him to realize, the more freely for the privacy he had, all that he had conceived: to covet the things of heaven, strive after the spiritual and meditate day and night on the law of God.[75] Nor was the true manna from heaven lacking to this true solitary, for God in his kindness and bounty was ever preparing and raining it down on his needy servant.[76] (1. 2)

The practical effects of his enclosure, which will in turn impinge on the community, are felt at once. Wulfric, a prey to insecurities before his conversion, hesitant to the last about the way to take, sloughs off all vestige of self-doubt at the door of the cell. His patron and former lord, William fitzWalter, becomes his squire and arms him for battle, handing over his hauberk to the greater knight. Wulfric has entered the eternal lists; he gives orders now to those still fighting earthly battles. This is a theme which runs right through the *Life*. It was the recluse's privilege to speak truth to the great and Wulfric makes full use of it. When King Stephen calls to see him in the hope of a confirming word, the interview ends, after an incomplete confession, with the king presenting his cheek to the prophet to be struck and spat upon (3. 33). This could be seen as raising one's hand against the Lord's anointed, and it is doubtful whether prophetic liberty has been taken further.[77] Nor, except in

[73] Ps 118:131.

[74] Ps 1:4.

[75] Ps 1:2.

[76] Ps 67:11.

[77] Kings seem to have expected brusqueness of recluses. Robert of Knaresborough was terse to the point of discourtesy with John, who promptly gave him a carucate of land and the site of his hermitage. See Brian Golding, "The Hermit and the Hunter," 100. It is interesting that Anselm, as abbot of Bec, was permitted to rebuke King William II for his way of life, but as soon as the king appointed him to Canterbury and he acquired feudal obligations, he lost his power. See Southern, *The Life*, 64, 67, 68–69.

its physical aspect, was the incident unique: his verbal attack on the queen, after the latter's rudeness to Lady fitzWalter, is almost ferocious (3. 23). John insists repeatedly on Wulfric's courtesy, but it is more in evidence with the poor than the great.

The anchorite's role and influence in the community was a by-product of his spiritual life rather than something envisaged as its purpose. The initial obligations went rather in the other direction: Wulfric sought an encounter with God and counted on the community to provide the necessary conditions. As a priest he required access to a church and as a human being he needed shelter and some assurance that his necessities—food, light, clothing—would be provided. What was promised him we do not know. William fitzWalter must have given some undertaking and would have been faithful to it. Montacute at some point assumed responsibility for a daily pittance. The parish priest probably kept him in candles (2. 4). Little by little, a mutuality established itself between the neighborhood and its new holy man. Gifts came from further afield as his reputation spread, and we know that Wulfric's fame travelled fast and far, because within six or seven years of his enclosure word of his wonder-working had reached the court of Henry I and provoked a sneering suggestion that he was stashing away large sums of money. Drogo de Munci put his finger here on one of the paradoxes of the anchoritic life. The *Life* itself contains conflicting evidence. John's first concern is to establish the credentials of his hero-saint: Wulfric's withdrawal from the world is total; he is a true ascetic and his practices are extreme, going beyond what John thinks either necessary or prudent; he lives as one of Christ's poor, possessing nothing, dependent on others for his food, owing even his cape and his coverlet to the kindness of strangers.

The gifts we later learn of him receiving—loaves of bread, the occasional fish, cloth to cover a book, a new cape—are consistent with a life of poverty and deprivation, as also with an economy where property, from land to its most basic products, was still the main medium of exchange. Three stories, however, suggest a different, hidden reality: if Drogo de Munci is convinced that recluses are in the business of self-enrichment, no less cynical is a clerk called Robert of Cirencester, who, after failing to show the anchorite up as an ignorant rustic, tries to prove him money-grubbing. The assumption in both stories is the same: "Go to the man of God," the clerk tells two beggar women, "it's his business to give alms, the more so as he is loaded with money [3. 30]." Both clerk and courtier employ the word *pecunia*, hard cash, and the third story appears to prove them right. Wulfric's servants seem to have been mostly young, boys being cheaper to employ, but one clearly outstayed his childhood and turned into something of an entrepreneur at his master's expense. When Wulfric was finally prevailed on to get rid of him, he was found to have "numbers of sheep and cattle,"[78] as well as *gold and silver* and precious vestments (3. 25), having, one imagines, intercepted gifts in money and in kind and traded with them. It may be that this servant's profits grew with every telling of the story, but it still proves the obvious, confirmed by John (2. 17), namely, that visitors to a holy man, as to a shrine, did not come empty-handed, and that gifts were sometimes in hard currency.[79]

The question is not what Wulfric was given, but what he did with it. His coffer must have grown quite full at times but, again according to John, it was all redistributed.[80] Certainly we see Wulfric leaving Robert of Cirencester's coins untouched on his windowsill, where the beggars later pouched them, presumably at his invitation. Much in the way of books and vestments went to the parish church and more to Forde: indeed in John's eyes the dishonest servant compounded his sin by betraying "the poor men of Christ." If stealing from Wulfric was never a good idea, robbing churches and monasteries was profitable and relatively easy. Freebooters like

[78] Ælred, in the Rule written for his sister, evokes the spectre of the recluse who busies herself seeking pasture and a shepherd for her flock, and demands reports of numbers, yields and prices (Inst Ind 3). *Rule of Life for a Recluse*, in Ælred of Rievaulx, *Treatises and Pastoral Prayer*, trans. Mary Paul Macpherson CF2 (Kalamazoo: Cistercian Publications, 1971) 47.

[79] Clerics also received and gave relics. Wulfric amassed a considerable collection, enabling him to present a relic of Saint Augustine to a prior of the Canons Regular. See below, 217.

[80] H. Mayr-Harting, "Functions," 343, offers the interesting suggestion that Wulfric may have acted as "a repository, a kind of primitive banker." Unsurprisingly, the *Life* furnishes no evidence either way.

Henry, later of Waverley, did it. So did mercenaries: those brought by Henry II on a premature attempt at conquest "plundered the poor"— otherwise known as living off the land—"profaned the sacred," taking gold and silver vessels for resale, and stole Wulfric's horse, no doubt to carry the booty, but of course they were shipwrecked on their way home (3. 18).

What John makes clear is that Wulfric's way of life remained outwardly unchanged through these vicissitudes. If his asceticism became a little less extreme, this signaled not a falling away but a growth in spiritual wisdom (1. 6). In the neighborhood he was still seen as leading a life poorer and harder than all but the indigent, and this fact was essential to the veneration in which he was held; indeed it was part of his function. For the ascetic practices freely undertaken for the love of God were also, indirectly, the price the anchorite paid for authority in the village, where his austerities proved his holiness and the life of the parish "was enhanced by the residence of one among them who had chosen this difficult way."[81] It was not only the wisdom and healing hands of the resident holy man which benefited the community; the villagers were enriched by his prayers, his presence, the having of him among them. Had Wulfric not carried out his part of the bargain, his occupancy of the cell at Haselbury would not have lasted for twenty-nine years nor would his reputation have outlasted him for thirty more.[82]

Since the community in which Wulfric was embedded consisted mainly of the rural poor, it is worth looking at how he served this constituency. There are a number of stories which turn on food, particularly that staple of the poor, the loaf of bread. The loaves in question are always entrusted by the giver to a servant who falls into temptation on the way and hides one or more for his own future use: the loaf turns to stone (2. 13), or on one occasion, when being cut for distribution to some hungry children, drips blood (2. 14). Pasties, similarly diverted, are found crawling with mag-

[81] Ann Warren, *Anchorites and their Patrons*, 282.

[82] On the spiritual services rendered by anchorites to the community, see the different chapters in *Anchoritic Traditions*, particularly P. L'Hermite-Leclercq, "Anchoritism in Medieval France."

gots (3. 26). On the basis of these stories Wulfric has been seen as vindictive. In fact, he has no part in the corruption of the food. He is not shown as in any way responsible or even aware of it. It is presented as the consequence of sin, and when the horrified and repentant thief returns to the cell to confess his fault, he is not only forgiven, but the loaf or other food, made whole again, is broken and shared, or given to him for the hungry children, or for a poor man with whom the stolen pasties had been left, and the sinner leaves instructed, absolved, and with the holy man's blessing. These are homilies in action. So too is a lesson in neighborliness given to two men who refused a helping hand to free a loaded wagon from the mud (3. 12). Wulfric teaches the community by word and example; he is listened to because God's power is seen as being at work around him.

The anchorite was also the *vir Dei*, the man of God, perceived as channeling, deflecting, or focusing God's power, whose lightning bolts could be hurled by a recluse's curse. One did not cross such men with impunity; there was an Old Testament aura about them. Living alone, they needed authority of a sort, both for their own safety and to teach and drive home their lessons. But the power, once loosed, was beyond the anchorite's recall: he forgot himself at his peril, and at that of others. Wulfric's moment of impatience with a mouse resulted in its instant death (1. 30). The cellarer of Montacute was in another class; he had long been a thorn in Wulfric's side, grumbling at the boys who went to collect their master's dole, giving short rations or none at all. One day he called in unexpectedly and Wulfric had the table "liberally spread as hospitality required." Conversation was stilted. Not long after, the cellarer again sent the boy home "carrying nothing but blasphemies and curses." Wulfric exploded: "May God this day take that man's food away who has taken mine from me!" Sure enough, that very day the cellarer was swept away in a flood and drowned. This time Wulfric was horrified and, "battering the ears of God and his friends alike with his lamentations over him and pricked by repentance, he shouldered the blood guilt of the other's death." Yet when the same friends asked him why he had done it, his only response was: "That was what I had to do and what I needs must say" (2. 15). Wulfric, on John's showing, was moderate compared to some recluses.[83] A clerk who was notably rude and offensive and later developed acute bellyache went back to the man of God and "humbly confessed his folly, receiving healing and absolution in return," though he was also warned to reverence God in his servants from then on (3. 30). Similarly, a serving woman who was convinced she was suffering from a dire complaint and was told by Wulfric that she was pregnant railed at him furiously and called him a liar. She too returned and met with pardon and comfort (3. 13). But visitors soon learned not to underestimate the saint: cryptic remarks, mysteriously linked to alarming events, could leave them in a state of fear and awe (3. 34).

An accurate assessment of the social spread of Wulfric's visitors is impossible. The *Life* is not representative: there is always a tendency for stories to circulate within social groupings, and the well-off and well-born had easier access to the monks and clerics who formed the majority of John's informants. Even the stories of dishonest servants come from their noble mistresses (2. 13; 3. 26): establishing the identity of witnesses was an important factor in a Life intended to advance a cause for canonization, and the higher up the social scale, the easier these were to trace. Where the corroboration of a servant is required, a distinctive nickname or surname is given in place of the baptismal name (2. 6; 3. 47). Some village tales entered the monastery in the heads of prospective lay-brothers who brought their memories and stories with them (3. 4; 3. 5). It is clear, however, from the sweep of the *Life* that Wulfric was a man of many friendships and extensive acquaintance across a wide range of social classes. His friendships with women are shown, perhaps surprisingly, as being both numerous and close. Indeed John makes a point of saying that he "enjoyed the pure friendship of many [women]" (2. 26). He knew, or knew of and was known to, at least three named female anchorites, one of whom he

[83] Robert of Knaresborough offers a not untypical example, cursing the rector who attempted to extract tithes from his lands; the priest died in agony and Robert is not said to have shown regret (Golding, "The Hermit," 103 and 109). Godric of Finchale, on the other hand, was exceptionally patient and gentle.

had counselled and directed and esteemed above all other women he knew.[84] He greets as his "sister" a certain Richelda, described as the mother in religion of Christina of Wareham, but not herself enclosed (3. 7). Lady fitzWalter was his "very dear friend, being herself a sweet and holy woman" (3. 23). An unnamed woman came annually all the way from Kent to talk with *suum illum dilectum salvatorem*. Returning after his death as the result of a dream, "she held him lifelong and did not let him go,[85] reviving . . . the faith of their former charity and the original covenant between them, keeping both to the end" (3. 46). Women sought and found healing at his hands, others came for counseling, all, except the queen who was given a tongue-lashing, met with kindness and attention to their needs.

In all of this Wulfric has John's sympathy and approval. John himself is clearly fond of the anchoress of Wareham, whom he refers to as "my Christina" (2. 29), and finds something to praise in almost every woman he introduces—this in an age when clerical misogyny was common. The one, not altogether surprising, exception is the maidservant who finds herself pregnant by the child committed to her charge and later attempts infanticide. It is not these offences, however, which inspire John to tax her with "a woman's shamelessness" but her abuse of Wulfric for telling her she was pregnant and bidding her to "take good care of [her] womb." The whole matter appears to get sorted out by consultative process, completed by confession and absolution. Whether seigneurial justice is involved in any way is not made plain. It is a remarkable story (3. 13).

Wulfric counted friends and acquaintances among both higher and lower clergy, and if his religious sympathies went first and foremost to the white monks at Forde, he was happy to see Walter, after much shilly-shallying, set off for Glastonbury, and he referred to the black monks of Winchester as brothers, *fratres nostri* (3. 20).

[84] Odolina, 3. 2; Christina, 2. 27, 2. 29, and 3. 7; Matilda and Gertrude, 2. 27–29; possibly Aldida, 3. 26. The presence in the *Life* of five women recluses against one man (John of Winterbourne) confirms what is known of the predominance of women anchorites over men, at least in towns.

[85] Song 3:4.

His relations with Cluniac Montacute are an untold tale: all that survives are two dramatic incidents linked by the long thread of a daily dole, and a lot of pussyfooting on the part of John, who seems to have given Montacute a wide berth.

The *Life* reveals a preponderance among his visitors of lay over clerical and vowed religious of roughly 2:1; of men over women of 3:1, but if only the lay are counted that ratio drops to 2:1 in favor of the men. This contrasts with John's informants, where monastic and clerical predominate over lay. These figures certainly need adjusting for the reasons mentioned above, the lay/religious ratio upward and that of men to women downward. The proportion of poor to rich among his visitors was also surely higher than would appear from the *Life.*

7. Biography or Hagiography?

John wrote a Life, but with qualifications: it was undertaken for the glory of God and the benefit of the faithful, and this in his eyes was its justification. By definition it falls into the category of Saints' Lives, or hagiography, where to the plotting of a career in terms of verifiable facts is added the element of edification, like a chemical which alters the nature of the original substance. The *Vita Wulfrici* embodies the three aims of the hagiographer: to teach, to delight, to praise the subject. So much for the category, but reality is always more fluid. Biography and hagiography remain part of a continuum and a medieval Life may be situated at one of many points on its sliding scale: Eadmer's *Life of Saint Anselm* has been likened to "an anecdotal account of a man who was also a saint,"[86] tending therefore to the biographical. A particular Life may well be located by different scholars at varying points on the scale: the case of Christina of Markyate springs to mind.[87] The most extreme position, which sees all hagiographical writings as a collection of *topoi,*

[86] Benedicta Ward, *Miracles and the Medieval Mind. Theory, Record and Event, 1000–1215* (London: Scolar Press, 1982) 171.

[87] See the wide range of views in *Christina of Markyate, a Twelfth Century Holy Woman*, ed. Simon Fanous and Henrietta Leyser (London: Routledge, 2005).

offers a fit-all formula which, when measured against individual texts, may be found over simple and of limited use in deepening understanding.[88]

Clearly, those writing the lives of men and women deemed holy saw these lives in terms familiar to themselves and interpreted them in the light of established traditions. Indubitably too the biographical data that fitted the template were given emphasis and arranged and added to as seemed "likely," "proper," "in keeping." But the reduction of everything to the "genre," so that one ends up with a purely literary phenomenon, fails to take into account the complexity both of that genre and of the underlying historical reality. Lives at a given time in a particular social context tend to follow norms, whether of conformity or of rebellion; this is true of all periods. Again, the nonconforming will themselves be aware of following a different path and claim the authority of predecessors. And the fact that they are following a waymarked route will be seen by them and others as their justification for rebelling, particularly in a period like the Middle Ages, when deviation from the social norms was ill viewed and the only acceptable form of nonconformity was the way of self-denial, of ascesis, embraced for the love of Christ. It had been consecrated and rendered safe by the desert fathers. Anyone in the twelfth century who had sat on a pillar, immured him- or herself in a cell, lived as a wild man in the woods, or indeed chosen celibacy for any other reason would have been treated as a criminal or a lunatic—or possibly a heretic, which would have been worse.

John was bound to present for admiration Wulfric's ascetic practices: they were one of the building blocks of the genre. But they were also the reality, for there was no point in shutting yourself in a cell unless you intended to live an ascetic life.[89] These men and women were, after all, in training to be athletes of Christ, and

[88] "We must take care to avoid *a priori* reductionism, for solitary enclosure as the expression of religious feeling is not a simple or ahistorical phenomenon," L'Hermite-Leclercq, "Anchoritism in Medieval France," 114.

[89] Wulfric's regime, as regards fasting and sleep, does not appear to have been much more extreme than that of Saint Anselm when a monk at Bec. *The Life*, ed. Southern, 14–15.

athleticism tends to be competitive, if not with others (which would be frowned on as at odds with humility), with oneself: there is always the higher peak to climb. John uses again and again the word *aemulatio*. It is likely that Wulfric's practices grew more extreme in the telling, but not inordinately so, I think. If his asceticism had not been remarkable, no one would have told stories about him in the first place: averagely ascetic anchorites were not noteworthy.

If the key being used to interpret experience, one's own and that of others, is Scripture, then a certain pattern is going to be found. Meaning is sought for and found in patterns and the key will determine which patterns are unlocked. This applies whether or not it is the key to truth or merely to a particular psychological conditioning. Therefore the lives of the saints will of necessity reflect these patterns; indeed the saint, while alive, may well take certain decisions which shape his or her life in accordance with an unfolding pattern. The hagiographer will also be using the same key to look for patterns in the life, and they will emerge.[90] This is a different process from taking a template and reshaping a life to fit it, like Procrustes mutilating his victims until they corresponded with the dimensions of his bed. Of course a hagiographer might be a Procrustes when a gulf of time and facts could only be bridged by invention, but this was not the case with John of Forde and Wulfric.

John understood himself to be writing a Life. At one point he says he is giving a faithful account of what was *digne mirari*, worthy of admiration and wonder, in (Wulfric's) outward being and doing (1. 2). The words *digne mirari* must be allowed their weight but should not be given more. There was nothing remarkable, let alone admirable, about Wulfric's early years of which John gives a bare and seemingly factual account. And if the *Life*'s later tone is laudatory, room is found for incidents in Wulfric's life which had shocked his contemporaries and continue to trouble John; indeed

[90] This dialectic is not dissimilar to that of the apostolic church tracing the foreshadowing of Christ's life in the stories and prophecies of the Old Testament, and Christ himself growing into self-understanding within the awareness of these foreshadowing types and patterns. See Henry Wansbrough, OSB, *The Use and Abuse of the Bible: A Brief History of Biblical Interpretation* (London: Continuum, 2010) 3–5, 10–17.

the prior derives a certain comfort from the fact that the anchorite has human weaknesses, "trusting," he says, "to find refreshment in their shade when beset by my own" (1. 21).

Veritas—truth—is a word John's pen traced frequently, in respect of himself, of his witnesses, and of Wulfric. In differing contexts he puts forward as alternatives *falsitas* and *pueriles fabule*. Truth, as understood by John, comprises "facts" but goes beyond them. After weighing the evidence for the cutting of the hauberk, of which he has heard differing versions, he comes to a reasoned conclusion which he holds to be the truth (1. 10). Here the outcome might be debatable but the process, by modern standards, is sound. On this level it can be said that John makes conscious and consistent efforts to come at the truth: he chooses his witnesses with care and sometimes double-checks their reports. Occasionally he even lets a doubt seep through: "In case any reader's faith should falter under the weight of such a sign, Brother William, the hospitaller, claims to have heard it from the holy man himself, who also told the venerable abbot of Waverley . . . that he had fed forty people with a single loaf; but whether these were the same we have just been talking about or possibly others, I would not make so bold as to determine" (2. 11). The story of the pilgrim's staff brought back by a helpful wave elicits a similarly ambivalent comment: "This outcome was attributed by the man of faith [a noble of consequence] not to chance but to the power of God's saint" (3. 9). There, as in the following passage, faith serves almost as a substitute for evidence: "All this was told me by one of our brothers who hails from thereabouts, a young man who gives much cause for hope, and with the firmness of his faith he prevailed over mine. But to make good any possible lack in it, I sent to the faithful in those parts, by some of whom I was introduced into the very truth of the matter" (3. 17).

But behind all John's uses and understandings of the word "truth" stands what he calls *ipsa veritas*, "truth itself," or better, "truth in person": "The anchorite John, of Winterbourne in the county of Dorset, a man who has kept from youth to a holy way of life, tells the story I am about to write and he calls to witness truth in person, whose presence in his testimony we do not question as the anchorite lives with him in intimate friendship. Christina, too, the venerable recluse of Wareham, who has this truth in the safest of safekeeping [*custodia tutissima*], and of whom I more than once made careful inquiry, gave this story her full backing" (2. 27). The truth John is speaking of here is Christ, the way, the truth, and the life, whom Wulfric sought "in truth and so deserved to find him faithful, as the truth is in Jesus" (1. 2).[91] Here is John's ultimate statement about the *Life*: "We know that even if [Wulfric] does bear witness to himself, his testimony is true,[92] for it is not he alone[93]—truth itself gives him from heaven a testimony greater than that of John.[94] It follows that those who heard these things from him, those who were worthy of his continuing friendship, are for us such trustworthy witnesses to what happened that we can rely completely on the Lord in regard to them, whose word can be safely taken as putting an end to controversy and establishing the truth. We unfold a tale taken from them on trust and passed on in that trust for the benefit of the faithful" (1. 13). Christ, then, visible as holiness of life in Wulfric and in John's chosen witnesses, is the ultimate guarantor of what we read in the *Life*. We are no longer on literary ground here; there is a much more complex process at work than a passing of themes, like reach-me-down clothes, from one generation of saints' lives to the next.

John's purpose with Wulfric's life was with its meaning, but there had to be a life before the meaning could be drawn out of it. These tales are not comparable to fables, which also serve as basis for a moral. In the fabular tradition, the moral comes first; the story serves to illustrate it. Hagiography gives us the meeting, not of a fiction and a moral truth, but of two realities: the human, with known and limited potentialities, and the divine that erupts into it in the form of power (healing, prophecy, wonder-working). In the interpretation of Scripture, the key to hagiographical texts, the allegorical and anagogical meanings depend on the precedence of the historical. For

[91] Eph 4:21.
[92] John 8:14.
[93] John 8:16.
[94] John 5:36.

the writers of these Lives there was always the temptation, regularly given way to, to manipulate and "heighten" the historical life so that it might better incorporate desired meanings, which were seen as taking precedence.[95] Yet John's reverence for truth included a care for factual accuracy which he strove for in the light of his time and with the means at his disposal. One walks this tightrope with an awareness of the drop on either side, but given John's witness to his own understanding of truth, as well as to his aims and methods, a respect for the general historical authenticity of the *Life* in the form of a presumption in its favor would seem a prerequisite to making sense of the whole. Just as a theatrical representation requires a suspension of disbelief, perhaps a suspension of unbelief is a helpful preliminary to the reading of a work of hagiography.

8. Wulfric as Wonder-worker

> ". . . in acts of healing, in the casting out of demons or the telling and foretelling of the mysteries of God."

A reader taking a cursory look at the *Life* might carry away the impression of a succession of miracle stories strung like beads on a thread between biographical bookends. The reality is somewhat different. If we define a miracle as a manifestation of power, believed to be divine, *praeter* or *supra naturam*, then there are just over a hundred such incidents in the *Life*, spread unevenly through the text: there are long chapters devoid of signs and wonders and some where healing and prophecy walk side by side. If, on the other hand, we think of a miracle primarily as the marvelous—that is, inexplicable—healing of a physical ailment, there are only eighteen; and this figure itself begs a question, for we marvel according to our degree of knowledge and our ability to explain, and the

[95] Walter Daniel gives a revealing, if slightly tetchy, justification of this process: "For what are the facts? Is it supposed that the dead body of Ailred did not shine when it was washed? It was a light to all of us who stood by. And how? Much more than if a carbuncle had been there. . . . You must pardon me, therefore, if I magnified the incomparable, as it deserved, by using a permissible hyperbole." Walter Daniel, *Epistola ad Mauricum*; Powicke, *Life*, 77.

twelfth century marveled, if not more readily than the twenty-first, certainly at different things.

But the marvelous was not necessarily of God. Since the devil could also circumvent the laws of nature, or give the impression of doing so, miracles were no guarantee of holiness; it was holiness, rather, that authenticated the miracle. This, if not always the view of the sick and suffering, had ever been that of the Church, and was fully shared by John. When he exclaims: "O high humility of blessed Bernard, more precious to me than a thousand miracles" (2. 26), he is reflecting Bernard's own teaching, summed up in the latter's comment in his Life of Malachy that the saint was himself his first and greatest miracle.[96] The emphasis throughout the *Life* is on the anchorite's virtues, his sanctity; John marvels at Wulfric's signs not per se but as pointing to the grace of God at work in his saint. The reflective passages which, particularly in Books 1 and 2, seek to draw out the meaning of these signs use them as a series of illustrations to the pages of Wulfric's inner life; John knows his readers will focus on the compelling illuminations but hopes they will also read the text.

The same saint's Life can offer more than one angle on the miraculous. John gives not only his own view but refracts through his lens the views of Wulfric and his visitors. People came, he says, for a variety of reasons, "ranging from a hoped-for grace of healing to a reverence for holiness," and not least to consult him, as one with direct access to God, "about the dark uncertainties of things they had to bear" (1. 11). As for Wulfric, his understanding of his role and of the power that flowed through him changed—probably over time, though since chronology was not a determining factor in the arrangement of the chapters, it is hard to be precise. Certainly, he began by charging people not to speak of graces they experienced (1. 11). Two things seem to have altered this: a first

[96] *Et meo quidem judicio primum et maximum miraculum quod dedit ipse erat*, Bernard of Clairvaux, *Vita Sancti Malachiae* 43, *Sancti Bernardi Opera*, vol. 3, ed. J. Leclercq and H. M. Rochais (Rome: Editiones Cistercienses, 1959) 348. Ælred of Rievaulx and Baldwin of Forde make the same point about holiness being more to be desired and emulated than miracles. Ward, *Miracles*, 25–26.

dream interpreted by the theologian Robert Pullen, who told him that God had gifted him with the grace of healing and the power to work signs (1. 11), and a second, monitory, dream in which he was rebuked for his diffidence and told to speak out confidently and bid others do the same (1. 12).

Sometimes John presents Wulfric as an innocent, like a child at play and barely aware of what he was doing (1. 10); this distancing enables John to create a space for God to work and preserve Wulfric from suspicion of self-seeking or self-aggrandisement: "And clearly this man too, child that he was, spoke like a child, thought like a child and reasoned like a child, setting no value on these phenomena, nor on himself in relation to them, quite unconscious as he was of being revered. Hence, since to him they were not acts of power but trifling matters without significance, he recounted them to the holy-minded with the simplest of smiles, so that unadorned truth took away every suspicion of boasting" (1. 13). Yet in other situations and perhaps also as time passed, he is shown as well aware of his power and taking on occasion a certain grim pleasure in its surprise effects (3. 34): a reaction reminiscent of childhood, but not a sign of holy simplicity.

The birth, childhood, and death of saints are often enveloped in a miraculous aura.[97] John is admirably brief in respect of the first two, which are accompanied by nothing remotely supernatural. We are prepared for Wulfric's approaching death by the sudden disintegration of the hauberk. Its donning had marked the start of his life as a warrior of Christ; its cutting to size had been his first "sign"; he is bidden to lay it aside a full year before his death, a sign to him that his warfare is at an end and that he will die "out of harness," like an old horse put out to grass. When the time comes, his prophetic gift remains, insofar as he foretells the hour of his calling and warns Osbern to expect trouble over the burial (3. 42), but John's account is straightforward, moving, and unadorned.

[97] Ward, *Miracles*, 169, 173, 174, 178; also *The Book of Saint Gilbert*, ed. and trans. R. Foreville and G. Keir (Oxford: Clarendon Press, 1987) 11 and 125–29. John is of course familiar with the phenomena and includes a secondhand account of an extraordinary fragrance which accompanied the opening of the tomb of Matilda of Wareham (2. 29).

Miracles, writes John, "constituted the strenuous exercise of this man" (3. 39). Presenting them was in turn no small exercise for John. He was divided between the need to bring out the extraordinary in this man's life as reflecting his holiness and to rein it back and show it as but a natural and secondary concomitant of that holiness; thus we find him writing: "That an hour's ecstasy should be experienced by a good man and a friend of God, who habitually sang his way through the whole Psalter with unwavering attention will indeed astonish no one. It is more the remarkable stability in an exceptional soul that I for my part admire and reverence" (2. 19). Many of the stories can be read, and are perhaps best understood as the perception, interpretation, and description, in an appropriate and common language, of lived experience within a given context.

The "signs" and miracles related in the stories fall into three categories, which may be set out as follows:

1. **Healing** **17**
   - demonic possession: 1. 12; 1. 17; 3. 3; 3. 7 **4**
   - dumb: 2. 14; 2. 15; 3. 10 **3**
   - blind: 3. 15 **1**
   - fever: 3. 8 **1**
   - intestinal disorder: 2. 12; 3. 2; 3. 4; 3. 6; 3. 47 **5**
   - cut hand: 3. 5 **1**
   - unspecified: 3. 15; 3. 46 **2**

2. **Prophetic** **45**
   - Insight. Knowing the thoughts and/or lives, past and present, of those who come to him: 2. 20; 2. 28; 3. 4; 3. 5; 3. 7; 3. 11; 3. 13; 3. 14; 3. 27; 3. 31; 3. 33 **11**
   - Foreknowledge: 1. 17; 2. 20; 2. 22; 2. 25; 2. 27; 3. 1; 3. 2; 3. 3; 3. 7; 3. 16; 3. 17; 3. 18; 3. 22; 3. 23; 3. 28; 3. 30; 3. 32; 3. 33; 3. 38; 3. 40; 3. 41; 3. 42 **22**
   - Knowledge of events at a distance: 2. 6; 2. 25; 3. 12; 3. 20; 3. 21; 3. 24; 3. 26; 3. 32; 3. 34; 3. 35; 3. 36; 3. 37 **12**

3. **Manifestations of God's power or presence** **42**
    - to do with light: 2. 2; 2. 3; 2. 4; 2. 5; 2. 6 **5**
    - steel cut, links parted: 1. 9; 1. 10; 3. 14 **3**
    - water warmed: 1. 25 **1**
    - a wave returns a pilgrim's staff: 3. 9 **1**
    - bread multiplied: 2. 11 **1**
    - water changed into wine: 2. 7; 2. 8; 2. 9 **3**
    - wine changed into blood at consecration: 2. 19 **1**
    - visitors deemed in retrospect otherworldly: 1. 1; 1. 20; 2. 10; 3. 45 (to Osbern) **4**
    - consequences of theft from or marked disrespect for Wulfric, usually, though not always, independent of him: 2. 13; 2. 14; 2. 15; 2. 16; 3. 25; 3. 26; 3. 30; 3. 34 **8**
    - dreams and revelations, vouchsafed to Wulfric: 1. 11; 1. 12; 1. 18; 2. 11; 3. 19; 3. 29 **6**
    - dreams and revelations, vouchsafed to others: 1. 26; 1. 27; 2. 12; 3. 3; 3. 7; 3. 10; 3. 14; 3. 46; 3. 47 **9**

In all these instances Wulfric is presented as a channel of divine power, but in varying ways or degrees. The healings are a response by word or gesture to a request; sometimes the request is received and responded to intuitively or "prophetically" and the healing takes place at a distance. The healing miracles are relatively few in number, and while the symptoms described are physical, it is possible in some of the cases to posit underlying psychological causes or natural outcomes to self-limiting conditions.

Three of these healing miracles consist in the restoration of speech to a mute, and the variations on the theme offer insights into the often complex substructure of the "simple" miracle story. In the first, the dumb man—reluctant or indifferent—is "brought" to Wulfric, who prays and lays his hand on him,[98] after which the man speaks clearly and in two languages (1. 14). This is a story which can be read in psychological terms. The man might have lost his

[98] Mark 7:32.

speech as the result of some shock or trauma, and any recovery from that state would have brought back whatever languages he spoke before. Circumstantial detail is at a minimum as John's interest is in the squabble sparked off between Brihtric and Wulfric.

The second story follows immediately on the first and could not be more different. The dumb man comes with a group of friends, stays behind of his own accord, and presents himself for a blessing. Kneeling at the window for Wulfric to make the sign of the cross, he suddenly protrudes his tongue as far as he can, so that the anchorite's hand touches the back of the tongue in passing. The man rushes off to rejoin his friends, leaving Wulfric unaware that anything has happened. The rest of the story is of exuberant joy. The man tells his friends, his family, the whole village. At last someone asks him whether he thanked his healer. Penitent, he goes back "with peace offerings of praise and acts of thanksgiving." His faith, says Wulfric, giving him another blessing for good measure, has made him whole.

There is no suggestion that these men are deaf mutes, merely that they are unable to speak. The second is entirely self-motivated and his impediment apparently physical. The third case is that of a deaf mute brought in the train of a noblewoman staying as a guest at the manor house. His function, if any, is unclear; he is presented as almost childlike and the thought of a cure has crossed nobody's mind. He wanders out on his own and falls asleep outside Wulfric's door. A dove is seen by some bystanders to fly out from the cell and introduce its beak into the sleeper's ears and mouth.[99] On awaking, he can both hear and speak. He goes in and says to his mistress, who has been looking for him: "Here I am," and when she asks how he comes to be speaking, he tells her that Wulfric came while he slept and laid a finger on his mouth. There is clearly a story behind the story of this man of unknown age, part of a noblewoman's retinue, almost of her baggage, in a state of noncommunication and dependency.

In the other two categories, the prophet as seer and as mediator of divine power, Wulfric appears as a more specifically liminal figure,

[99] Mark 7:33.

occupying a frontier land between realities, particularly in regard to the first of the two where terms like "clairvoyance" and "telepathy" have today a wider, if contested, currency than "prophecy." Henry of Waverley remembers the sharpness and penetration of the holy man's gaze (2. 20). Others, to their discomfort, find their inmost thoughts laid bare (3. 11). One of his boys complained that his master knew his least peccadillo "as if he were the inseparable comrade and witness not only of his steps but of his very thoughts" (3. 24). Less was more: Wulfric, seeing nothing, saw all; because his gaze was turned inward, walls were no obstacle to his seeing.

The last section is too complex for easy definition. The cutting of the hauberk is the result of an initiative taken by Wulfric, the parting of the links his response to requests; both involve instructions or gestures and in these particulars resemble the healing miracles—indeed the links confer benefit, even healing, on their recipients. In others of these signs (with rare exceptions like the cursings of the cellarer and the mouse), Wulfric is almost a bystander, at once essential and passive. Things happen because of him, but he is not seen to provoke or even invite them. By and large they are presented as God's response to the holiness of his servant, who is rewarded by visible signs of divine favor, or defended by warnings and punishments visited on any who treat the Lord's prophet with contempt.[100] The underlying theology here is that of Romans 12:19: "Beloved, never avenge yourselves, but leave it to the wrath of God, for it is written, 'Vengeance is mine, I will repay, says the Lord.'" It is no coincidence that in the story of the cellarer (2. 15), where Wulfric appears to transgress this law, John first has him offer the man the best he can put on the table, thus fulfilling the prescription in the next verse: "To the contrary, 'if your enemy is hungry, feed him; if he is thirsty, give him something to drink.'" And when, after further provocation, Wulfric looses his lethal word and the cellarer is later that day swept away in a flood, John backs away from the obvious conclusion, calling once again on Saint Paul:

[100] Ps 104:15; 1 Chr 16:22.

> Now this is slippery ground where I personally watch my feet, and I would advise you to do the same for fear of stumbling in the still prevailing darkness. I say this to forestall any rush to premature judgment[101]—whether to predict this man's eternal death or the salvation of his soul when and if God should so decide—and arriving at an over-hasty verdict about a death which consists at present in the destruction of the body. It is, moreover, the height of blind presumption and a temptation passing human strength to seek to draw boundaries in matters which lie for now beyond our mortal day, and which, referred to the hearing of a higher court, are the preserve of God alone.

Realizing, however, that he has to take up a position, John turns to Christ's teaching on the punishment in store for "whoever causes one of these little ones to sin": "better for him to have a great millstone fastened round his neck and to be drowned [like the cellarer] in the depth of the sea."[102] But even Scripture cannot armor John against his own unease. He prefers to think of the cellarer's death as serving to heal Wulfric's wounded soul, "by teaching him, through penance for his lapse, to lament the death of an enemy, at the same time arming him with the virtue of charity against any like occasion in the future."

There was, however, to be another juncture when Wulfric showed himself unforgiving, in circumstances less personal and much more mysterious. He refused point-blank to receive a man who was standing in despair on the far side of the bridge which led into Haselbury and which Wulfric, by his boy, forbade him absolutely to cross. The boy came back upset and pleaded with his master. A noblewoman, dismayed by the human drama being played out on the sidelines while she was seeking spiritual counsel, added her voice to the boy's. But Wulfric, "setting his face"[103] and hardening it like adamant and flint,[104] said: "I will not spare and I will not take pity,"[105] and reinforcing the inexorable judgment: "I neither

[101] 1 Cor 4:5.
[102] Matt 18:6.
[103] Ezek 4:3.
[104] Ezek 3:9.
[105] Jer 13:14.

wish nor am able to take pity" (3. 1). Here again John takes refuge in Scripture, taking the story as an *exemplum* of the Last Judgment, when there will be no crossing of the bridge. "Is this not," he writes, "the face of the judgment to come . . . when finally, as they weep and wail, they will hear from the throne of the implacable judge: 'What I have written, I have written.'"[106] He can no more come to terms with the story on the human level than could the woman present, wife of Alan de Faleisa, who never ceased as long as she lived "revolving in her heart the scene of this terrible judgment, and as she in turn related it to others, she became herself a sign and a portent[107] for all who heard these things." The reader too is left baffled by Wulfric's refusal to receive a man who is plainly seeking forgiveness for some grave sin. Assuming that the anchorite's prophetic gift gave him knowledge of the evil done, and that he lacked the authority to grant absolution, he could have given counsel and directed the man to the bishop. The story remains enigmatic; the fact that John had difficulties with it speaks for its authenticity and for the honesty with which he handled his source material, and confirms his own broad tolerance and compassion.

9. Holy Man or Saint?

The holy who during their lifetime had been channels for divine grace and power became even more effective after death. Indeed, had they not, their sanctity might have been called into question and their chances of canonization would certainly have been compromised. If John sent on three separate occasions to check out the story of a healing which took place fifteen years after Wulfric's death, it was for fear that someone might be thinking "that death had unstrung blessed Wulfric's hand and weakened his power" (3. 47). It must have been a matter of relief to John to come on this story which he was able to authenticate so satisfactorily by interviews with the principal witness. He appends three *post obitum* stories in all, but the other two are not so well provided with

[106] John 19:22.
[107] Isa 20:3.

the features expected in miracles connected with a shrine, and in neither case was the witness still available for questioning. Both stories were passed to John by Walter of Glastonbury, the first originating with Osbern, the second with a woman only identified as coming from Kent. In the first there was no healing, just the sudden appearance in the church of a strange pilgrim who persuaded Osbern to hand him the only objects belonging to Wulfric that remained to him, namely, the saint's porringer and spoon. Pricked almost instantly by sharp regret, Osbern ran out of the church to catch the elusive pilgrim, only to find he had disappeared without trace. He quickly concluded from the suddenness of his coming and going, a certain fierce beauty, the authority of his words, and the secret knowledge he revealed that this was some angelic being. This incident is essentially about grieving and loss. Osbern is alone in the church at Haselbury; Wulfric has gone, his spoon and porringer are then taken, the visitor disappears with them and cannot be found; Osbern and the villagers are left running around like ants in a disturbed nest; and John himself is puzzled by it all.

The second story (3. 46) reintroduces an unnamed woman from Kent, who once sent Wulfric some silk for covering a book (1. 27). We learn that a close friendship existed between her and the holy man and that she made annual visits to Haselbury, which ceased only on his death. Now she has fallen ill and Wulfric tells her in a dream to resume her visits, for she will find healing only at his place of rest. Much more is made of this spiritual friendship lasting beyond the grave than of the unidentified illness and it is in no way typical of healings at shrines.

In the Prologues John makes no secret of his heartache at the thought of the empty cell, the unknown grave, the silence over all. Osbern's role in this state of affairs has been considered,[108] and these glimpses of him in the church at Haselbury years after Wulfric's death add a few brushstrokes to an unfinished picture. The priest cuts a strange and lonely figure in the first story (3. 45). He starts by assuring the "pilgrim" that he has nothing belonging

[108] Above, 31–32.

to the anchorite save "objects consecrated to sacred use." At once the visitor's courtesy turns into something more threatening. He points to a chest holding Wulfric's dish and spoon. "*Surge*! Get up," he says, "and give them to me." Was Osbern deliberately concealing precious keepsakes, or had he forgotten their very existence? It is unclear. But the order is given with such compelling authority that he jumps to his feet and hands over dish and spoon without a word spoken. By the time he has relocked the chest and felt the first pang of regret, his visitor has vanished. John looks vainly for a meaning to this story, which leaves a lingering aftertaste of fairy tale. Any attempt to deconstruct it must surely lead back to Osbern's inner wrestlings with his psyche.

The last and longest story (3. 47), the only one to which John is able and careful to fix a precise date, introduces a couple from the hamlet of Hurcott near Ilminster, a man named Wudeman and his wife Liviva. The husband has a dysenteric illness and has given large sums to doctors who now despair of him. His wife finds herself standing one night in a dream in the church at Haselbury, where a noble-looking man with white hair tells her to collect some dust from the grave of the man of God: mixed with water and given him to drink, it will cure her husband's illness. The husband, dubious and skeptical of dreams, dissuades her from any action. Time passes and the dream returns. This time to the north of the altar she sees a splendid tomb and prepares to kneel reverently beside it, but the occupant stretches out shod feet and tries to kick her away. As she stands quaking, the "ancient" reappears and rebukes her for dilatoriness.[109] On waking she hurries to Haselbury, where Osbern and William fitzWalter's widow listen to her story with tears of joy. Unguided, she makes her way to the unmarked grave, scoops up the dust, and takes it home. Her husband recovers, word spreads, a number of people come to her and she uses the rest of the dust to cure their ills, enabling John to conclude in sweeping mode: "So the whole church of God will have known that blessed Wulfric

[109] The identity of the different figures—presumably Wulfric—is left unclear, as it surely was in the dream.

is in the glory of God the Father and is ready if anyone calls on him; indeed, before he is even invoked, he says: 'Look, here I am.'"

This story, with its dreams full of menace, is disquieting and moreover untypical of the living Wulfric, whose courtesy is often emphasized and whose kindness to the sick is a recurrent feature. There are echoes here of the "vengeance" miracles of saints to whose relics insufficient honor was shown, stories associated with cults fostered by religious houses, useful for keeping pilgrims in order and encouraging generosity.[110] More important are certain narrative inconsistencies. Why is Osbern moved to tears of joy, when he has done all he could to discourage visits to Wulfric's resting place? Probably because human nature is inconsistent, and he was torn between fear and longing. But joy at knowing that Wulfric was still present and active among them was soon conquered by the fear of losing "the treasure" that was his bones, and the reburial John has already written of (3. 44) was now hurriedly carried out. How Osbern kept this secret is a mystery. The pressure to reveal and honor the resting place must have increased once the news of the miracle spread, as John says it did. Yet the excitement subsided again and the silence rolled back in, which suggest that cults, to establish themselves, needed more than folk-memories and local piety.

Thus far, we have tiptoed round a central question: was the *Life* written with the express purpose of obtaining Wulfric's canonization? The argument for introducing this question from the outset was strong but would have meant its piecemeal examination under a variety of as yet unexplored headings. After a round tour of the work, one may hope for a better perspective on the problem. To set it in its historical context: a succession of reforming popes, starting with Gregory VII, lengthened through the eleventh and twelfth centuries the reach of Rome across western Europe. In England the Norman Conquest abetted this process of centralization by

[110] "Reginald [of Durham], in his account of the miracles of Saint Cuthbert, . . . stresses the importance of the shrine with its formidable patron. Those who mock the saint or doubt his powers are punished by Saint Cuthbert. The severity of the punishment is proportionate to the honor of the saint rather than the severity of the crime." Ward, *Miracles*, 63.

cutting off the church in its upper echelons from its Anglo-Saxon roots: at the death of William I, Wulfstan of Worcester was the only native bishop remaining in his see. The veneration of local saints and particularly the establishment of new cults were seen as problematic by imported prelates short on empathy with an alien past and who had Rome as well as Norman kings looking over their shoulders. Lanfranc, and to a lesser degree Anselm, discouraged or suppressed a number of local cults, and the English church played a prominent part in fostering the tendencies of successive popes to take the process of canonization into their own hands.[111]

Five years after Wulfric's death, Alexander III, the first of the great canonists, was elected pope, and over the following half century the establishment of new cults came under much stricter control. Investigation became more thorough and protracted. A number of canonizations, including that of Saint Bernard, were postponed at the Council of Tours. Saint Bernard made it ten years later in 1174, but Malachy of Ireland, whose cause was put forward at the same time, was rejected by Alexander on grounds of *fastidium*—too much of a good thing.[112] By the time that John was writing his *Life*, a whole legal process had been set in place, elements of which are clearly reflected in the Prologues and indeed to some extent in the way the text is structured. In papal canonizations it was usual for a written Life to be presented and for the support not merely of a single bishop but of the higher ecclesiastical authorities to be obtained. Miracles were essential, including a number which had taken place after the subject's death, proving that he or she was indeed in the presence of God. These must in turn be supported by the testimony of named witnesses, and by the turn of the century, Innocent III was requiring that a number of witnesses "be produced in person at Rome."[113] A list of twenty witnesses, all named bar two, who knew Wulfric and spoke with John in person, many of whom he refers to as "still alive today," can be found on page 245.

[111] Kemp, E.W. *Canonization and Authority in the Western Church* (London: OUP, 1948) 53–65; R. Foreville, *The Book of Saint Gilbert*, cviii.

[112] Kemp, *Canonization*, 90.

[113] Kemp, *Canonization*, 105; and Foreville, *The Book of Saint Gilbert*, cvii.

The dedicatory Letters addressed to Bartholomew and Baldwin respectively take on a more formal appearance when read in this context. The impetus still comes from John and the unnamed abbot, who address not Wulfric's diocesan but their own, whether because protocol demanded, or friendship invited, is not made clear. Bartholomew not only encourages, he offers, according to John, to put his own hand to the work should it need amending.[114] John may well have been referring here to juridical niceties of presentation with which a canonist like Bartholomew would be familiar. Later, when forwarding the *Life* to Baldwin, John speaks of it as "amended" ; was this by Bartholomew's correcting hand or authorial second thoughts? Probably the first: the *Life of Gilbert of Sempringham* was similarly *emendata*, post factum, by the chancellor of Lincoln.[115] The bishop of Exeter also convenes to the panel of judges his confreres of Bath and Worcester: Bath because Haselbury fell within that diocese and Worcester because Baldwin, then the incumbent, was a man of mark who would carry weight in Rome. It all fits very well. Bartholomew unfortunately dies, but Baldwin meanwhile has been elevated to Canterbury and can carry the torch alone. John, one senses from his Letter to the primate, has little doubt that he will do so. The case of Becket is brought forward to encourage him: so recently martyred, so swiftly raised to the altars. The examples of William of York and Godric of Finchale are less compelling: the archbishop of York slips into the calendar in 1227; Godric, of humble birth and mode of life, still waits. John is aware that these two are not in the same class, calling Thomas *beatissimus*, whereas William and Godric are merely *beatus*, the term he applies regularly to Wulfric. John's Letters are written on the same pattern as the Prologue addressed fifteen years later to another archbishop of Canterbury, Hubert Walter, in the cause of Gilbert of Sempringham,[116] identical themes being developed by both writers, though John is somewhat less verbose. It seems certain

[114] . . . *episcopus voluntatem non solum probavit sed et accendit et instruxit; seque emendando operi supremam manum impositurum repromisit.*

[115] Foreville, *The Book of Saint Gilbert*, 8.

[116] Foreville, *The Book of Saint Gilbert*, 2–10; even the use of Becket is paralleled.

that if obtaining Wulfric's canonization was not his only reason for writing the *Life* it was a driving factor.

We then have to ask why he was not successful. A comparison of the outcomes of requests for canonization put forward by English bishops between the mid-twelfth and mid-thirteenth centuries is revelatory. Holiness and miracles were claimed on behalf of all the candidates. What seems to have tipped the balance was class, "deediness," and the clout, not least political, behind the successful. The four Englishmen canonized by papal bull between 1161 and 1203 were respectively a martyred primate, a former bishop of Worcester, a king, and the founder of an order (Becket, Dunstan, Edward the Confessor, and Gilbert of Sempringham). In other words, they all had high-profile public roles and the last three had the weight of a reigning king behind their cause.[117] While another bishop and two archbishops were added to the calendar before 1350, not a single recluse made it to sainthood during the entire period, despite the fact that a number had Lives written about them[118] and some had active local cults to which a blind eye was turned. Robert of Knaresborough, who died in 1218, is even accorded a courtesy *sanctus* in a bull of Innocent IV in favor of the Trinitarian friars, and his cult was allowed to flourish in the neighborhood, as did that of Godric under the auspices of the monks of Durham, who built a priory church to house his shrine. Like Wulfric, these were of English origin and, like his, their followings were mainly local. Kings may have turned aside on occasion and paid their respects, but they remained rare visitors.

If John's project took form in a rose-tinted dawn following Becket's triumphant canonization in 1173, the cold light of history now shows up his hopes as unrealistic. There is no indication that the *Life* went further up the ecclesiastical ladder than Canterbury. Whether Baldwin took any steps at all is impossible to say, but even with Wulfric's cause at heart he would have been hard put to promote it. Between his enthronement in 1185 and his death in 1190,

[117] King John had a devotion to Saint Dunstan and Henry II had good reasons for pressing the claim of the last Anglo-Saxon king of England. He was also an energetic supporter of Gilbert of Sempringham.

[118] Godric of Finchale, Robert of Knaresborough, and Christina of Markyate.

there were four successive popes in Rome, and when he himself was not locked in struggle with the monks of Christ Church, he was on the road preaching the crusade. He left for the Holy Land in March 1190, together with Abbot Robert of Forde, and died at Acre in November. Wulfric never stood a chance.

This is not to say that the *Vita* should not be accounted a success, even in John's terms. His stated aims, as also Wulfric's prophecy (3. 40), may be said to have been triumphantly fulfilled. Despite the absence of a marked grave and presumably as a result of the popularity of the *Life*, less than fifty years after John wrote it, "innumerable miracles" were reported by Roger of Wendover[119] as taking place at Haselbury. Without other fanfare Wulfric crept into the Sanctoral, and pilgrimages to his cell continued until the Reformation.[120] It would be pleasant to think, as seems likely, that they started during John's lifetime.

Roger of Wendover was the first of a procession to pillage the *Vita* for stories concerning Wulfric. Latin chroniclers and compilers of saints' lives trawled through John's narrative, spurning the mystical dimension in the quest for the miraculous and the dramatic.[121] For an abridgement of the *Life* more respectful of its author's aims and written in English, readers had to wait until the seventeenth century, when a compendium by Dom Jerome Porter, titled *The Flowers of the Lives of the Most Renowned Saints of the Three Kingdoms*, was printed at Douai in 1632.[122] Even if a few copies came to England

[119] Roger was summarizing excerpts from John's *Life*, under the year 1154, the starting date of his chronicle, and appends this invaluable comment. See Roger of Wendover, *Flores historiarum*, vol. I, ed. H. G. Hewlett (Rolls Series), 1887.

[120] For the later use made of the *Life* and the development of the cult, see Bell, *Wulfric*, lxiv–lxvii.

[121] For further details on the use to which the *Life* was put, see Bell, *Wulfric*, lxiv–lxvii. A much later work, not apparently known to Bell, is *The Customs, Superstitions and Legends of the County of Somerset*, by Charles Henry Poole (London: 1877, 2nd ed. St. Peter Port: The Toucan Press, 1970), which has a remarkably accurate four-page condensation of the essentials of John's *Life*, quoting in Latin word for word a sentence from 3. 22—one of the least "startling anecdotes" in the *Vita*. Poole writes in a footnote: "Many of these legends I gleaned from the *Acta Sanctorum*." Poole, *Customs*, 94–98.

[122] The part devoted to Wulfric is given by Bell as an Appendix to the *Life*, 174–85.

and circulated among recusant families, it is most unlikely that the contents of this work filtered back into surviving folklore. But lore of some sort was still extant in Haselbury at that time, for Thomas Gerard of Trent, who published in 1633 his *Particular Description of the County of Somerset*, concluded his entry on that village with the following passage: "before I part hence I will shew you that the elder Lords had neere the Church a mansion house now wholly ruined, in place of which a farme house is risen up; that they will tell you many strange stories of St Wolfricke, whose Cell remaines unto this daye on the Northside the Chauncell which I should rather you should inquire of the inhabitants than looke for here."[123]

We can no longer inquire of the inhabitants about those particular stories; others, however, were being told in Somerset as recently as 1900. Ruth L. Tongue, a collector of folktales, reports hearing three as a child.[124] One combines elements found in John's *Life* in 1. 1 (Wulfric's love of hunting), 1. 9 (the cutting of the hauberk), and 1. 17 (the man who did homage to the devil): stories which had found their way into all later medieval abridgements of the *Vita*, and thence filtered back, probably quite late on, into the oral tradition. A tale about a mouse and another turning on a greedy boy and loaves of bread, which is longer and much more developed, carry reminiscences of John's material, but are sufficiently different to suggest the possibility of an independent filiation. The provenance of "Wulfric and the Greedy Boy" (the tale is reproduced in the appendix on pages 251–54) was given as oral and said to be traceable to the late seventeenth century, but doubts have been raised as to the reliability of this.[125] It is fairly clear that just as John's written work emerged from oral sources, it in turn, through homilies and pilgrims' tales, fed back into an oral

[123] Thomas Gerard, *The Particular Description of the County of Somerset*, 1633, ed. Rev. E. H. Bates (Somerset Record Society 15, 1900) 78.

[124] "St. Wulfric and the Devil" and "St. Wulfric and the Mouse" can be found in Ruth L. Tongue, *Somerset Folklore*, ed. K. M. Briggs (London: The Folklore Society, 1965) 188–89; for "St. Wulfric and the Greedy Boy," see Katharine Briggs, *British Folk-Tales and Legends* (London: Routledge, 2nd ed., 2002) 303–5.

[125] In email correspondence with The Folklore Society.

flow, but whether that flow ever carried flotsam independent of written sources is a matter of speculation inviting further research.

10. The Writing of the *Life*

In the Letter to Bartholomew, John presents himself as Christ's poor man of Forde, someone coming as it were from nowhere, without background or context adequate to his task. In fact, not only was he well schooled, he was living in a community which valued and fostered intellectual activity. Baldwin, who had just left for Worcester, had written industriously during his abbacy and encouraged, if not John, one Roger of Forde and a certain Maurinus to try their hands at poetry and prose.[126] Attitudes to literary composition—of the right kind—were favorable; there were those in the cloister who could give advice and there was also a good library at John's disposal,[127] in which saints' lives would have had a place, besides being read out in the refectory.

John was a novice then, but he knew what he was about, and gave the shape and structure of his book much thought. He was someone too who straddled two cultures: the oral vernacular and the written literary, each with a tradition of storytelling. The one was native to the boy, the other had been acquired by the man; the *Life of Wulfric* was their meeting ground, where the first took a new and fixed form of life in the second. Part story, part homily, part document promoting a cause, the *Life* draws on many ways of seeing, hearing, and recording. John, by training a man of the pen, belonged to a generation which was busily collecting the material floating free and sifting it into categories—chronicles, histories, lives, sagas, romances—in which it might be given permanent form, its scene-shifting halted. In Wulfric's world, by contrast, the spoken word had pride of place; books decorated the margins of life, rather as life would soon decorate the margins of books. In the

[126] Christopher Holdsworth, "John of Ford and English Cistercian Writing 1167–1214," *Transactions of the Royal Historical Society*, 5th Series, 11 (1961) 125–26.

[127] Holdsworth, "John of Ford," 126–27.

Life, Wulfric's world passes into John's. With one exception, everything that John writes down, every scrap of information, comes to him by word of mouth. Only the abbot of Malmesbury, a man who had a secretary, and monks or hired servants, to carry a letter once written, submits his evidence in writing; it contains perhaps the least convincing anecdote of the book (3. 15).

Yet despite the importance that John set by "living memory" and the credit accorded to witnesses, particularly those who had "seen with their own eyes," he felt obliged to put all these memories down in writing with a view to presenting them, gathered and organized, to a wider audience, probably indeed to a tribunal. The oral tradition was seen to be insufficient: no longer fit for purpose, it had in some sense failed. And indeed, for whatever combination of reasons, it had failed Wulfric since, in his case thirty years after his death, it flowed only underground. But training and habit are not so easily set aside. John had received most of his education and formation orally, and writing remained, to a degree, an artificial medium. It is the "listener" he addresses more often than the "reader."[128] As well as the *litteratus*, quill in hand, he is also now the remembrancer telling stories, now the preacher delivering his homily, complete with *exempla*, to an audience whose interest he has at all costs to retain: "For the day, as you see, is drawing towards evening and I am most reluctant to keep you listening until after sundown, anxious as I am to offer you, not tedium, but pleasure" (2. 29). All storytelling, whether oral or written, is an art and this particular formula an artifice, but it drew on a reality entirely recognizable to men and women living in community, whether manorial hall or monastic refectory.[129]

Biographies normally follow a chronological plan, but as the focus in Lives of the holy is on being rather than doing, this does not work

[128] 1. 17; 1. 19; 1. 30; 2. 23 against 2. 12.

[129] Walter Daniel, in his "Letter to Maurice," presents his *Life* of Ælred as being read aloud to two prelates who subsequently criticize it, and Maurice is asked to read them Walter's letter rebutting their criticism: *Ista, mi pater Maurici, lege, queso, duobus prelatis illis*; Powicke, *Life*, 66 and 80–81. Southern assumes from the punctuation that Eadmer wrote with a view to his work being read aloud, *The Life*, xxvii.

very well,[130] and John, showing considerable originality, looked for a different kind of structure. Using the youth and death narratives as end-stops, he divided the material he had collected into three themed sections, which he clearly expected the reader to interpret, rather as a saint's life may be read from a stained glass window.[131]

BOOK 1 has rightly been seen as "the narrative of formation,"[132] the tale of Wulfric's calling and novitiate. Wulfric himself is portrayed as "reading" his encounter with the stranger in the forest as a call to change his life: just like the king of England, the King of Kings required a new coinage and was preparing to beat it out of the precious metal found to hand. The following chapters describe this process: the embracing of solitude, the hours of prayer, the struggle with temptation in its many forms. This struggle is depicted as a *militia*, a warfare (1. 3), a metaphor used by Saint Paul[133] which has run and run, never to greater effect than in the age of chivalry. Hence the adoption of the mail shirt or hauberk, the body armor of the warrior class, which Wulfric added to the scratchy hair shirt,[134] not for effect (he wouldn't have the hauberk sent to London to be shortened for fear of drawing attention to himself [1. 9]), but because its weight, and no doubt its heat in summer, added enormously to the discomfort. He was, however, as was John, keenly aware of its symbolic significance. In the early stages of his reclusion, the hardening of the body and strengthening of the spirit which its wearing procured were his protection in his

[130] It is nonetheless the pattern generally adopted. The *Vita Ailredi* has no obvious structure other than the chronological, which Powicke finds at times "strangely confused," *Life*, 45, n. 1.

[131] This Dom Maurice Bell missed, deeming the division into three books purely arbitrary, and numbering the chapters consecutively in consequence, *Wulfric*, lxxxii. Marsha Dutton drew attention to the significance of the structure in "John of Forde's *De Vita Beati Wulfrici Anachoretae Haselbergiae*: A Model for Cistercian Contemplative Life," *A Gathering of Friends*, 76–92.

[132] Dutton, "John of Forde's," 80.

[133] Eph 6:13-17.

[134] Haircloth was a sign of penitence from biblical times onwards (sackcloth and ashes). Worn next to the skin, it was a traditional form of penance well beyond the Middle Ages. Monks were laid on haircloth strewn with ashes when dying, *Vita Ailredi* 48; Powicke, *Life*, 62.

warfare with sin,[135] and its falling spontaneously from his shoulders a year before his death (3. 41) told him that he had nothing more to fear save death itself, where Christ would be his armor.

This first book unfolds a tale of conversion and gradual purification through physical and spiritual trials. It also contains Wulfric's first signs and healings, notably ones which mirror the stages of his own inner journey. The shortening of the hauberk (1. 9), described by John as the first of his signs (his equivalent to the miracle at Cana), is followed by two exorcisms (1. 12; 1. 17). The healer cannot cure in others what he has not yet overcome in himself, and Wulfric, "still unskilled from lack of practice in these matters," is tentative at first, enabling the devil to stand his ground until the anchorite invokes the threefold power of the Trinity. The second tale is one of the longest and most dramatic in the *Life*, and, although the devil puts up a great fight and Wulfric calls on Brihtric to assist him, the saint is in charge throughout. Slotted between these exorcisms are the two healings considered above (pp. 55–56), where Wulfric gives or restores to two dumb men the grace of communication which he himself enjoys in so rare a degree (1. 7). The adversary visits a solitary in all manner of guises, and Wulfric was long troubled by lust (1. 21). It is contempt that eventually sends the devil packing and allows Wulfric later to tell a monk of Forde, surprised to find him laying his healing hand on a woman: "Having my hand on that woman's breast was no different from having it on this wood" (1. 24).

It is clear from the above that the structure imposed by John was thematic, not chronological: meaning was paramount. The events in the last two stories can be dated to eighteen years or more after Wulfric's enclosure. He himself told the first of them to Henry of Waverley, not, surely, at the time of the latter's conversion, but after he became abbot of Tintern around 1147. Book 1 draws to an end with a gradual easing of purgation and a beginning of consolations: instances of coming and going between heaven and earth (1. 18; 1. 20), the water he bathed in miraculously warmed (1. 25), dreams prompting the sending of much needed gifts (1. 26; 1. 27). A lighter

[135] 1. 5; 1. 6; 1. 9.

touch is introduced in the last pages with Richard the scribe (1. 28; 1. 29) and the story of the mouse (1. 30). This closing tale allows Brihtric to reenter as the perfect foil. Priest and anchorite sometimes do service as a comic turn, and John was uncomfortably aware of this: he devotes an earlier chapter to shining a theological light on their relationship, showing them as complementing one another and alternating between themselves the roles of Martha and Mary (as opposed to Laurel and Hardy) (1. 16).

BOOK 2 begins with a meditation on Wulfric's mystical life, which develops the Martha-Mary motif in the context of the anchoritic vocation: the balance to be struck between service and contemplation, the two faces of love. Wulfric is now a fully fledged holy man whose life is divided between watching with Christ by night and pouring out by day the riches he has received. The theme is thus set in the first chapter. This is to be the book of spiritual consolations, received and given; what was adumbrated in Book 1 becomes here almost the norm. It is also the book of Wulfric's illumination in the spirit, illustrated by the lamps and candles which are the focus of the early chapters (2. 2–6). These are followed by seven stories centered on either bread or wine, a series oddly broken into by a healing (2. 12).[136]

It is in this book that Wulfric's life at Haselbury is gradually peopled. Apart from some mostly nameless extras, the cast of Book 1 is very small: William fitzWalter, Brihtric the priest, Brother William, and finally Richard the scribe. Now the world starts knocking at the recluse's window, and not necessarily the sick in search of healing. Osbern makes his first appearance, followed by Alfred of Lincoln and his mother Bence, Lady fitzWalter and her daughter Beatrice, and a scattering of other neighbors (2. 4–13). The circle widens to embrace the collective, in one chapter the king's court, in others the monks of Forde and those of Montacute, with whom relations are on the one hand good, on the other tense.[137] The last ten chapters are given over to the stories of Henry of

[136] John rarely does things without reason and it may be that I am simply not seeing the obvious.

[137] 2. 15; 2. 16; 2. 17–18.

Waverley, reformed sinner, long-term friend and Cistercian abbot, and the recluse Matilda of Wareham, both of whom Wulfric ushered into the religious life, and whose subsequent holiness (and in the case of Father Henry the connection with Saint Bernard) served as a warranty for Wulfric's own: *even* Saint Bernard was known to have sought Wulfric's intercession. If Book 1 is focused narrowly and intensely on Wulfric himself, Book 2 shows the recluse "in community" (a community of which he is both guide and servant), still growing in wisdom and grace, but in ways which foster interrelatedness, which make him more than himself.

BOOK 3 is the least structured and, as regards the main body of anecdotes, the least interesting. It starts, however, with the third of the judgment or "cursing" stories, where Wulfric is shown to take an active part in the bane of another. In Book 1 this other is merely a mouse that Wulfric curses for nibbling a hole in his new cloak, whereupon it comes scurrying out and dies at his feet. The reader is meant to laugh and side with Brihtric, who wishes his friend would curse the rest of the mice in the county. Wulfric, however, is deeply upset. "If I didn't think it would displease my Lord," he says, "I would pray to him for this one, that he might bring it back to life." Halfway through Book 2 we have the story of the cellarer of Montacute (2. 15).[138] This time he does not precisely say, "Perish the cellarer!" but he invokes God's intervention in terms that leave the Almighty little leeway. The cellarer can also be seen as bringing his death on himself by his arrogance and persistence in his sin. Wulfric, although he appears to regret the cellarer less than the mouse, again repents his own anger and impatience, and John, who saw room for improvement here, says that Wulfric "grew gentler after this and better at loving his enemies" (2. 16).

In real life this may have been true, but in John's *Life*, with its lack of chronology, the reverse seems to obtain, for Book 3 opens with the unsettling tale of the man who was forbidden to cross the bridge (3. 1).[139] John shows a subtle mastery of his medium here. There is no authorial presence at this stage, merely the bare bones

[138] See above, 43.

[139] See above, 58.

of narrative and Wulfric's own words. His harshness bites into us through the terror it arouses in the boy and the woman, who are the unwilling witnesses to this event. There follows an allegorical "reading" on the pattern tradition applied to Scripture. We may object that divine judgment cannot properly be foreshadowed in human terms, nor can metaphor be used to justify human actions. But story and commentary exist on different planes, acting as reflections,but not otherwise interconnected. The fact that David was a murderer and an adulterer does not preclude him being seen as a "type" of Christ. John here is offering an eschatological reading which increases awe, while leaving the story, *qua* story, harsh and repellent.

This opening chapter, portraying Wulfric in the full severity of the Old Testament prophet, is followed by a rare statement of intent. The next stories are to show the prophet's "gentler face," with his twin gifts of healing and prophecy going hand in hand, and indeed the next thirty-six chapters (this is the longest of the three Books) illustrate the prophetic gift in all its variety. The prophecies extend from public issues—the death and captivity of kings, the failure of the second crusade, the departure from Haselbury of the Canons Regular—to the most mundane: a minor injury, the arrival of the lord of the manor, a pilgrim's staff thrown back by a wave. Some could be ascribed to coincidence, others to an uncanny knowledge of what is going on in other people's heads; for most there is no explanation. There are eight healings and seven deaths, natural or violent, "seen" or foretold. Overall these are signs representing and conveying a holy man's liminality, his living athwart two realities, able to move in and out of time and space, to watch over all who look to him, healing their ills, easing their passing, ensuring, as may be, their salvation. The stories are narrated virtually without commentary: this is by far the least rhetorical of the books and has the fewest scriptural references. In this, and in the care taken to provide named witnesses to virtually every story, these short and often less compelling chapters stake their claim to inclusion as the solid rock on which any case for canonization must be based.

The emphasis on narrative flow continues, but in a broader bed, through the chapters covering Wulfric's death, burial, and translations. John displays to the full here his powers as a writer, which are considerable. The same talent for telling a tale, giving it pace, anchoring it in the real with enough concrete detail, and enlivening it with dialogue was already manifest in Henry of Waverley's conversion story. The tale of the man who had paid homage to the devil (1. 17) is another excellent piece of dramatic writing, with fifteen scriptural quotations forming an underlying harmony, at once deepening the meaning and enriching the imagery. The sweep of the last chapters enables John to employ these gifts again and bring the work to its climax and a fitting close.

The absence of any chronology for the significant years of Wulfric's life had the happy effect of obliging John to search for a different structure: hence this much more "composed" work than is usual in the genre. He is, however, a hagiographer first and an artist second. He lacks the artist's ruthlessness with his material. As John shuffles his pack of stories and sorts them into themes, from time to time we hear him say: "Goodness, what shall I do with this one?" He forgets which characters he has already introduced,[140] presents them in chronological disorder, and fails to adjust his narrative in ways which would give the appearance of a smooth progression down the years. But these were not priorities for him and cannot be said to mar the reader's pleasure.

John is good at bringing out humor and conveying humanity, and we owe to his skills a small gallery of portraits scarcely paralleled in medieval saints' lives.[141] Reginald of Durham does well by Godric, and had the advantage over John of knowing his subject intimately over a long period. Yet John recreates Wulfric from the memories of others with an extraordinary consistency of tone, and has the wisdom, after commenting on the saint's taciturnity, to keep his utterances brief and oracular (unlike those attributed

[140] An example of an anecdote written before there was any general plan and probably before the project was even approved is 3. 20, which opens: "William fitzWalter, as the lord of that village was called, came one day to see the man of God." Given the central role of William fitzWalter in the earlier events of Wulfric's life, this opening makes little sense.

[141] Pauline Matarasso, "John of Forde as Portrait Painter," *A Gathering of Friends*, 43–63.

to Godric). However like or unlike he was to the original, John's Wulfric is certainly somebody we know and won't forget. The same can be said of Henry of Waverley and Osbern, to a lesser degree even of William fitzWalter. John does not interfere with his cast, even when they puzzle him; he lets them be themselves.

Among them it is not incongruous to place John himself. Indeed at one point he launches into a confessional moment, seen and interpreted through a dense weave of scriptural allusions, which calls to mind the *Meditations of William of Saint-Thierry* (1. 19). But mostly he is a surprisingly self-assured authorial presence, given the overstated modesty of the Prologues. Were he not so patently nice, he might come over as intrusive, but how can we fail to like a man who admits to cringing under criticism, just like the rest of us (1. 30)? The characteristic which comes over most consistently is his generosity of spirit. He searches out the best in everyone and shows an extreme reluctance to sit in judgment, even putting in an impassioned plea to be spared that role in his own order (2. 21). There is an occasional generalized reproof aimed at monks who wander abroad too much (1. 8), are extravagant (2. 22), or, worse, search out weaknesses in others (2. 21). Otherwise those whose behavior falls short are almost always left nameless. "I knew someone—still alive today . . ." is a phrase that enables John to deplore the fault without pointing the finger. Even the cellarer of Montacute is granted anonymity. Rare too are monastic writers who claim the superiority neither of their order nor of their state. In John's pages there is generous praise with no hint of criticism for Walter of Glastonbury, who chose Glastonbury over Forde. Lay men and women, "tangential and incidental" in the *Life of Gilbert of Sempringham*,[142] here rub shoulders with monks and clerics without any underlining of difference. Those who show themselves to least advantage tend to be monks or clerics,[143] whereas ordinary people are praised as religious, God-fearing, and devout. At a time

[142] Brian Golding, *Gilbert of Sempringham and the Gilbertine Order c. 1130–c. 1300* (Oxford: Clarendon Press, 1995) 8.

[143] The cellarer of Montacute, the future procurator of Glastonbury (3. 30), a man of unknown status, but almost certainly a clerk (3. 34).

when the chances of salvation outside the cloister were often represented as remote, John's breadth of sympathy, fostered perhaps by his sources, is impressive. He may not be a great writer, but he is a good one of his kind and, like Father Henry, a most congenial companion on the way.

11. The Song of Songs: Thematic Unity

After the relative success of his *Life of Wulfric*, at least within the limited aims of ensuring until the Reformation an afterlife on earth for its saint and a slot in compilations of the Lives of the holy, John of Forde slipped, as a writer, into virtual oblivion. His sermons on the Song of Songs, written to complete the commentary begun by Saint Bernard, never emerged from under the shadow of that greater work. Time had, in any case, moved on—the thirteenth century would see the triumph of scholasticism, and John, at his quiet monastic amble, was overtaken in his own lifetime. For centuries he was left to sleep. The *Vita Wulfrici* received its first edition in 1933 and has been little studied since, and one suspects not greatly read. The substantial commentary on the Song—one hundred and twenty sermons preserved in a single manuscript—was not published until 1970 and was translated into English in 1977. Now that his whole surviving *opus* is in at least one vernacular,[144] it is to be hoped that he will receive attention as a spiritual writer. It has been the first concern of this introduction to set John and his subject in the context of their time. To treat adequately of what was closest to John's heart, namely, his understanding of the contemplative life as he perceived it mirrored in Wulfric, lies outside these parameters. One possible starting point might be to suggest that the reflection in the mirror was a two-way process. John was inspired by what he heard of Wulfric; he also projected onto the anchorite his own understanding of the spiritual life.

The material received by John, including happenings, doings, and sayings, was almost all in the form of stories. Wulfric's own accounts

[144] John of Forde, *Sermons sur le Cantique*, trans. Pierre-Yves Émery (Paris: Éditions du Cerf, 1999–), are currently appearing also in French.

of what might be seen as his inner life come in narrative form: he struggles with a troop of devils; a virgin appears and dismisses them with a sweep of her sleeve; his candle burns all night but, like the burning bush, is not consumed. It is John who "reads" these and interprets them for us, and, interestingly, in ways and terms which adumbrate his later work. The long meditative passages in Books 1 and 2 in which John imagines and bodies forth the spiritual commerce between Wulfric and his God contain the themes he was to develop in his Sermons on the Canticle.[145]

The importance of the Song of Songs in the *Vita*, and hence in John's understanding of the contemplative life as early as 1180 or thereabouts, is incontrovertible: the work contains forty references to its eight short chapters, passed only by those to Isaiah (46) and the Gospels of Luke (43) and John (48), all many times longer, and of course to the Psalms (101), unique for variety of content and its place in the monastic office. These allusions to and quotations from the Song of Songs are interwoven with others to the marriage of the Lamb (Rev 19:7), Christ as the bridegroom (John 3:29), and the Gospel parables of the wedding feast (particularly Luke 12:36). The beautiful reflective chapter which opens Book 2 begins and ends with key quotations from the Song of Songs, enclosing the one from Luke 12:36 on the coming of the bridegroom. It is in Books 1 and 2, which present Wulfric's being rather than his doing, that these conjunct themes are mainly developed, although already in the first Prologue John speaks of Wulfric "reclining . . . at the great table of the Lamb's marriage feast," and at the end, as Wulfric waits for death, John has him running "to meet Christ coming from the wedding feast to fetch him to it" (3. 41).

Yet anyone looking for a foreshadowing in the *Life of Wulfric* of the later *Sermons on the Song of Songs* will be struck by the absence

[145] These passages, which could be claimed as the chief beauty of the book, are the very ones that later summarizers dropped in favor of "startling anecdotes" of the more lurid variety. See Bell, *Wulfric*, lxviii, who writes pertinently of John of Tynemouth: "He has given us everything that the historian does not want." One might add, "and the seeker after truth."

of wisdom as a developed theme.[146] Once only is the assimilation between Christ and Wisdom made, and then implicitly: as Wulfric winkles the rings off his hauberk with nimble fingers, John sees "God's wisdom graciously at play in her father's presence and as playfully bantering with the simplicity of her faithful people" (1. 10; Prov 8:30). Christ, the Father's wisdom, is presented here as condescending to simplicity, Wulfric's as well as his visitors', and herein lies the clue: the guiding thread of the *Life* is not divine wisdom but holy simplicity. Elsewhere wisdom appears personified only as a metaphor for Saint Bernard, seen as the mirror image of Wulfric's simplicity (2. 26). Simplicity being the theme, it is truth that becomes the touchstone, since John has need of truth as an absolute to authenticate his narrative; so while in the *Sermons* Christ is "wisdom itself,"[147] in the *Life* he is "truth itself," *ipsa veritas* (2. 27), and it is as Truth that the Bridegroom of the Song visits the soul of his beloved Wulfric. This melody, simpler and more linear, as is appropriate, than the full orchestration of the later Sermons, a melody which comes and goes only to return again, echoing the dynamic of the Song, gives to the *Life* its unity and meaning, and in John's eyes surely its true justification.

[146] On the place of wisdom in John's theology, see Hilary Costello, "John of Forde and the Quest for Wisdom," *Cîteaux, Commentarii Cistercienses* 23 (1972): 141–59.

[147] Costello, "John of Forde," 145.

TRANSLATOR'S NOTE

Providing a translation of the *Vita Wulfrici* has been complicated from the outset by the lack of the first essential: an authoritative text. The only edition to date, that of Dom Maurice Bell,[1] is not the reliable critical edition it aspires to be. In the absence of a good printed text, the translator is thrown back on the manuscripts, of which there are four extant, dating from the late twelfth and early thirteenth centuries. One is in the Cambridge University Library, catalogued as Add. mss. 3037, to be referred to as C; one is the Eton ms. 109 (E); two are in the British Library, Cotton Faustina B. iv (F) and Harleian 320 (H). The business of dating manuscripts and establishing the relationship between them, if there is more than one, falls properly to the editor and I shall not venture onto that ground. There is a new edition of the *Vita* in preparation in which these questions and others will be covered, and it is my hope that its publication will coincide approximately with that of the translation.

On discovering the limitations of Bell's edition, given as a redaction of the Eton ms., but closer in fact to a conflation of E and F, and made more confusing by the eccentric *apparatus criticus* which accompanies the text, I took the precaution of checking it against the manuscript it purported to reproduce. Since then, Dr. Keith Day, whose forthcoming critical edition is currently with Brepols, has generously allowed me to consult his redaction of C, which, in his well-argued view, is closer to John of Forde's original.

[1] *Wulfric of Haselbury, by John, Abbott of Ford* (London: Somerset Record Society 47, 1933), hereafter Bell.

It should be said that the differences between the two best mss., C and E, do not for the most part affect the work of translation. A large number are cosmetic: variations of spelling, or the placing of adjectives before or after their qualifying nouns, are irrelevant to the translator who will be taking other and greater liberties. There are those, however, which significantly affect the sense. So while keeping E as the basis of this translation, I have on a number of occasions used a divergent Cambridge reading where that gave a clearer ring of truth. These instances appear in the notes.

In this I have been guided by two seemingly contradictory aims: to start as close as possible to John's *ipsissima verba*, while yet avoiding too literal a translation where the text ends up sidetracked in a linguistic no-man's-land. The translator's skill is exercised in the attempt to integrate different and sometimes opposing fidelities: to the word and to the wider meaning. John was anxious not to bore his "listeners" or present them with something "insipid," and I have tried to ensure that his work continues to interest and engage today. Latin syntax is not that of modern English, so I have not been afraid on occasion to turn sentences back to front, if this resulted in a prose that ran more smoothly and was more convincing. With the same end in view, I have changed some punctuation and introduced paragraphs where the sense suggested them. At the same time I have respected to the very best of my ability every perceived nuance of John's text and where possible his use of repetition, alliteration, and other stylistic means to which he had recourse to render his work attractive and persuasive. It has been said of Saint Bernard that, when he entered Cîteaux, he gave up everything except the art of writing well.[2] John is not in the class of Saint Bernard; he was nonetheless a conscious stylist and could tell a lively story. As a translator, one hopes to please the reader, but still more one's author.

The scriptural references indicate the presence in John's narrative of a phrase from the Vulgate. These run the gamut from an unconscious or semiconscious reminiscence to an exact quotation.

[2] Étienne Gilson, *La théologie mystique de saint Bernard* (Paris:Vrin, 1934) 19.

Some of the more meditative passages are spun entirely out of threads from the Vulgate—loose quotations grammatically tweaked to tell a new tale, while they continue to sing their own accompaniment. John's familiarity with Scripture gave him a sense of total freedom in relation to it. He could take the verse from Lamentations, *videte si est dolor sicut dolor meus*, sung during Holy Week, and apply it, with a minor adjustment, to the pain of toothache. No monk would have read this without a wry smile. I have had to take similar freedoms to enable the narrative to flow in English; among them, recourse to various translations including at times my own, particularly in the Psalms, where there is a wide gap between the Vulgate and the original Hebrew on which modern translations are based. I have tried throughout to integrate the scriptural voice without losing it but am conscious that some echoes have been sacrificed to clarity, and anyone wishing to savor to the full this counterpoint should turn back to the Latin of the two originals. The reader may also find it helpful to follow up John's allusions if the text seems less than clear: a passing reference to the Song of Songs, transparent to his contemporaries, may be opaque today, particularly when it involves an unexpected change of sex, as when Wulfric, for example, mutates without warning into the *sponsa Christi* of the Canticle.

Specific problems of translation have been covered in the notes as they have arisen, but some, of a general or recurring nature, are perhaps best looked at in advance.

1. John refers relatively infrequently to Wulfric by name, and very rarely without the prefix *beatus*, although on a few occasions he uses instead the affectionate *noster*. His designation of predilection is *vir Dei*, man of God, followed by *vir sanctus*, holy man. I have followed John's practice in general, but not slavishly.
2. Some words are slippery in that they carry more than one meaning. Many words of course are translated now one way, now another according to context, but with words like *virtus*

and *salus* different meanings can subsist to some extent side by side, or one may be predominant and the other underlying.

3. *Virtus* is both "virtue" and "power"; at one end of the gamut the power can be naked and armed. In Wulfric the power is spiritual and therefore the meanings lie intimately conjoined; a translator accepts regretfully the need to choose.

4. *Salus* is another such word, where the meanings "salvation" and "health/healing" are comfortably twinned in Latin but in English impose a choice. Where there is physical illness the choice is clear, but whatever the context, the subsidiary meaning should always be held in the mind.

5. *Puer* can be age-related or class-related, and may be both. Wulfric's servants are likely to have been boys, particularly in the early years; we hear of one who larked about when running errands (3. 25), and one, termed *puer*, who is also said to be his only *minister*, and so, by inference, a boy. There is, however, one who robbed him extensively and was clearly a grown man, as were Godric's servants, whom Reginald of Durham refers to as *ministri, servi, famuli*. For Wulfric's servants, I have used alternately "servant," "boy," and "lad." For those of his benefactors, also called *puer*, "servant." Wulfric is God's servant—*servus*—but also Christ's *parvulus* and *puerulus*, his "little one." At one point John uses *servus* of both Wulfric and his servant in the same sentence as a form of wordplay.

6. *Vir potens* in the *Life* can be anything from a knight upwards; a magnate should logically be *potissimus*, but it is to William fitzWalter, who certainly was not, that John applies this superlative (3. 22). *Dives*—rich—is almost an equivalent, since wealth gave power, and land was the source of both. Women are more often called rich, as they rarely exercised power directly.

7. The Pauline opposites *caro–spiritus*, together with the corresponding adjectives *carnalis–spiritalis*, figure frequently in the *Life*. *Caro* is no longer automatically rendered in modern Bibles as "flesh." I have used sometimes "flesh," sometimes alternatives, as seemed best in the context.

THE LIFE OF BLESSED WULFRIC, ANCHORITE OF HASELBURY

WRITTEN BY THE VENERABLE JOHN, PRIOR OF FORDE

Letter to Bartholomew, bishop of Exeter

Letter to Baldwin, archbishop of Canterbury

BOOK 1

1. 25. How the cold water in his cell would be suddenly warmed
1. 26. Of a coverlet sent to him through a revelation
1. 27. How another revelation brought covering for a book
1. 28. How his scribe's carelessness got a prophet's chiding
1. 29. Of the monk who was cured of insomnia
1. 30. Of the mouse that died from a thoughtless curse

BOOK 2

2. 1. On keeping vigil
2. 2. Of the lamp that was relit
2. 3. How it happened again
2. 4. Of the candle which burned without being consumed
2. 5. Of the heavenly light which appeared as he prayed
2. 6. Of a similar consolation
2. 7. How water was changed into wine
2. 8. The same sign, yet somewhat different
2. 9. A third instance
2. 10. Of the bread and wine of heavenly provenance
2. 11. Of the loaf miraculously multiplied
2. 12. How he healed a virgin while she slept
2. 13. How a stolen loaf was made hard as stone
2. 14. Of the loaf which dripped blood
2. 15. Of the terrible death of the monk who was a thorn in his side
2. 16. Of a judgment on another defamer, his repentance and healing
2. 17. Of his hospitality and almsgiving
2. 18. Of praise for the Cistercians and some criticism too
2. 19. Of the sacrifice of the altar consecrated without water
2. 20. Of the conversion of Abbot Henry of Waverley which he foretold
2. 21. [Of Abbot Henry's way of life]
2. 22. Of some debts whose rapid resolution he foretold
2. 23. Of Abbot Henry's reverence for the man of God

2. 24. Of the schism under Pope Innocent to whom blessed Bernard lent support
2. 25. Of a fault of blessed Bernard's which the holy man expounded before it was told him and declared that it had been remitted
2. 26. Of the mutual embrace in which wisdom humbly accepted simplicity's bold rebuke
2. 27. Of Matilda, a recluse of Wareham, whose conversion, life, death, and future glory he foretold
2. 28. Of Matilda's patience
2. 29. How Matilda valiantly withstood the temptation of hunger

BOOK 3

3. 1. Of an instance of severity shown by blessed Wulfric
3. 2. Of signs in which healing and prophecy went hand in hand
3. 3. Of a demoniac cured on the road
3. 4. Of a lay-brother cured on the road
3. 5. Another tale of the same
3. 6. Of a priest who fell ill on the road and was healed on invoking him
3. 7. How a woman brought to him by a revelation was told its meaning and received healing
3. 8. Of the healing of Samson of Lincoln
3. 9. Of the staff that was blessed, lost at sea, and amazingly recovered
3. 10. Of the dumb man healed while he slept
3. 11. Of the monk whom he convicted of certain thoughts
3. 12. How he refused to show his face to men who had shown no kindness
3. 13. Of the woman to whom he prophesied that she was pregnant
3. 14. Of a chance remark which met with a jocular riposte
3. 15. How he healed a man whose eyes had been put out
3. 16. Of one who came late to mass
3. 17. Of the woman whose death he intimated mystically
3. 18. How he foretold the judgment of the Hiribelli

HERE BEGINS THE PROLOGUE[a] TO THE LIFE OF BLESSED WULFRIC, ANCHORITE, ADDRESSED BY THE VENERABLE JOHN, PRIOR OF FORDE, TO THE LORD BARTHOLOMEW,[b] BISHOP OF EXETER.

To the reverend father and lord Bartholomew, by God's grace bishop of Exeter, from brother John, Christ's poor man of Forde, yet his son by grace of adoption,[1] good days in full and blessed measure. Your deliberation and good pleasure, reverend father, that the life of blessed Wulfric should be set down in writing[c] for the glory of God and the profit of the faithful must surely be taken as a response from God, by the indubitable rule of faith whereby we trust the speaker as being himself the Beginning who also speaks to us,[2] courteously imparting to us by the word of his grace[3] the beginnings of all devout desires together with their continuance and happy outcomes. And blessed Wulfric did indeed deserve well of this world for his works of power, the benefit of healings, the message of salvation,[4] the unveiling of God's mysteries, and, what is better than all these, his example of outstanding holiness; for all these things the world is still in his debt. And yet it must wring pious hearts to hear that, although he was with us only yesterday, today it is as though he had never been,[5] and the venerable name of this most holy man, interred as it were with his ashes, still fails to figure on a tomb.

But what are these things to him? He is content to be remembered only in heaven, being as far removed from our wretched condition as he is above our thirst for fame; indeed, while he was still a sojourner among us, the world and all its glory[6] was trod-

[1] Rom 8:15.
[2] John 8:25.
[3] Acts 20:32.
[4] Acts 13:26.
[5] Job 10:19.
[6] Luke 12:27.

den beneath his feet.[7] What likelihood of him returning now to exalt the things he then held in contempt, and build up what he formerly knocked down?[8] Drunk on the stream of everlasting delight,[9] he does not crave our beggarly pleasures nor thirst for our water,[10] reclining as he now does at the great table of the Lamb's marriage feast.[11] Rather, his own hope now fulfilled, he gives us of his overflow and makes good our poverty out of his profusion. Nevertheless you will have done well in releasing the church from its debt and paying on her behalf a due of glory to God for his saint, it being entirely proper that God be thus glorified in his saints,[12] and expedient too for the church to glorify him in them, lest she be found ungrateful.

For the rest, since the treatment of so great a matter is too important to be left to the light-mindedness of youth, you decided to refer the business to the lord bishops of Worcester[d] and Bath.[e] This step was taken with all prudence and good sense, but your gravity weighs heavily on me and the measure, which indeed serves truth, works to my disadvantage. How so? Are not these eminent churchmen who are to be my judges also the judges of this world of ours? And when I come before the tribunal of their threefold authority, and they and the whole church with them fix their attention on my words, will not the light that is in me become darkness[13] in the brilliance of that light, and I perforce be left not only mute but looking foolish?

Nonetheless, such is my faith in the God of my mail-shirted saint, the Lord God of hosts,[14] that when I give my testimony to the truth before these kings I shall not be put to shame,[15] knowing who it was who said, "The truth will make you free."[16] The God whom I

[7] Ps 8:8.
[8] Job 12:14.
[9] Ps 35:9.
[10] John 4:13.
[11] Rev 19:7.
[12] 2 Thess 1:10.
[13] Matt 6:23.
[14] Isa 22:5.
[15] Ps 118:46.
[16] John 8:32.

serve in his saint is able[17] to change these judges into advocates and witnesses, so that every word about my Wulfric spoken by these three witnesses will stand.[18]

Stand, did I say? No, run, and run swiftly,[19] even to the very end of the earth.[20] Who will there be to tell me that these are bringing this gracious name before kings and gentiles and the sons of Israel[21] and giving it for an oath to God's elect?[22] How my eyes will rejoice should it ever befall me to see this modest little mountain raised up to Jesus Christ on the peaks of these three higher mountains,[23] that the Lord may be worshipped on his holy mountain[24] and from there answer our cry.[25]

But in the meantime it seems to me that I would be best advised to send to yourself, as one of those judges, my case to be prepared: particularly since the work is yours, undertaken at your wish, finished under pressure from you, embellished by your title, and sealed with your authority. Who would hesitate to lean on your name? More, who would dare to take from you what you have such manifold claims to? Receive therefore that which is not mine but yours, or, rather, held in common with Christ and all who are in Christ,[26] and, by that standard of freedom and equity which you have customarily applied in other cases, adjudicate mine too. I want you, as an incorruptible judge, to demand a reckoning of every idle word. Let your eye spare nothing now, nor show any pity,[27] so that mercy may be mine on the impending day of judgment: the judgment day, that is, of the human race. For I do not want whatever crumbs of glory I

[17] Matt 3:9.
[18] Matt 18:16.
[19] Ps 147:15.
[20] Acts 1:8.
[21] Acts 9:15.
[22] Isa 65:15.
[23] Isa 2:2.
[24] Ps 98:9.
[25] Ps 3:5.
[26] Acts 4:32.
[27] Ezek 16:5.

may hope for from this trifling work to be handed out to me here and now; better that I should wait in silence till that day of days.[28]

Lastly, to Him in whom is stored up the reward of all good works I commend this paltry deposit of mine, lest perchance the spirit of vanity should blow on it and bring my glory down to dust. The grace of our Lord Jesus Christ be with all who listen to these things in a religious spirit. Farewell.

Here begins another to the lord Baldwin, archbishop of Canterbury

To the most reverend lord and very dear father in Christ, Baldwin, by God's grace archbishop of Canterbury and primate of all England, from brother John, Christ's poor man of Forde, the spirit of counsel and fortitude.[29] The little work about the life of the blessed man Wulfric, brought forth as given from above[30] and also amended, cannot in my opinion be better sent for testing, nor, once proven, dedicated to another than yourself. No judgment of it will be more discriminating than yours, whether in its reasoning or in the authority of its verdict. I know that in this book I have tried to avoid the disfigurement of falsehood, and trust that I have also escaped it, insofar as in a matter of this sort, which rested more on the testimony of faithful men than on the power of reason, truth has been able to guide and evaluate itself. As for the fruit of the work, God, the Judge,[31] will make provision as best pleases him; for I am confident that I have taken my principal purpose—devout most surely and sincere—from blessed Wulfric's own devotion: namely, to glorify God and build up the church; also to offer her saint, well-nigh forgotten like one who is dead,[32] to her lips and teeth for rumination.[33a] For who, not lacking all religious feeling, could hear without both marveling and groaning how such a man,

[28] Lam 3:26.
[29] Isa 11:2.
[30] John 19:11.
[31] Judg 11:27.
[32] Ps 30:13.
[33] Song 7:9.

who in his day was in name and in glory[34] a sign and example to the church of God, has almost vanished from human memory, and how that sacred head, the vessel of such great virtues, to this day dishonored and exposed to the common lot, has lain sleeping in base dust? Although this matter has moved me long and deeply, and piety, with its undertone of grief, urged me to break the invidious silence, I have subdued these pricks of zeal till wish and piety should be confirmed by authority and rule. Then the late revered bishop of Exeter, consulted by the lord abbot,**[b]** not only approved my wish but gave fresh impetus and guidance; he even promised to put the finishing touch to the work himself before referring the whole to you for a final examination. But the bishop, destined for life everlasting, was released from human concerns before the matter could be seen through as agreed. You, though, live on and have no choice but to honor the debt laid on you by that good father.

However, the subject in and of itself has a better and more felicitous reason for calling upon your name (or rather submitting itself to your honor without your even being aware of it), since the Lord has so ordained it that whatever the English church possesses of virtue or of grace belongs in your treasure-vaults. All the glory of the king's daughter,[35] whether blazing inwardly for God, or outwardly lighting up the world, is your glory, so long as you also glory in the Lord.[36] Whether it be the most blessed Thomas, his purple newly conferred and freshly tapped again from his very veins;[37c] or blessed William of York,**[d]** he, too, illustrious in northern parts; or blessed Wulfric and Godric,**[e]** men honored and held dear for their simplicity, all things are yours and you are Christ's.[38] Yes, our age has this by no means paltry comfort: a veil to cover its nakedness and spare it further shame in the eyes of an earlier generation, that of the ancient fathers; for God has blessed us and our days are not empty[39] nor our land barren. I have said too little: we have that in

[34] Jer 13:11.
[35] Ps 44:14.
[36] 1 Cor 1:31.
[37] Song 7:5.
[38] 1 Cor 3:23.
[39] Job 7:3.

which we may positively glory with our fathers, because here and now the branch of the Lord is beautiful and glorious and the fruit of the land is our pride.[40] Here and now, say I, the mountains drip sweetness[41] just as in those former times; if only there were also valleys to receive it! If only in our days and regions some could be found who did not disdain to open their mouths to the refreshing drops that flow from the eternal hills. But if a soul loathes[42] the word of truth, if someone stuck up and fastidious fancies he can sniff at manna, profane holy things, trample on pearls and honey-combs, even if I keep silent, he has one who will judge him.[43]

To ward off people of this pernicious species I am compelled to use the cover of your protection, or at least to invoke it and thus weight my words with fear, lest they presume to profane, dishonor, and abase the sacred tokens I present to you and, if it please you, entrust to your keeping. And not only that: do you yourself accept these offerings with the reverence and honor due to them and not unfitting to yourself, and having taken them, embrace them and hide them in your heart like a sweet-scented bundle, a bundle of myrrh. Lastly, if something should need cutting, let it be corrected after free and fair examination. I shall profess myself well done by, should my judgment issue from yourself, indeed should anything at all of mine deserve to feel the file of your correction and abridgement. Although, of course, I have no need to trouble myself further with these matters, since this is no longer my affair but yours and that of the church entrusted to your care. What was mine I have made wholly yours, transferring it to you: henceforward do as you want with it, or rather as the wisdom given you by God may dictate. May your holy fatherhood flourish in the Lord.

[40] Isa 4:2.
[41] Joel 3:18.
[42] Num 21:5.
[43] John 12:48.

HERE BEGINS THE LIFE OF BLESSED WULFRIC, ANCHORITE OF HASELBURY,

WRITTEN BY THE VENERABLE JOHN, PRIOR OF FORDE

1. 1. Of his calling and conversion

Blessed Wulfric, a man of modest English stock, was born, reared, and lived in Compton,[a] a village eight miles from Bristol, where he also served for several years as priest. He was ordained when still a youngster, well below the usual age, and more, it is thought, out of shallow immaturity than from any spiritual desire, as one who did not yet know the Lord[44] and was activated more by the natural self than by the spirit. As priest he certainly did not abstain from hunting and hawking, and prior to his calling spent his time among people in thrall to worldly vanities; but by the breath of God's grace these bonds were loosed in a trice.[b] For out of the blue one day while he was thus engaged, soldiering energetically in this lunatic pursuit of his, a fellow appeared—a poor man by his dress and aspect—who begged him meekly for a new coin. There was a fresh minting in England then, in the days of King Henry I, but being new the coins were still uncommon. When Wulfric replied that he did not know whether he had a new coin about him, the other said: "Look in your purse and you'll find tuppence halfpenny there."[c] Left speechless by this reply, he searched in his pouch and, finding just what the other had said, devoutly offered what was being asked.

This was the beginning of the grace[45] which God dispensed to his beloved Wulfric as a foretaste of the blessings of his sweetness,[46] having seen and singled him out like another Nathanael under the fig tree.[47] There is good reason to believe that this stranger was an angel of the Lord, pointing towards the new man[48] he was asking for in terms of a new currency. Certainly Wulfric himself, hark-

[44] 1 Sam 3:7.
[45] John 2:11.
[46] Ps 20:4.
[47] John 1:48.
[48] Eph 4:24.

ing back later to this story, used to say: "He was no man, for all he seemed one." In the end, what the one had been asking and the other giving was made plain when the stranger took the coin he had requested with the words: "He for whose love you did this will repay you. And I in his name foretell to you that soon you will leave this place for another, and thence you will move shortly after to a third; there at length you will find rest and in a narrower dwelling-place persevere with God to the end; and thus at the last you will be called to join the company of the saints."

All this took place in a village called Deverill,[d] where God's holy man first exercised his priestly office. Holy thus far by predestination only, but from then on properly so called; for the God who was calling him breathed into his nostrils the breath of life,[49] and by ways and means known to himself gradually kindled in his new creation[50] a hatred of iniquity,[51] a contempt for vanity, and a love of truth and of the highest good. Recalled not long after to serve as priest in his birthplace by its lord, the well-respected William,[e] he became one of his familiars, eating always at his table. Such members of that household as are still alive bear witness to this day to the resolution with which he girded his loins[52] and seized on the virtue of abstinence with total commitment, eating no meat whatever, save when respect for his table companions required it, some of whom he had to humor. Just as the light which rose in the darkness went on gleaming in its midst,[53] so bright tokens of holiness spoke of the plenitude in Christ which was to come. For the blessed man, who aspired now with his whole heart after solitude and purity of life, made these his own in that very hall—even on feast days, which was yet more remarkable, being harder; and as he prepared to leave Egypt he was already girding his loins[54] and eating the Passover lamb—in other words innocence and holiness—in Egypt itself.

[49] Gen 2:7.
[50] 2 Cor 5:17.
[51] Ps 118:163.
[52] Prov 31:17.
[53] Isa 58:10; See John 1:5.
[54] Exod 12:11.

Meanwhile he worried away about bringing to birth the purposes he had conceived through the Holy Spirit and had for some time been carrying within him, and was held back, as often happens with those striving after higher things, by doubts about which form of religious life would best nurture his brood of aspirations. But here too the Lord came to his help and pointed the way. Under the guidance of the Holy Spirit, and counseled and assisted by the knight just mentioned, he moved to another village of his called Haselbury, some thirty miles east of Exeter. There in a cell abutting on the church, which had been empty for some time, and without the usual induction by the bishop and no solemn blessing,[f] but only the inward authority of the Holy Spirit, he buried himself with Christ,[55] shortly to be transformed with him in a sort of resurrection glory: in newness of life,[56] in cheerfulness of spirit, in the power of signs,[57] in the grace of prophecy. But all this was attained at the cost of much toil and sweat,[58] with great affliction of body and spirit, and with God's grace going before.

1. 2. Of the grace of the inner man

And so the man of God, having entered into the rock to hide from the face of the Lord and the glory of his majesty,[59] began to build for himself an inner solitude, straining to penetrate to the hiddenness of that face[60] as to a still farther solitude, and, panting with open mouth, to draw the Holy Spirit[61] into the very depths of his being. Otherwise, to condemn the body to such close confinement while leaving the soul outside, as is the way of some, is a deplorable folly. Solitude of that sort is the shadow of the Old Covenant,[a] not the truth. That was not blessed Wulfric's way, indeed not.[62]

[55] Rom 6:4.
[56] Rom 6:4.
[57] Rom 15:19.
[58] Ezek 24:12.
[59] Isa 2:10; See Exod 33:22.
[60] Ps 30:21.
[61] Ps 118:131.
[62] Ps 1:4.

On the contrary he began to feel he had found a vast space within these narrow bounds, allowing him to realize, the more freely for the privacy he had, all that he had conceived: to covet the things of heaven, strive after the spiritual and meditate day and night on the law of God.[63] Nor was the true manna from heaven lacking to this true solitary, for God in his kindness and bounty was ever preparing and raining it down on his needy servant.[64] For since he sought the Lord in truth, he deserved to find him faithful, as the truth is in Jesus,[65] and with the Holy Spirit to interpret and bear witness to the truth,[66] he made full and faithful trial of the hundredfold promise,[67] and of the water welling up to eternal life.[68] And the Lord gave his saint the choice gift of faith to quench all the flaming darts of the evil one,[69] because he was of a trusting spirit, looking to God in confidence and leaning on him in any and every need. Indeed, with a special tenderness and intimacy of love, he called the Lord God his Lord in his native tongue. This purity of faith was refined, and one might say overlaid with gold, by a certain holy and sincere simplicity which had been his from his mother's womb,[70] but by the sanctification of the Holy Spirit this gift of nature was made a gift of grace. For it was through this loyalty and gentleness of his that the Lord made him holy,[71] so that the grandeur of faith might be tempered by the humble simplicity engrafted on it, and that in the distribution of graces the second might be shored up by the first, the first hidden and safeguarded in the other.

As regards his inner life and how far it is licit to peer through the keyhole into the holy of holies, I have touched on these matters rather than followed them through, leaving the rest to that

[63] Ps 1:2.
[64] Ps 67:11.
[65] Eph 4:21.
[66] John 5:33; See Acts 14:3.
[67] Matt 19:29.
[68] John 4:14.
[69] Eph 6:16.
[70] Job 31:18.
[71] Sir 45:4.

advocate from whom nothing is hidden, not even what is behind the veil,[72] and for whom not a hair can fall from the bride's head,[73] which does not receive from him its meed of praise. My share of homage—if I am found worthy of paying it—is to loosen the strap of his sandals,[74] or, more exactly, to show how graceful were the sandaled steps of the king's daughter,[75] that is, to give a faithful account of what was worthy of wonder in his outward being and doing, both at the outset and as he progressed.

1. 3. Of the outset of his new life and the rigor of his abstinence

And so blessed Wulfric, having entered on the terrain of more open warfare, began to act boldly[76] in the power of his God and waited with high courage for the assault of him who is as prompt as he is practiced at countering the success of zeal; indeed the saint actively incited and challenged him to battle. He started by mortifying what was earthly in him[77] with strict fasting, straining and striving to wring out all natural comeliness and restore to himself the beauty of holiness through extremes of abstinence and watching. And indeed the bloom of youth and, speaking in human terms, good looks that passed the ordinary, were dried up in no time at all as the breath of the Lord, blowing on him,[78] blew it all away, until, with the skin barely clinging to his bones,[79 a] the wasted flesh bodied forth no longer the carnal man, but the spiritual. It was oatmeal bread and porage, also made of oats, that formed his choicest fare, though even these this most frugal of men picked at rather than ate, to the point where his servant swore that he carried much of it away in the state in which he had brought it. Like

[72] Song 4:1.
[73] Luke 21:18; See Acts 27:34.
[74] John 1:27.
[75] Song 7:1.
[76] Acts 14:3.
[77] Col 3:5.
[78] Isa 40:7.
[79] Ps 101:6.

one of the Lord's Nazarites[80] he refused to touch wine or ale or any strong or intoxicating drink, except on major feast days, when he would take some wine if it was offered, but more in honor of the feast than to reinvigorate the body. Moreover, in case all this should cause his strength to fail him (or rather, so that it might ebb slowly by degrees, as though he were left hanging on a cross), he drank a sort of beverage which we call "bersisa,"[b] lest either his simplicity or his zeal (each of which is very liable to be led astray and Wulfric had in the highest degree both these qualities which belong to the more perfect). . . .[c]

1. 4. Of his watches and his bed

That his diligence in watching was total and tireless was known to those who kept a searching eye on him, and he himself, when asked by some of his closest friends, confessed in all simplicity to spending entirely sleepless nights, except for the occasional brief nap to which human weakness now and then drove him. This catnap he would take, or better, snatch or nibble at, not in bed, but with his head leaning against the wall or elbow propped on the altar step; then, waking as though he had done some wrong, he went straight back to the common round, stronger for the break.

At other times during the day, after taking some refreshment, he would pay what was owing to nature in the matter of sleep, but parsimoniously, as with dues meted out by weight and measure.[81a] Such sleep he took in bed: but the bed in question was a place of torment rather than rest, being made of branches interwoven to form a wattle hurdle, which turned him, as its maker, into the murderer of his own body. However, on the order of Robert, the late revered bishop of Bath,[b] and with his senses already disciplined and old age advancing, he tempered this racking to some extent, lest he be thought either ignorant of the spiritual good of obedience or not to have learned by experience that it is better than sacrifice.[82]

[80] Num 6:2-5.
[81] Wis 11:21.
[82] 1 Sam 15:22.

He accustomed himself too to supporting his head on a bolster stuffed with hay, but the bishop, far from obtaining this relaxation of discipline by request, had to extort it by virtue of obedience.

1. 5. Of rough clothing and cold baths

Again, he contented himself with simple clothing over a clinging hair shirt. But it was not long before habit hardened him to the latter's use and he began to hanker after a shirt of mail. The knight mentioned earlier, made aware of his desire, fell in reverentially with the holy man's bold wish, hoping to win a share in the triumph by supplying the warrior with his armor. He handed over his own hauberk, as to a mightier knight than he, and dedicated this piece of military equipment to heaven's recruit. And so the soldier newly harnessed advanced to the spiritual battle, and having changed the arms of the world into weapons of righteousness[83] became a source of terror to his foes. Thus armed and armored did he fight by day.[a] At night he plunged himself cold and naked in a tub filled with cold water and there, like Christ's little slave-boy, would offer to the Lord the psalms of David from start to finish, singing to him with drum and psaltery.[84b]

After each new baptism he bloomed afresh with a beauty of innocence in which there was nothing base, and, like a flock of shorn ewes that have come up from the washing,[85] emerged from the water whiter than milk. Putting back on his shirts of hair and mail (noble both, but the second emphatically nobler), he spent the rest of the night office, cheerful and devout, in hymns and prayers punctuated with frequent genuflections. For a long time this enthusiast for God persevered with tireless vigor and rigor in that harsh discipline, dousing the stimulus of the flesh, in his case acute, in the mighty waters.[86]

[83] Rom 6:13.
[84] Ps 149:3.
[85] Song 4:2.
[86] Exod 15:10.

1. 6. Of the devil's snake-bite

While a passion[a] as relentless as hell[87] was thus contending in the cause of chastity with more mettle than prudence, up in the heavens a kite knew its time[88] for tempting and desiring and taking possession of the man of God. One night when he was getting out of the vat as usual and brushing off the water with his hand, he found a snake hanging from his thigh.[89] Seized with fear, the holy man grabbed hold of it, pulled it off, and flung it to the ground. Examining it by the light of the lamp, he saw the body lying headless, a development that left him stupefied with terror. On coming back to himself he vomited with much retching all the venom which that poisonous snake had squirted in, and healing thus the wounds he had received he was soon restored to health. But as long as he lived he bore in his flesh the reminder of this event and would show to those he knew well the scars of the wounds which the venom-bearing teeth had sunk in him, as though they were the stigmata of Christ's passion[90] and his own battle honors.

So it was that excess of zeal was reined back and brought within the limits of discretion, while the holy man learned that the purity striven after was more to be looked for from the grace of God than won through intemperate physical training.[91] And so, released by heaven from a form of choice—and chosen[b]—torment, he turned more readily to other spiritual exercises and compensated richly for the harm done by the earlier warfare with the great benefits of that godliness which avails in every way.[92]

1. 7. Of the grace and freedom of his conversation

Let me say something about how he appeared to others: when called out to converse, he presented himself very graciously like a

[87] Song 8:6.
[88] Jer 8:7.
[89] Acts 28:3-5.
[90] Gal 6:17.
[91] 1 Tim 4:8.
[92] 1 Tim 4:8.

bridegroom coming from his chamber,[93] and, drawing as it were on a well-stocked pantry, proffered spiritual counsel filled with authority and grace.[94] As his knowledge of divine letters was not great, it was out of that sanctuary of God, his own heart, that he brought forth living words, inasmuch as the Lord's anointing was teaching him everything.[95] His precepts, like loaves fresh from the oven, were potent with his grace and virtue,[96] and to those who heard them they gave off a delicious smell,[97] redolent of heavenly purity and delightful simplicity of heart.

Moreover, when talking he was no respecter of persons, but contented himself with calling any and everyone by their plain name,[a] omitting, whether by design or artlessness, the styles and titles of the great. Worshipper of God alone and lover of simplicity and truth, he would not or could not worship men; on the contrary, by robbing the great princes—kings even—who visited him, of the glory of deceptive designations, he tacitly told them that they were but men.[98] And this was a good opportunity for teaching those who carried more than the usual weight of worldly success and fawning plaudits: disburdened, at least for an hour, by the lover of truth, they saw themselves plain in that clearest of mirrors. He rebuked the powerful, whoever they were, with as complete a freedom as when he took the visiting King Stephen severely to task for seeming to carry the sword in vain—in that being more easy-going and lenient than was right he failed to execute judgment and justice in the land.[99b]

[93] Ps 18:6.
[94] John 1:14.
[95] 1 John 2:27.
[96] Ps 102:20.
[97] Ezek 16:19.
[98] Ps 9:21.
[99] Jer 23:5.

1. 8. Of his striving after silence

Very sparing of words, he was well able to exercise self-control in speaking[100] and place his hand over his mouth,[101] to the point where even religious men were given brief access to his plenty. Having dealt succinctly with the business he had been called out about, as soon as he felt his interlocutor sliding to other matters, he would shut the window and retire inside his cell. So just as one thought one held him fast, the lover of solitude would slip from one's grasp and, like some angelic vision, vanish as suddenly as he had come. To the worldly minded this may perhaps have rendered him less human, but the spiritually aware will have wholly forgiven one called back by an inward fragrance,[102] drawn irresistibly, yet so delightfully, by its sacred and secret rapture. None of this, in a word, will surprise those found worthy of being brought into the king's chambers[103] and who have heard the bridegroom's zealous concern and urgent pleas for the quiet of the bride.[104] May all those who have devoted themselves to the spiritual life be roused to greater fervor by such depths of charity in the Word of God and such heights of virtue in the man of God, and not readily entrust for long to human eyes that face which Christ so ardently desires for himself. I have no regrets at having introduced this topic: it may remind some members of our order to go out more rarely and for graver reasons, and when they do, to conduct themselves with greater discretion and reverence.

1. 9. Of the cutting of the hauberk[a]

It was around this time that Wulfric, beloved of God, first won renown in the world through a manifestation of the power of the spirit. Known until then to God alone, he broke like a new and saving dawn on the consciousness of humankind. It happened like this:

[100] Prov 25:28.
[101] Wis 8:12.
[102] Song 1:3.
[103] Song 1:3.
[104] Song 2:7.

as the mail shirt he had donned to do battle in God's cause slapped heavily against his knees, impeding the rhythm of his genuflections, he sent for the knight, his aider and abettor in this warfare, and discussed with him the excessive length of the hauberk. "It can be sent to London," suggested the knight, "and cut back to whatever measurement you specify." "That would involve a lot of bother and delay," replied the saint. "Besides, one couldn't avoid the danger of ostentation." The knight tried again: "Well, look," he said, "Exeter is near: it can be sent there if you say so." "There is no need. Just take the shears yourself and do the job with your own hands, now, in the presence of God." The other, flabbergasted, was looking at Wulfric as though he were mad, when he was struck by a divinely inspired thought: Wulfric, he said to himself, cannot be deceived, nor yet want to deceive. And so the holy man, strengthening the faith of the wavering knight with words of faith from his own rich store, handed him the shears which had been fetched from the latter's house, and having run a thread through the links of the mail to mark the limit of the resection, he laid the shirt across the windowsill in front of him. To the knight, still hanging back and muttering to himself about the outlandishness of the task—and it was indeed something weird and wonderful he was being asked to set his hand to—the other said: "Take courage[105] and see that you stay calm. Look, I am going to pray to my God about this matter; as for you, just get on with the job in faith."

Accordingly the soldiers both set to, one to prayer, and the other to cutting, and the work prospered in their hands.[106] The knight had the impression he was cutting not steel but stuff, so easily did the shears run through the now yielding metal. But before the work was finished, the saint left off his prayer, and the knight too had to stop his cutting. The shears had been driven by the power of prayer, and when it ceased they sensed at once and refused to respond any longer to the knight's pressure. When he squeezed still harder, the iron broke in his hand, although not right through. At that moment the holy man returned from prayer and asked how

[105] Acts 23:11.
[106] 1 Macc 2:47.

the work was going. "Well, until now," said the knight, "but just as you came back, the shears broke and seized up." "Don't let this upset you," said the other, "take up the shears again and finish the job begun in the power of faith[107] you had before." So the knight, having recovered his firm faith in the word of power, completed the task with similar ease. This was the first of the signs blessed Wulfric worked:[108] itself a potent commendation of the power of God and of his own faith realized through the medium of another man.

1. 10. Of how he would detach the rings

The working of this great sign was celebrated with due honor far and wide. Meanwhile the mail shirt he had donned out of a wonderful zeal for the love of God, and had then cut by a marvellous power of faith, he was now proceeding to share out among his visitors as a remedy for their various ailments. With no less simplicity and faith, and without recourse to shears, he would winkle the links one from another, the Holy Spirit giving such skill to his fingers that no sign of a scratch was left on any. The unravelling took neither toil nor time, each link remaining entire and the parting being effected with a wonderful and divine facility.[a] The matter was momentous, yet he gave the impression of someone at play, or even performing conjuring tricks, as, while doing divine violence to the shirt, he innocently pilfered its links in a kind of spiritual thieving. And truly in her servant's fingers God's wisdom was graciously at play in her father's presence[109] and as playfully bantering with the simplicity of her faithful people, a simplicity which has learned, as regards the mysteries of faith, to be content with faith alone and pure.

This ritual eventually became such a matter of course to the man of God that he seemed to have it not so much to hand, as the expression goes, as at his fingers' ends, so that by overdoing this miracle he almost did away with admiration. Not that there

[107] 2 Thess 1:11.
[108] John 2:11.
[109] Prov 8:30-31.

was anything that envy or disbelief could possibly misrepresent, since the fact that it was done openly meant that the watchers had to believe their own eyes, while daily reenactments renewed the truth and added to the power. And still to this day these rings can be found throughout the district in the keeping of the pious who treasure them as a gift—a testimony to holiness or a guarantee of health—either way a sacred and sure deposit.

So much I had from Brother William,[b] the hospitaller of Forde, and Dom Walter,[c] a monk of Glastonbury, not to mention others whom it would take too long to name. Some accounts of the cutting of the hauberk and other matters appear to vary, but the differences are merely circumstantial. I think, however, that after long scrutiny and from what I believe to be the more dependable testimony of proven honesty and age, I have got hold of the truth. As for what follows, it was told me by Brother Joseph, a man no less trustworthy and advanced in years and an intimate of the man of God in his lifetime, and he in turn was repeating what he had heard from the venerable Brihtric.[d]

1. 11. Of a foreglimpse of signs in a dream

Around that time the man of God had a vision, as follows. It seemed to him that he was sitting in the outer cell, with a receptacle full of oil in his hand, and suddenly Jesus was present with all the blessed company of apostles, and Peter, their leader, said to him urgently: "Look! Here is the Lord. Get up, make haste and follow us." He jumped up at once and, impatient of any check to his ardent desire to follow, with a brusque gesture let fall the receptacle he was holding, spilling the oil down his clothing and onto the floor.

He revolved this dream long and often in his mind, opening it to many unable to interpret it, until finally there came a certain Robert, surnamed Pullus,[a] who later—doubly fitted to the office by his life and learning—was made chancellor of the city of Rome, a high position which he filled to admiration. He was the one to provide an interpretation consistent with the vision, saying: "God has appointed this place to be glorified through you by the grace of healings and the working of signs: this is the oil poured out by your own hand in this spot and on your clothes." And the dream was indeed true and its interpretation sure,[110] for from then on the hand of the Lord was upon the man of his right hand[111]—were it in acts of healing, in the casting out of demons, or the telling and foretelling of the mysteries of God. And through all this, as much in grace and holiness as through the wonder of miracles, he showed himself an apostolic man.

So it was that, just as his interpreter foretold, he was inwardly filled by the Holy Spirit like a vessel brimming and spilling over, so that his name might be, at God's call, an oil poured out.[112] From then on men and women of every kind started to flow towards him, not just from round about but from great distances, led there by a variety of reasons ranging from a hoped-for grace of healing to a reverence for holiness. The fragrance of the prophetical gift drew some: these came to see, to speak with, and to hear the words of a man with the spirit of prophecy, through him to question the Lord directly, and to consult him about the dark uncertainties of things they had to bear.

Amidst all this the man of God stood filled with such humility and so grounded in simplicity, that, the more remarkable the signs, the more firmly he cleaved to the truth, counting the signs for nothing. This passionate lover of evangelical humility shook from his hands every tribute of human praise, and strictly charged those who experienced the grace God worked through him to tell no one.[113] Thus does God, who gives glory to the humble, go out to meet humility on the way.

1. 12. How he healed a demoniac and was given authority to speak of his own powers

Among the first to come in hope of the grace of healing was a certain demoniac, brought by others; him the man of God ordered

[110] Dan 2:45.
[111] Ps 79:18.
[112] Song 1:2.
[113] Mark 7:36.

to stand at the back[a] while he said mass, so that the unclean spirit might be blown away by the sight of the sacred elements and by hearing the words of power. But the man possessed was plunged into sleep where he stood by his evil invader, who effectively stopped his ears, so that like the deaf adder he might not hear the voice of the charmers.[114] And as our charmer was still unskilled from lack of practice in these matters, the spirit used this wile to make repeated sport with his simplicity, until at last the power of exorcism in the name of Father, Son, and Holy Spirit inhibited it and it left.

Afterwards the saint insisted again and again, both to the man who had been delivered and to those who were taking him—or more correctly now accompanying him—home, that they must at all costs hold their tongues about the words spoken. And this was done. But once the party had gone their way, a heaven-sent sleep fell on the man of God, and he saw a figure of venerable aspect standing in front of him, who said: "What were you trying to do by forbidding those men to proclaim the works of the Lord?[115] Take care not to do it again, but speak confidently of the works of power the Lord will do through you, and bid others do the same." So the man of God, on awaking, lost no time in obeying this vision and command from heaven, but sent his servant hurrying after them with the message: "As to what I told you, don't keep quiet. On the contrary you must declare to everyone everywhere the glory of God that you saw and experienced." From then on the man of God spoke out, as though sent by the Holy Spirit,[116] and recounted freely yet humbly the works the Lord performed through him, albeit only to religious ears.

1. 13. Of his deeply rooted humility

We need at this point to consider more deeply how great in the Lord's sight must have been the humility whose burden of glory

[114] Ps 57:5-6.
[115] Sir 18:2.
[116] Acts 13:4.

was judged to be not for private bearing only but worthy of exposure to public view and hearing. Certainly, to be adorned with virtues is in itself a noble virtue, but the virtue of virtues is not to be weakened by the virtue and oppressed by one's own praises, or at least not crushed by them. A woman in whom the heart of her husband trusts,[117] to the extent that he hands over stewardship to her, so great is his confidence, is properly termed strong. And strong, too, are those who are prompted by the Holy Spirit in the midst of all this honor to glory not in it, nor in themselves, but in the Lord.[118]

I say this much because of a general surprise that the man of God did not keep silent about his own works, these being matters about which one should utter nothing or next to nothing,[119] as it is both unseemly and highly dangerous to sing one's own praises. But such critics have perhaps failed to note either the intimate command of the Holy Spirit, or those qualities which blessed Wulfric had in so singular a degree and which freed him from all trace of pride and boastfulness, namely, simplicity and truthfulness in all their purity. Children in their simplicity are, as we know, left free to speak their minds without restraint, and bodies still immature may display their nakedness unblushingly. And clearly this man too, child that he was, spoke like a child, thought like a child, and reasoned like a child,[120] setting no value on these phenomena, nor on himself in relation to them, quite unconscious as he was of being revered. Hence, since to him they were not acts of power but trifling matters without significance, he recounted them to the holy-minded with the simplest of smiles, so that unadorned truth took away every suspicion of boasting.

What is more, the very artlessness of his admissions lends no small weight to the credibility of what took place; for if we accept human testimony,[121] no witness should be more acceptable than he, for none could be more faithful. We know that even if

[117] Prov 31:10-11.
[118] 1 Cor 1:31.
[119] 2 Cor 12:4.
[120] 1 Cor 13:11.
[121] 1 John 5:9.

he does bear witness to himself, his testimony is true,[122] for it is not he alone[123]—truth itself gives him from heaven a testimony greater than that of John.[124] It follows that those who heard these things from his lips, those who were found worthy of his friendship, are for us most trustworthy witnesses to what happened, as we have confidence in the Lord concerning them,[125] whose words can safely be taken as settling contention and establishing the truth. We unfold for the benefit of the faithful the tale commended to us, and with the same faithfulness with which it was passed down; and honoring as we do the footprints[126] of the holy man, may we strive first and foremost to maintain his reverence for the truth. It were better to have kept silence than to let that very truth, while in our hands and with our conscience as witness, be jeopardized in even the least degree.

1.14. Of a dumb man cured and an argument with Brihtric[a]

Among his friends and closest of all to the holy man was Brother William, the lay-brother hospitaller of Forde. A man of the highest general repute, but in our opinion highest of all in that, having spurned in the very flower of his youth the pomp of the king's court, he reigns prosperously to this day in the poverty of Christ. Once he had clasped Brother William closely to his heart and was loved as greatly in return, the man of God held absolutely nothing back from him, clearly deeming him worthy to be let into his chambers[127] and made privy to his hidden treasures.[128] He would discuss with him such matters as the mysteries of God's kingdom[129] and the blessed hope of the saints, how graciously God's mercy

[122] John 8:14.
[123] John 8:16.
[124] John 5:36.
[125] 2 Thess 3:4.
[126] Isa 60:14.
[127] Song 1:3.
[128] Isa 45:3.
[129] Mark 4:11.

had gone before him[130] and how favorably followed after—spiritual things to the spiritual, matching the subject to the man.[131]

One day Brother William called on him as was his habit and asked him how he was: "I am well," he replied, "except that our priest Brihtric has exasperated me with his reproaches, and has wasted the day so far in quarrelling." "Whatever could have provoked so mild a man to anger, above all with you?" "A dumb man was brought to me," he replied, "and I prayed to my Lord for him and laid my hand on him, whereupon the man spoke properly and without impediment, not only in English but in French as well. This upset the priest so much he couldn't contain himself for indignation and went for me in a burst of anger,[132] saying: "Look, I have served you all these years,[133] and today I've proved plainly that it's been a waste of time. It would have been enough to loosen this stranger's tongue so that he could speak; instead you have kindly provided him with a double function for it. You have never given me the use of French, and when I come before the bishop[b] and the archdeacon I have to stand as mum as any mute." Brother William laughed at this, and he in turn made the miracle, played down lightheartedly, merrier still at his retellings.

1.15. Of the Curing of Another Dumb Man[a]

A not dissimilar cure is said to have been worked by the man of power on another mute. This fellow came to him from the castle of Bampton,[b] not brought by a stranger, but of his own accord in a group, and when the others left after receiving a blessing, this man stayed behind and presented himself to the man of God to be blessed. It happened that, as the saint was making the sign of the cross on the mute's face, the latter opened his mouth wide and the saint touched the back of his tongue, which he was sticking out as far as he could, and loosed it, all unknowing. The man went

[130] Ps 58:11.
[131] 1 Cor 2:13.
[132] Ps 47:8.
[133] Luke 15:29.

joyfully back to his fellows, no longer mere companions but seized on as witnesses of the wonderful—whether as power or joy. With happiness for spur they set off at once for home, singing now with full hearts in the ways of the Lord, for great is the glory of the Lord.[134] Entering his family home, he hailed them all with his new voice, scattering new and thankful greetings everywhere he went. Questions about what had happened gave him plenty of exercise for his newly loosened tongue. Again and again he opened his mouth to repeat the same story but could hardly satisfy his avid listeners, and the tongue that was now bearing witness to itself more than made up for its long silence. But when at last they asked him if he had given glory to God in the presence of his saint for the great grace received, he admitted not having thought of it: in the excess of joy, he had quite forgotten to give thanks. His friends gave him some wise advice and sent him back to his healer to apologize to him for his ingratitude and make, albeit late, thank-offerings.

So he made his way back, contrite of heart and with peace-offerings of praise[135] and acts of thanksgiving. His happiness restored by a second blessing from the holy hand, he was fortunate enough afterwards to hear the saint say: "It was not my power, my son, for I was unaware of what happened; your faith has made you well,[136] so not to me but to God's name give the glory.[137]

1. 16. In praise of Brihtric

I should be afraid of doing that good and worthy man Brihtric, whom I mentioned earlier, an injustice if, while laying bare his faults, I were to say nothing of his many and great merits. In fact, he much resembled blessed Wulfric in simplicity and humility, serving God day and night like him with psalms and prayers; and insofar as his ministry allowed him, he kept perpetual watch in his church. Indeed, in order to devote as many hours as possible to

[134] Ps 137:5.
[135] Ps 50:19; see Num 29:39.
[136] Mark 10:52.
[137] Ps 113:1.

solitude and emptiness, when dinner time came he rode home on horseback, so that, the meal over, the animal would be there ready to take him back at once.[a]

So close was the spiritual twinning between these blessed men, this pair of pigeons,[138] that they were always seeking in a friendly way to outdo each other in reciprocal subservience and humility. Brihtric assisted the other as he might a superior, humbly giving him "Sir," while blessed Wulfric, for ever belittling himself in comparison, would say that Brihtric was the true anchorite of that place, whereas he, constantly exposed to conversation, could more properly be called the parish priest. Thus it was that these two seraphim, calling one to another,[139] went about serving, assisting, and giving each other precedence in Christ,[140b] who was himself in their midst, their life, and jubilation. You could say that the priest had been made in the image and likeness[141] of his friend and been provided for blessed Wulfric by the Lord to be a comfort and a helpmeet fit for him;[142] but enough of this for the time being.

1. 17. Of the man who had paid homage[a] to the devil and was wonderfully restored

One day when Wulfric was occupied at some task in the Lord's presence, he was suddenly roused by a strange vision. He called Brihtric to him and said: "Fetch the cross and holy water as fast as you can and hurry to the man the devil is holding prisoner in the ford outside the village. Sprinkle him with holy water and bring him back to me." Rushing off with all speed as he was bidden, Brihtric did indeed find a man seated on a horse in the middle of the ford, but apparently fixed to the spot and quite unable to move either forwards, backwards or sideways. Long since seduced by the devil, as he later confessed, through greed for money and

[138] Luke 2:24.
[139] Isa 6:3.
[140] Rom 12:10.
[141] Gen 5:3.
[142] Gen 2:18.

power, he had placed himself of his own accord under the yoke of a malign bondage and, speaking face to face with his slave-master, had made a covenant with death and a pact with hell.[143]

It so happened that, while the strong man, fully armed, was brooding over his prey and enjoying for the time being a wholly untroubled reign, a stronger assailed him.[144] Breaking into the gaoler's house without his knowing in the form of a spirit of repentance, he infiltrated a disturbing fear into the depths of that captive soul. The prisoner quaked to see the extent of his wretchedness and, shuddering with all his being at the prospect of the eternal fire which would soon engulf him, scanned the horizons to see if anywhere on earth there might be one who could redeem or save him.[145] He reflected that it would take someone strong to do this, since his enemies were exceedingly strong and he himself was in their hands.

At long last he lifted his gaze to blessed Wulfric, said to have healing in his hand,[b] and resolving to go to him he lost no time in organizing his journey. But no sooner had he imprudently revealed this to one of his household than there appeared beside him that familiar enemy of his in a well-known guise, accusing him of betrayal and threatening him with savage punishment if he tried anything like this again. This taught him to keep silence and guard the door of his mouth from the one lying in his bosom,[146] for he had noted many a time that his inmost thoughts, unless he betrayed them by some word or gesture, remained hidden from that lurker. Despairing, he held his tongue, and silently despaired the more for having to keep the misery seething in his breast from bursting out. Then, after concealing for some while his intention of doing penance, he braved the danger, and pretending to head for Cornwall took the road to the man of God. The Lord's mercy accompanied his penitent from the far north of England right to the ford we mentioned earlier, where it appeared for a space to desert him.

[143] Isa 28:15.
[144] Luke 11:21-22.
[145] Ps 7:3.
[146] Mic 7:5.

Now it was up to blessed Wulfric to defend his frontiers and lands in this battle that he would prosecute to the end. The devil, knowing his time was running out, arrived in fury, glaring at his prey with ghastly eyes. Unable to keep his hands off the man he shook him violently, saying: "What's this, you traitor, that you were about to do? You are trying to dissolve our pact, but it's in vain, for you'll pay the price of one or other betrayal, the one by which you once renounced God or the one by which you are now thinking of renouncing me." The man sat there dumbstruck and disempowered; caught between everlasting death and longed-for freedom, he was racked with the fears and torments of a woman in travail.

Blessed Wulfric meanwhile, who had seen his son fleeing to him for refuge when the young man was still a long way off, was moved with compassion,[147] and as he could not run to meet him, he sent his angel of mercy in the venerable person of Brihtric, whom he directed in this embassy in order to prepare the other's way to him.[148] Nor was the priest to proceed in modest style, but with the triumphal sign of Christ's cross going before and vested for celebrating the great sacrament in which a captive of sin was to pass over into the body of Christ, in which a man would once again be ransomed from the devil's hand, as happened long ago, and the mystery of human redemption celebrated, as it were visibly, in one individual. So the minister went to this great work in the spirit and power of his master, and, by sprinkling the man with holy water in the name of Jesus Christ, he rescued the prey[149] and put the robber to flight. Having thus drawn the captive out of the mighty waters,[150] with triumphant rejoicing the priest led captivity captive[151] and presented him to the man of God, who, like another Moses, had been holding up his hands to the Lord while his Joshua was doing battle.[152]

[147] Luke 15:20.
[148] Mark 1:2.
[149] 1 Sam 30:8.
[150] Ps 17:17.
[151] Eph 4:8.
[152] Exod 17:8-13.

Meanwhile the partridge that gathers a brood it did not hatch[153] followed behind, and seeing his erstwhile serf now standing beside the man of God, he stretched out a hand and grabbed him, while the other shouted out: "Ah! my foe is seizing me![154] Help me, I beg you, man of God!" Wulfric immediately took his hand and pulled with power, and with the enemy still hanging on to the other hand a prolonged and desperate tug-of-war ensued. Our penitent was waiting to see who would prove the stronger, when the man of God with one hand took some of the water he had blessed (while still holding on to the captive with the other), and threw it in the enemy's face, and thus, though not without a violent convulsion, evicted him from the innermost recesses of his dwelling. Our new man, still terrified and shaking like someone who has just escaped from the very jaws of death, was courteously admitted to the inner cell while his wound was dressed, and he vomited all the poison he had swallowed at the holy man's feet; then, like a stag that has been released, its antlers grown back, he no longer feared his foe.

Who meanwhile can describe the joy there was among these angels of God—Wulfric and Brihtric, that is—over that repentant sinner,[155] or the shouts of joy and victory in the tents of the righteous[156] giving thanks to the Lord for his goodness, for his mercy endures forever?[157] Their exulting was like the rejoicing of angels in heaven, like the glorying of conquerors and friends of God, indeed like the revels of victors when, the booty taken, they divide the spoil.[158] These too divided their spoil, first giving glory to God, as was altogether most proper and courteous, and then compassionate care to the sick and wounded man, laying up for themselves this latest fruit of righteousness for eternal life.[159]

Let the listener note how great was the holiness, how tried and approved by God, that was invoked from the ends of the earth by

[153] Jer 17:11.
[154] Tob 6:3.
[155] Luke 15:10.
[156] Ps 117:15.
[157] Ps 106:1.
[158] Isa 9:3.
[159] Matt 6:20; see John 4:36.

that abyss[160] of wretchedness, and lastly how great was the power which came so mightily to its aid. Clearly in this great undertaking nothing was lacking: neither the prophet's vision, nor a father's care, nor the warrior's valor; nor, at the end, a mother's tenderness, the physician's healing skills, the teacher's precepts.

Finally, since the penitent absolutely refused to leave the holy man's side until he had received the life-giving sacrament which would no longer allow him to doubt that he was one body with Christ, he drew near for holy communion. Asked whether he believed, he replied: "I do truly believe that I, a sinner, see here the body and blood of Christ under the appearance of flesh and blood." The holy man said in reply: "Thanks be to God. But now let us pray together that in its former likeness you may deserve to receive it."[c] Thus did he send him away in peace, communicated and filled with faith and the consolation of the Holy Spirit.[161] These things I heard from Brother William and others, to some of whom the holy man had recounted them in person.

1. 18. Of an experience of ecstasy in prayer

Anyone asking how a penitent might gain access to that holy inner room would have learned that the saint had a door between his cell and the church, through which he used to pass when going to celebrate vigils before the altar of Saint Michael to whom the church had been dedicated. He was standing one night before the altar in prayer, when there suddenly stood beside him an angel of the Lord[162] who ravished his soul from his body, or so it seemed, and bore it to heaven, where he showed him the glory of God and the hope of the saints. Leading the soul back a little later, the angel gently restored it to its body, found standing in front of the altar, seemingly abandoned. The saint was left to regret the short duration of such felicity and his swift return, while keeping ever in mind the glimpse of eternal years[163] given him as a pledge of everlasting life.

[160] Ps 41:8.
[161] Acts 9:31.
[162] Acts 27:23.
[163] Ps 76:6.

No one will find this hard to believe who has read how Saint Ambrose, while leaning on the altar, assisted at the funeral rites of Saint Martin,[a] or, to favor you with a more sublime example, how the blessed apostle was taken up to heaven and to paradise, whether in the body or out of the body he himself confessed he did not know.[164]

1. 19. Of his total absorption when singing the psalms

That an hour's ecstasy should be experienced by a good man and a friend of God who habitually sang his way through the whole Psalter with unwavering attention will indeed astonish no one. It is this great stability in an exceptional soul that I for my part wholeheartedly admire and reverence, I who have rarely managed to concentrate my unbroken attention for the space of one or even half a psalm. I have sinned a sin against God[165] and so have become unstable and myself forsaken my God,[166] wherefore my heart has forsaken me too.[167] And truly since God has driven me from his presence[168] no place keeps me long; but nor does anyone invite me in and I am become a burden to myself[169] as well. In psalms and prayers I seek to be reconciled to my God, so that all things may be reconciled to me; but I am thrust out, excluded, rejected with upbraiding, as though one were saying to me and my like: "Dogs outside!"[170] I confess that at the last I find some small consolation touching God's judgment and my own incapacity by saying, as I talk to myself: "Who has gathered the wind in his hands?"[171] Only the Father of spirits[172] can do this, he who commands the winds and the waves and they obey him.[173] Thereupon I flee from the

[164] 2 Cor 12:2.
[165] Lam 1:8.
[166] Jdt 8:18.
[167] Ps 39:13.
[168] Jer 15:1; see Gen 4:14.
[169] Job 7:20.
[170] Rev 22:15.
[171] Prov 30:4.
[172] Heb 12:9.
[173] Luke 8:25.

wrath of God, a fugitive and a wanderer in a foreign land[174] until the days of repentance and the time of my exile are fulfilled; and so the spirit returns to God who gave it,[175] in whom alone is lasting happiness and the quiet repose of the spirits of the blessed.

However, my being like this gives me no grounds for disbelieving that such a man as he can attain to what is beyond me. My weakness, common enough, cannot prejudge that special freedom of the saints which any may receive at Christ's hand in the measuring of gifts. Moreover, should anyone be slow of heart to believe,[176] we know that no guile was found in the mouth of him[177] who said to one of our monks lamenting his own weakness during a visit: "As for me, I feel myself carrying through with unbroken attention from 'Blessed is the man'[178] to 'Let everything that breathes praise the Lord.'"[179a]

I have known someone—alive today—who refused to believe the people making these assertions, arguing that a simple man was less self-aware and, not being of an exploring mind, had nothing important enough to occupy it, and this was why he had advanced these claims. Not long after, a divine judgment overtook the speaker—yet what a merciful one it was! For on coming to the night office, he had a new and never repeated experience: he had been so abundantly filled, he said, with the gift of the Holy Spirit, as to concentrate on every verse with consummate ease and delight, singing in spirit and in mind as well.[180] He showed himself more accommodating on the subject after this and he never again felt secure when arguing with someone asserting a truth. But I fear my maunderings on these matters may offend your gravity, and that by letting abundance run riot I have become burdensome where I intended to be pleasing and serviceable. And yet, as you have begun, do bear with me,[181] and if you profit in no other way,

[174] Gen 4:14.
[175] Eccl 12:7.
[176] Luke 24:25.
[177] 1 Pet 2:22; see Isa 53:9.
[178] Ps 1:1.
[179] Ps 150:6.
[180] 1 Cor 14:15.
[181] 2 Cor 11:1.

by listening you will at least exercise your patience, as Wulfric's charity commends us to do.

1. 20. Of a heavenly visitation

It happened one day that the man of God sent the boy who was his only servant to the forge to get a staple[a] made, needed for closing the door. After the lad had left, locking the outer door and taking the key with him, the holy man remained alone and gave his mind to the things of God. And suddenly a man with a venerable white head inspiring awe attracted his attention by tapping in the usual manner at the window, and, forestalling him with a sweet-savored blessing[182] and a message of salvation,[183] sat down in a manner at once familiar and courteous.

When the visitor had asked the holy man how it went with him and the other had said, well, thanks be to God, they conversed sociably for a while on spiritual matters. It arose that the man of God, on being asked whether he had confessed all his sins, replied humbly: "Indeed, I think so." Whereupon the other, disclosing a particular sin, said: "You never mentioned this one in confession, but do so now as soon as ever you can." When the holy man, astonished at this, admitted that it was so, his interlocutor added: "Know that your dwelling-place is made ready in heaven and lacks only one staple to bring it to completion." At this the man of God marvelled even more, but being too awestruck to ask the other who he was, he turned his eyes to his altar as though to give thanks or ask for grace, and when he looked back at the window the man who had spoken with him was gone, and he understood that this had been a divine showing.

Nonetheless, lest his own conscience, or that of any who came to hear of it, should entertain private doubts over the credibility of what had happened, he took care to ask the boy, who came back soon after, if he had locked the door on leaving. "I locked it when I went out," he said, "and I found it just as locked when I got back."

[182] Ps 20:4.
[183] Acts 13:26.

He sent him accordingly to fetch a priest, not the one mentioned above, but another by the name of Segar,[b] three of whose sons were monks at Forde, while a fourth was a lay-brother in the same house. To Segar he revealed this sin as bidden from above, and after receiving absolution he gave him a sequential account of the divine vision.

This priest, who faithfully kept silence with regard to the sin confessed, as faithfully betrayed the holy man in respect of his glory, lauding and honoring one found worthy of the company of heavenly spirits—not through visions and riddles any longer, but openly[184] and in daylight. What does not yet shine out clearly enough, even today, is whether this visitor was one of the angelic host, or—a far greater honor—the Lord Jesus Christ himself, the king of glory, especially as signs of his coming seem clearly to announce him. For to turn aside to the garden enclosed[185] and, before entering, ambush the solitary retreat lest the presence of a stranger prove an obstacle to its delights; next to enter through closed doors[186] and, knocking, rouse the one at rest; to stand behind the wall, gazing in at the window, looking through the lattice,[187] and then to show one's face openly, bringing words of peace and salvation: unless the bride is mistaken in her observations, these are signs that the bridegroom is approaching—signs that compel belief. Moreover, who has a better claim than the searcher of hearts[188] to question and examine the paths of a man and light up that darkness[189] in him which is hardly known to himself, and then to suggest the counsel of confession, sending the penitent to the priest after first consoling him with the promise of eternal life? This is the ancient of days[190] himself, whose converse is with the simple, and because he does not long abide the human gaze, in a blink of the looker's eye and for a little while he slips away.[191]

[184] Num 12:6-8.
[185] Song 4:12.
[186] John 20:26.
[187] Song 2:9.
[188] Wis 1:6.
[189] Ps 17:29.
[190] Dan 7:22.
[191] John 16:16-18.

But one to whom divine consolations were sumptuously dispensed had to be plagued as well by visions arousing horror, and blessed Wulfric had his share of these, that he might be tested to the full in both respects.

1.21. Of visible assaults by demons

So it was that in the deep silence of the night a great troop of evil spirits foregathered and hemmed the innocent man in, as though intending to bring a case against him. Discussing among themselves what should be done with this fellow who opposed them with all his strength, who dashed their counsels, snatched their spoils, destroyed what they built up and rebuilt what they destroyed,[192] they soon came to a unanimous decision: the man deserved to die;[193] driven out of his dwelling and church, he should suffer as greatly as he had offended.

Grabbed by the hands of that sinister crew, he was dragged first into the church and then bundled roughly through it without any show of reverence or pity. They were about to throw him out of the church when a holy virgin, suddenly appearing, threw the whole muster of fiends into confusion with the glory of her coming,[194] and boldly asking why they presumed to harass an innocent man like that, she dispersed them like chaff with the wide fold of her sleeve. That very day the holy man had commemorated a certain blessed virgin in celebrating his mass, and it was she who took his case out of the hand of his enemies.[195]

On another occasion, when he lay ill, the adversary came in, and glaring at him with his dreadful eyes he swung the staff he was holding high in the air and struck the saint hard three times. But the latter replied unmoved: "Be off with you now, foul fiend, for you have no further power over me. Nor would you have any at all unless it had been given you from above."[196] In these wrestling

[192] Jer 1:10.
[193] Matt 26:66.
[194] 2 Thess 2:8.
[195] Ps 30:16.
[196] John 19:11.

matches the holy man was not once bested[a] by the adversary. When it came to the turning point in a contest, he had now the under, now the upper hand, but as it is written, "The enemy is wiped out in ruins for ever,"[197] the fiend yielded always the final victory to God and his saint. In the end the holy man got a hold on his enemy and gave him a good whipping, and before letting him go he made him swear an oath that he would never again return.

So it was that the holy man was found faithful in both respects, and as he had not indulged in the sillier sorts of jubilation when things went well, so did he prove steadfast in graver cruces and come through unscathed. Yet there was one form of molestation practiced by the enemy which was worse than all the others. When the holy man went to empty his bowels, his adversary would be waiting and would stroke his genitals with a caressing hand. For eighteen years he was troubled by this temptation, as he secretly confessed to the venerable Henry, abbot of Waverley—tormented beyond measure and past withstanding, to the point where he so loathed the privy that he would often use a pot. In the end, when he was ready to be delivered from the disgrace of such a servitude, on finding the enemy waiting for him as usual when he went to obey the call of nature, his spirit rebelled and he began to rail at him, saying: "Isn't it right that you, you wretch, whose desire it once was to be like the Most High, should now be a filthy thing that inhabits a stinking latrine?" To have this taunt thrown at him was more than the enemy could endure; weakened by so grievous a wound he took himself off and from then on ceased his harassment. Others admire blessed Wulfric's feats of strength, and so do I; but I boast more gladly of his weaknesses,[198] trusting to find refreshment in their shade when beset by my own.

1. 22. Of the bodily ills inflicted by the enemy

To enable God's saint to be shown to us tried and tested in every way, the adversary was given power over his flesh.[199] Making a mean

[197] Ps 9:7.
[198] 2 Cor 12:5.
[199] Job 2:6.

use of this, he struck him in the upper arm with a loathsome sore[200] that went right to the bone, where the putrefied flesh swarmed with maggots and matter came bubbling out. But the saint, by embracing this heavenly judgment with thanksgiving, transformed the tempter's weapons into weapons of patience and rejoiced in them like one who has found great booty.[201] Yet he took steps too to care for his health, having candlewicks laid in the runnels where the matter ran down like water through a conduit.[202]

No sooner had he recovered from these sufferings than he challenged Leviathan to greater combats. The latter, openly relishing his hour of vantage, sent an invisible fire—straight from hell as it seemed—to inflame the flesh of the holy man, who likened it to being consumed by flames so fierce as to pass all imagining. Convinced that he would soon be reduced to cinders, he sent for the priest and hastened to commend his soul to God and him. After some hours of this excruciating agony, the invisible torturer altered the torment, but the endurance of Christ's champion, the patience of his martyr never changed. The flame was taken away as suddenly as it had come and the saint started to stiffen with rigor as freezing cold crept through his body and he waited resignedly[203] for the passing of this hour. His body given into the devil's hand, he froze and sweated from morning till evening in this alternating torment, giving to those who fear the Lord some intimation[204] of the judgment to come, with its passing from snowmelt to scorching heat.[205]

1. 23. Of his public confession of a nighttime delusion

It happened that the feast of Easter was drawing near,[206] for which blessed Wulfric was sanctifying himself as usual in solemn expectation, anticipating the renewal of spiritual vows. But when the sacred

[200] Job 2:7.
[201] Ps 118:162.
[202] Job 3:8.
[203] Lam 3:26.
[204] Ps 59:6.
[205] Job 24:19.
[206] Luke 22:1.

night[a] shone bright—the night which is as bright as day[207]—that disturber of solemnities, the enemy envious of peace, inflicted a dream on the holy man and by means of this dream triumphed over the frailty of the flesh. Whereupon the lover of holiness, who found it hard to accept even so slight an impairment of his purity, reddened still more on account of the great solemnity of the day and paid then and there, in shamefaced confusion before God, for the tarnish on his chastity.

But it was not enough for this striver after perfection that only God and he should see his shame: with the whole congregation assembled, he must perforce walk out of his cell into the public space and start addressing them, turning his eloquence against himself.[208] "This," he said, "is what befell me, wretched Wulfric, pressed by my own sinfulness, in this most holy night; thus did my adversary deceive me, unhappy man that I am. I confess my sin to God and to you. I entreat God's mercy through your intercession and over and beyond I bewail, before God and yourselves, this wrong by which the enemy did not forbear to shame me during this holiest of feasts." Thus was humility's great-souled follower given strength to bear the abuse endured by Christ,[209] and that without any care for his own modesty, the embarrassment of those present, or, lastly, his reputation for holiness diffused far and wide.

With that our great orator closed his speech, having won much goodwill from his hearers, and returned to his sanctum rosier than old coral[210] and worthy of hearing, "Your cheeks are as fair as those of the turtle dove."[211] Finally, since such great humility needs must be glorified, the flesh from then on delighted the inner man with such peace[212] that he seemed—distanced from all turmoil of this sort—to have entered into a pact with the spirit.

[207] Ps 138:12.
[208] Job 10:1.
[209] Heb 13:13.
[210] Lam 4:7.
[211] Song 1:9.
[212] Rom 7:22.

1. 24. From peace of the senses to life in the spirit

Sometime later it chanced that one of our monks, as he was entering Wulfric's cell,[a] saw him placing his hand on the naked breast of a woman who had some infirmity there. Turning away, he smirked while pretending not to have seen. The man of God carried on with his healing ministry regardless, and having closed the rite with a prayer he made the sign of the cross over the woman and sent her away in peace.[213] Then, after greeting the monk—a dear friend of his—in his own sweet manner, he asked: "Why that sly smile just now?" And as the man reddened, lost for an answer, he went on: "Having my hand on that woman's breast was no different from having it on this wood." For in the pursuit of that purity he had been striving after, he had donned a degree of incorruptibility in that regard, enjoying in happy anticipation what we too look for: "You have removed my sackcloth and clothed me with joy, that my glory may sing to you and I may not be stung with remorse."[214]

1. 25. How the cold water in his cell would be suddenly warmed

Regarding the holy man's habit, already mentioned, of taking cold baths in the early days of his religious life, people should know that his cell was later so richly endowed with the power of God that the water, however cold, turned warm as soon as it entered. For since it was in cold water that he had warded off for the most part the heats of the flesh, he became just like a wineskin in the frost,[215] as God in exchange granted his servant a kind of dominion over cold water.

1. 26. Of a coverlet sent to him through a revelation

It remains that many a time blessed Wulfric was frozen stiff with cold, so much so that a man from the neighborhood of Bristol

[213] Luke 2:29.
[214] Ps 29:12-13.
[215] Ps 118:83.

was bidden in a vision to send him the new coverlet of fox-skins he had laid on his bed. In this vision the Lord, as the man later bore witness, spoke to him, saying: "My servant Wulfric is tortured with cold, whereas you are lying here snug and warm. Get up as quickly as you can and make haste to send him your coverlet." So leaping up he called to his son and one of his servants and bade them set off that very same night and take the coverlet to the man of God. There was no hanging around: he jumped to obey the divine command and they obeyed his with equal zeal.[a] And as soon as they got to the holy man, they unfolded this revelation, and having respectfully presented the gift they had brought, they bore home the fruit of a blessing for themselves and the one who had sent them. This I had from Brother William and he from the holy man himself.

1. 27. How another revelation brought covering for a book

In a similar way it was revealed one night to a sick woman living in the east of England that she should take the holy man a piece of costly cloth for covering a book, and that healing at his hand would follow without a doubt. She took it[a] and was healed. The man of God gave pains to copying books either for his own use or for that of the adjoining church; and when fine cloth was lacking to cover a book, the Lord took care of the matter on his servant's behalf. I had this from Walter of Glastonbury among others.

1. 28. How his scribe's carelessness got a prophet's chiding

About this work of copying there is a story worth telling. The holy man once instructed his scribe to leave out a passage of the original, as he had it elsewhere, but the young man forgot the charge and when he came to the place took the easy course of carrying straight on. However, the power of the saint's command stood in the way of the pen and brought its running to a sudden halt. The scribe, still oblivious and blaming it all on the quill, sharpened it again and again until by degrees he had so whittled it down that he threw it aside in anger and disgust. The man of God, who had been at prayer all this time, knew in spirit what was happening, and on returning made a pretence of scolding the scribe. "Now, now, Richard," he grumbled, "is this how you chose to disobey your instructions?" Remembering too late, Richard began to smile at his accuser and, not without cause or subsequent profit, enjoyed the joke at his own expense. I had this from Richard himself.

1. 29. Of the monk who was cured of insomnia

This Richard was a scribe at Forde abbey, where he later became a monk and eventually a cantor.[a] He had a son at Forde, likewise a religious, who exercises his father's office to this day. As a young man the son was greatly troubled with insomnia, and just how punishing an affliction this can be to those of our profession his fellow-sufferers know. His father appealed to the holy man on his son's behalf. "Let each monk recite the Lord's Prayer for him three times," said the saint, "and he will be cured." "But why, sir, are you unwilling to pray for him yourself?" The reply came back magnificent in its simplicity: "I could have obtained this from my Lord on my own; how much more all of you?" Richard's son was healed from that very hour[216] and boasts that the grace given has never failed him since. It is not so much the power of the miracle worked as the simplicity of the answer which led me to add this story, although the work itself, of no mean power, is praiseworthy enough; it is outshone, though, by the grace of that simplicity in all its sheerness. This too from Richard.

1. 30. Of the mouse that died from a thoughtless curse

I will give another telling example of his faith, or, if you prefer, simplicity. The blessed man was sitting one day in his cell, attentive to God and himself, when a glance at his garment—a cape[a] just sent him by a prior who held him in regard—showed it to have been nibbled by a mouse.[b] He took this somewhat hard. "Perish

[216] Matt 8:13.

the mouse," he exclaimed, "that has damaged my cape like this!" With that the mouse shot out of the wall, scurried across, and fell dead at his feet. Such was the force in a passing word he had let fall carelessly and with no real intent, that the mouse, as though accused of a crime, came hurrying to submit to the death sentence and in dying gave glory to God and peace to his saint. Indeed you may see in the smallest thing the greatest proof of Christ's love, as here anticipating his servant so as to catch—almost reverently—that word thrown out so lightly, lest it fall to the ground,[217]and seal it with the power of a decree. But the man in his utter simplicity, humbled by that sign rather than letting it give birth in him to self-aggrandizement, sent for the priest, who remained a lifelong witness to all this, and humbly confessed to him that he had killed a mouse with a heedless curse. "If only," replied the priest, "you would be good enough to dispatch all the local mice with a similar malediction." "Far be it from me!"[218] exclaimed the holy man. "Once with one mouse was a very grave fault; and," he added, "if I didn't think it would displease my Lord, I would pray to him for this one, that he might bring it back to life."

Thus it was that extremes of high-mindedness and simplicity met in this man in a wondrous and delightful congruence and, each pleasing in itself, were doubly pleasing when combined. Yet in all this I am left fearful of trivializing things confided to me as proofs of holiness by publishing them without due reverence. I am well aware of the need to proceed here with zeal and ardor checked and managed by piety, so as to safeguard the holy man's honor without boring my listeners. This has led me to resolve that the tales left untold—and they are many and remarkable—should be prepared for another day, especially as I knew you to be fastidious in your tastes and quick to find fault if something insipid were presented to you. Moreover, I am not ashamed to confess that I fall short,[219] for I am pusillanimous when it comes to bearing criticism.

Here ends the first book

[217] 1 Sam 3:19.
[218] 1 Sam 2:30.
[219] Ps 138:16.

Here begins the second book

2. 1. On keeping vigil

Like one of the watchmen who go about the city,[220] blessed Wulfric passed his nights, as I said earlier, watching and waking in unsleeping love. While Jerusalem slept in the night of her weakness, he, her guardian, stood ever watchful on her behalf. Daybreak saw him go out to his work and his labor until the evening,[221] and sharing freely and ungrudgingly what he had freely received,[222] he disbursed the riches of salvation with an open hand. From every quarter people were drawn to him as to an ensign lifted up on high[223] or a horn of salvation in the house of David,[224] and he was the humble dispenser of this great treasure, its faithful steward.[225] And in the evening, after he had dismissed the crowds, he went up his own mountain by himself to pray;[226] and spreading his wings again in what for him was dawn,[227] he would fly away to his window like a dove and take his rest.[228] And truly as the night grew bright with the reflection of the true light, it shone resplendently on his delights,[229] for it was at night that he worked out his own salvation,[230] since by day he was working the salvation of others in the midst of the earth.[231]

But even at night he was concerned for others, drawing water with joy from the savior's springs[232] which he would pour out again in the morning for those who came to him and had nothing in

[220] Song 5:7.
[221] Ps 103:23.
[222] Matt 10:8.
[223] Prov 30:32.
[224] Ps 17:3; Luke 1:69.
[225] Luke 12:42.
[226] Matt 14:23.
[227] Ps 138:9.
[228] Isa 60:8; see Ps 54:7.
[229] Ps 138:11.
[230] Phil 2:12.
[231] Ps 73:12.
[232] Isa 12:3.

which to draw it for themselves, for the well is deep.[233] Blessed that servant whom the Lord found thus awake in whatever watch[234]—indeed, at whatever hour of the night he came. Do you think he could have come empty-handed to the one waiting for him, when he himself is full of grace and truth,[235] especially when returning from the wedding feast?[236] Surely that was the time, when blessed Wulfric was released from the cares of humankind and Christ no less at leisure, after a fashion, from worrying about the world—since everyone is then asleep or nodding off—the time for him to say to Wulfric's holy soul in the joy of his love, "My beloved is mine and I am his."[237]

2. 2. Of the lamp that was relit

It happened one night that the lamp which was burning in his cell went out. After he had called to his lad several times to come and relight it and the latter had answered him not a word, being fast asleep in a house some way away, the blessed man looked round to discover the lamp miraculously alight. At this, rejoicing in the Lord his God who had illumined him from heaven, he put heart and soul into singing the words: "The Lord is my light and my salvation, whom shall I fear?"[238] Still more amazing is the fact that the wick was playing no part and the flame continued quietly on some oily matter, doing service as both flame and wick. Sent as it was from heaven, it worked in a heavenly manner and at no cost, and because it had come as a free gift, the more freely did it perform its service. So it was that the Lord overheard the desire of his poor man[239] before the man's servant heard his master's voice; and awake on the instant to his own servant's little trouble even before he cried out, the Lord was there with light. So all that night

[233] John 4:11.
[234] Luke 12:37-38.
[235] John 1:14.
[236] Luke 12:36.
[237] Song 2:16.
[238] Ps 26:1.
[239] Ps 9b:17.

the holy man walked in the light of his God[240] and when morning came he doused the lamp as he always did. But he came to beat his breast over his presumption, for later, talking about it to one of our brethren, he said that he still regretted seeming to have misprized the heavenly gift, by not saving some or sharing it with those dwelling with him.[a]

2. 3. How it happened again

On another occasion, when he was celebrating as usual the solemn office of vigils, the light went out quite suddenly—a trick of the enemy, or God disposing?—either way the holy man had to break off, leaving God's work unfinished. At once he lifted holy hands[241] in faith to God, for that earlier instance, when the Lord had visited him with a grace beyond hope or prayer's labor, was fresh in his memory. Guided by the Lord's own teaching, in giving form to his wishes he now made bold to say:[a] "Since you, Lord, lit my lamp, my God, lighten now my darkness."[242] The Lord did not leave his servant to labor long here, but as though the words "Let there be light" had been spoken with power, he gave the nod, and at once there was light.[243] The aura of those vigils grew in the festive beams of heaven's light, for the heavenly radiance which lit the outward scene contributed in no small way to the illumination of the man's inmost being. But alas, as the saint lamented to one of his intimates, while he was celebrating mass his servant snuffed the lamp. This came from Brother William and Walter of Glastonbury as well as several others who had heard these things from the holy man's own mouth.

2. 4. Of the candle which burned without being consumed[a]

My zeal for brevity almost led me to omit, at the risk of appearing to short-change you, what I am bound to set down if I too wish

[240] Isa 2:5.
[241] 1 Tim 2:8.
[242] Ps 17:29.
[243] Gen 1:3.

to be found among the trustworthy stewards,[244] depriving you of nothing and keeping nothing back for myself. One night when the holy man had discharged the office of vigils in full by candlelight, he was surprised to see, on glancing at the candle, that it had got no shorter, and he began to wonder whether he had fulfilled his due charge. In case he had slipped up through drowsiness, he ended by repeating what he had just completed, and having paid afresh his measure of service**[b]** he observed that the candle was as whole as ever. Then he really began to marvel and ask himself what meaning this had for him and trying to work out whether what he was seeing was real or the stuff of dreams. What more is to say? He recited the office a third time right to the end, and having completed everything as usual—if anything more carefully than usual—he found the candle persisting in its wholeness. Then and only then did he recognize the doing as divine and gave thanks to the Father of lights.[245] So turning his eyes to this remarkable sight of a candle burning and yet not consumed,[246] he waited for morning light by the candle's gleam. It was then that the priest was fetched. "Osbern," said the saint, "isn't this the candle you brought yesterday evening?" "It certainly is." "And isn't it still as big as it was then?" To which the priest replied: "Indeed I see it is just as big and I'm amazed." "Three times," said the saint, "I have sung my night office right through by this light, and you see what my Lord has done." "What can I say," replied the priest, "save that it seems to be some joke on the part of the divine majesty?" "Thanks be to him," said the holy man, "thanks be to him; he is my Lord: let him do what he will with his servant." And while they were chatting together about what had happened, the candle was suddenly whisked away and they didn't see it anymore.

We should surely not be surprised if the darkness was not dark to him for whom the night, as we read, was as light as day,[247] and if the office of vigils, stretched out to unlooked-for length, turned

[244] 1 Cor 4:2.
[245] Jas 1:17.
[246] Exod 3:2.
[247] Ps 138:12.

night into day.[248] For at night he would recall to prayer his hands and mouth, which the world had the use of by day, and restore himself to himself, or better, as one returning from a journey to a distant land, refresh himself in the company of that one and only beloved who was his lover too. So it was that the evening, which called him back to blissful leisure hours, dawned on him in sabbath solemnity, and as the sun set it seemed to rise, a sun that truly knows no setting. Now was the time to say with the illustrious psalmist: "Awake, my glory; awake lyre and harp."[249] Now was the moment for the ardent devotee of Christ's charity to call in loving tones to the bridegroom: "Return, my beloved."[250] And so as the world lay sleeping, he, like one set over it, kept watch for the eternal light, judging that time the best for consecrating to his delights, upon which, now that his resting-place was sealed, none could intrude. And meanwhile who can tell how busy was the leisure in that little cell of his, how radiant were the nights, what blissful sleep in Christ those vigils knew, how resonant was that silence, what quiet was in the clamor? Was that cell not the wine cellar[251] that gladdened the very city of God?[252] Truly these things are hidden from our perception; Christ alone has plumbed the mysteries of his nuptials, and it is something to have brought you the mere fragrance of them.

Accordingly dawn would find the holy man struggling to rise from that couch of his festal holy days, as though the angel were saying to him: "Let me go, for the day is breaking."[253] And there were his brothers standing outside and asking to speak with him,[254] or rather a crowd of people rushing towards him to press their claims and tugging this way and that the hands consecrated for their healing. That lover of peace might never set his personal interest before the common good, or neglect for love of his own quiet the salvation of others, for which he was ever mindful of

[248] Job 17:12.
[249] Ps 56:9.
[250] Song 2:17.
[251] Song 2:4.
[252] Ps 45:5.
[253] Gen 32:26.
[254] Matt 12:46.

having been sent. Thus did day and night divide blessed Wulfric between them, or to put it better, thus did he and the world share his person out; best of all, thus did Christ have the whole man, who sought not his own interests but those of Jesus Christ.[255] I have written at length about the holy man's night watches, in case I appear to disregard the very things in which he most pleased God and was found righteous.

2. 5. Of the heavenly light which appeared as he prayed

For the rest, lest someone should accuse me of giving more space to my own opinions than to facts, let me set down two stories to which the one who saw and heard testifies in person.[256] One Sunday when Master Brihtric went to bless the water in the church the aspersorium was missing. His son Osbern had accidentally taken it home and now the troubled lad didn't know what to do. Then it flashed on his mind—he believes by divine inspiration—that he might for this once tender the aspersorium belonging to the man of God. On slipping through the door to the cell he saw a light of dazzling brightness over the center of the altar. Intent on this light, the saint was standing quite still in front of the altar step. The boy, filled with wonder, handed the aspersorium to someone else to give to the priest while he himself returned to his vision. Having silently closed the cell door till he could just peer in with one eye, he saw the light move slowly away towards the left-hand corner of the altar and thence, passing over the chest which stood beside it, go out through the north window. Later the holy man, when Osbern asked him in private what the bright and beautiful light was that he had seen above the altar, said: "Did you see it then, my son?" "I saw it, sir." To which the saint replied: "Ah, if you were here around midnight, you might often see the like, and smell besides a fragrance so wonderfully sweet[a] that all the world's delights would count for little in comparison."

[255] Phil 2:21.
[256] John 3:32.

2. 6. Of a similar consolation

It happened that this same Osbern, now a grown man and a priest, went to the church at nightfall, intending to sleep there as usual. Looking up as he drew near the churchyard gate, he saw the interior of the building so bright and sparkling with light that the brilliance pouring out through the windows lit the entire graveyard. Greatly alarmed, he began urging his servant—whom he called Taillefer[a]—to look across. But though the latter looked curiously enough he saw nothing unusual and thought that the priest was making fun of him. Osbern, realizing then that something divine was being enacted to which the other was not to be admitted, stood rooted to the spot in fear and awe. Reluctant to obtrude his presence, he stayed leaning against the perimeter wall and began to sing psalms out of reverence for the vision.

Now, had I been a friend of the bridegroom[257] standing there listening, I should have been able to tell you what our Moses was saying to the Lord on our own Sinaï[258] and what the Lord said in reply, always assuming these things were such as may be uttered by human beings.[259] As it was, Osbern watched intently until, quite soon, an angel enveloped in fiery flame came out through the window, leaving the church free for the priest to enter.

When morning broke, the man of God called to him and said: "What was that vision you saw yesterday evening, Osbern?" "A fiery flame inside the church, and no ordinary one at that." "Good," said the saint, "because my Lord came and comforted his servant,[260] and he often provides consolations of this kind. So I prayed to my Lord to open your eyes that you might look on these things and I was hard put to obtain it. But your lad was not found worthy of being admitted. And I knew this too: you were singing psalms," and he told him which, "while you waited outside the churchyard wall for the vision to end." Thus was the holy man showered day and night with consolations; and to save us being cheated of all

[257] Exod 19:19-21.
[258] John 3:29.
[259] 2 Cor 12:4.
[260] Isa 52:9.

knowledge of such blessedness, he was given a witness to glory to announce it to us.

2. 7. How water was changed into wine

In the main it was through four kinds of physic that our apothecary procured the healing of his fellow creatures: namely, holy water, bread which had been blessed, the laying on of a hand, and the sign of the cross. Bread and water blessed by him were potent in driving out sicknesses of every kind, and when sent to the absent frequently cured whole families of their diseases.[261] Lastly, that water blessed by his holy hand was changed into wine we learned for certain, trusting as we do in the assertion of one found worthy of attending. It happened like this. The man of God retained a priest who was a friend of his to share his meal and, it being Friday, kept to his customary fast on bread and water. The priest agreed to observe the same monastic practice; they sat down together to this solemn banquet, and Jesus, invited and also invoked in the words of the blessing, came himself to the wedding feast.[262] It is indeed quite clear that he came and was present, since he paused to wait on them and himself made good their lack of wine from his own fount. Thus the priest, after tasting the drink and marveling at the flavor, examined it carefully and proceeded to drink to the health of the man of God. When he too had tried the new wine, they passed the cup back and forth, drinking joyfully in the presence of the Lord. This came from Aylward of Haselbury, a reliable man, who was also there in person.

2. 8. The same sign, yet somewhat different

He dispensed the same fruit of the vine[263] on another occasion and with a gladness matched with reverence because he did this on a holy day and in a holy place, and not just to one or two persons but to

[261] Luke 6:18.
[262] John 2:2.
[263] Matt 26:29.

the whole congregation at once. The church, as we said, being dedicated to Saint Michael, the angelic man venerated the holy archangel with particular devotion, taking confident refuge in the shadow of his wings.[264] Indeed, inspired by this special love, the holy man had made it his yearly custom on this feast day[a] to go and celebrate mass at Saint Michael's altar before all the people, and after the celebration he would serve holy water to the congregation from a tin cup.[b]

It happened on one of these feast days that the water offered as usual to the people tasted of wine, though without any change in the original color. The faithful[c] looked at one another, seeing water but drinking wine. This double miracle, whereby the water retained its appearance while taking on a foreign taste, raises the question of the nature of the drink, the eyes giving one answer, the palate another. Thus at a sign of his mighty right hand, water received the grace now of healing, now of gladness, and what had been received was passed on again as gift to those receiving. A religious man among the seniors of our house says he heard this from many who partook of the same draught.

2. 9. A THIRD INSTANCE

I must not omit what I ought perhaps to have put first: that the lady of Haselbury when gravely ill sent to her beloved Wulfric, esteeming she should not be debarred from drawing salvation with the rest from the common fount.[a] And nor in her time of need did Wulfric stint his power. He sent out at once for water to be drawn in a ewer, and when it was fetched, blessed it in her intention. But her daughter Beatrice, who is still alive today as a witness to this sign, marveled as she bore it away at the rose-red color of the liquid and the way it sparkled in the vessel like wine: "I was sent to fetch water, not wine," she said. "Take whatever this is to your mother," replied the holy man; "it is what God has appointed for her healing." Whereupon the woman drained the good cheer of health from the cup of good cheer,[b] assuring everyone to whom she told the story that she had never tasted a finer wine and that

[264] Ps 56:2.

the good wine had been kept for her until then.[265] Afterwards the blessed man mixed the remaining wine with water and measured it out as a saving draught to the sick who came to him.

2. 10. Of the bread and wine of heavenly provenance

The man of God's servant, happening to go out one day on his master's business, locked the door behind him, and while the saint was giving his attention as usual to sacred study, a woman came in, habited like a religious. The man of God came at her summons, and they exchanged greetings and blessings. Then holding out a quarter of a white loaf and a flask of wine which we call a *justitia*,[a] she pressed them on him, saying: "For holy charity's sake, I beg you to accept and taste of these." Not judging it prudent or himself at liberty to reject so awesome and respectful an entreaty, he stretched out his hand to them and set them aside as accepted for his use. Then turning back, he looked and saw no one at all, and taking fright at the thought of the noonday devil[266] and wondering what sort of greeting this was,[267] he turned to the Lord in heart and mind, praying that Christ would not suffer his little one to be mocked. Reassurance swiftly followed and tranquility of spirit, whereupon he blessed the gifts and broke[268] and ate. In the same way he drew off some of the wine and savored it. He nonetheless sent some of each to Brihtric with the message: "In the Lord's name try these which have just been sent to me." Lastly the holy man reserved what was left for the use of the sick. Brihtric, who used to relate the story, commended exceedingly both the appearance and the quality of the wine, declaring that truly this fruit of the vine[269] was not of earth but of heaven. I heard this from the venerable Walter of Glastonbury, who claimed he had seen that flask many times and that it had stayed with the holy man to the end of his life.

[265] John 2:10.
[266] Ps 90:6.
[267] Luke 1:29.
[268] Matt 26:26.
[269] Luke 22:18.

2. 11. Of the loaf miraculously multiplied

There came to the man of God a woman of high standing, one Bence as she is still known today,[a] along with her son, Alfred of Lincoln, and a retinue of the sort and size that befitted so noble a lady. The holy man called to his servant: "Look," he said, "Bence is here and must eat under our roof. Have you got anything to set before her?" "We have nothing to hand, sir, save one loaf." "That will do," said the man of God; "set it on the table." So the woman sat down with all her company and they were served with this loaf, a sight more apt to whet the appetite than give hope of serious refection, particularly to people used to more refined and richer fare. But because such great faith must display its resources when put to the test, heaven's blessing came to the aid of holy poverty, so that when the guests had had their fill, they even found half a loaf left over.[270]

Later, when these had left, another sizeable group came to the door, wanting to see and speak with the man of God and receive his blessing—something highly valued in those days. The saint, with his usual gracious hospitality, invited these in turn to take their places at table and the same half loaf left over from the earlier meal was set before them. But because, as a holy man has said, faith cannot suffer loss, after the blessing had been given to those who were cutting and eating it, the loaf began to profit by its losses and, unable seemingly to grow smaller, it stayed as big as ever it was. In case anyone's faith should falter under the weight of such a sign, Brother William, the hospitaller, claims to have heard it from the holy man himself, who also told the venerable abbot of Waverley, Henry I, that he had fed forty people with a single loaf; but whether these were the same we have just been talking about or possibly others, I would not make so bold as to determine.

2. 12. How he healed a virgin while she slept

I must not pass over what happened to a certain young girl of Abbotsbury.[a] This was the sister of a devout man named Gilbert,

[270] John 6:5-13.

herself no less devout and God-fearing than he,[271] and the virgin's name was Emma.[272] Afflicted with acute abdominal pain and tirelessly nursed by her mother, she woke up one night and roused her mother too. "Oh, mother," she said, "don't worry any more about my illness; see, thanks to God and the holy man of Haselbury, I am cured! It seemed to me as I slept that I came to him and he received me and I drank holy water from a tin cup that he held out to me; and healing and peace came back to my belly." And to help her mother believe it all, she described the man and the place. I had this from one of our monks, a most trustworthy man, who was there at the time and frequented the household for many years. Finally, to bolster my readers' confidence in this story, I sent to the subject, who is still alive, and she confirmed that all had happened just like this. So it was not enough that blessed Wulfric should heal those who were present and wakeful; he went so far as to extend his generous hand to the absent and the sleeping. Although the virgin too had some share in the glory of this miracle, seeing that through the ancient privilege of virginity, healing now came to a virgin of itself,**[b]** instead of her betaking herself to healing. Thus consideration was given to both modesty and healing, balancing the agreeable and the wholesome, since a virgin receiving healing in the womb was freed from the necessity of venturing out.

2. 13. How a stolen loaf was made hard as stone

Not far from the holy man's cell there lived a woman, the mother of William of Chinnock**[a]** who is alive today and a witness to this miracle, and she herself was called Emmeline. She was unstinting in devotion towards the man of God, and was in the habit of sending him, among other little presents, two or three loaves from every batch baked.**[b]** The gracious gift having become like a rent to be paid at due times, she sent him one day three loaves by one of her servants. The fellow kept one loaf back for himself, stowing it in a secret spot, and carried on to the holy man with two. Having

[271] Acts 10:2.
[272] Luke 1:27.

handed these to the man of God, who received them courteously, he went back to the stolen loaf, and, pulling it from its dark hiding place, got out his knife and tried to cut it. When the knife made no impression, he put all his strength to it, but this got him nowhere, proving the loaf to be utterly inviolable. Dedicated to the holy man and destined for his use, it was keeping itself faithfully for him, at once pointing to and punishing the bad faith of the other. Plainly it could not bear to let a thief or reprobate profane or harm it but changed in the traitor's hand from loaf to stone.

So the thief, caught with and by his loot, confessed his guilt and misery to his mistress, whom he had sinned against first, and begged forgiveness. She lost no time in sending him back to the man of God together with the stolen loaf and another witness to the tale. When he had told him every detail and implored his pardon, the holy man replied: "So, my son, you didn't act well, seeing you disobeyed your mistress." Then, taking the loaf from his hand, he blessed and broke it with supreme ease and handed him a hunk still warm and steaming: "Here," he said, "eat it." He joined him in eating some of the bread himself and then, with a blessing, sent the man strengthened on his way.

Now we who sit at blessed Wulfric's table have, along with the fullness of evangelical refreshment, three loaves of bread, and in these three loaves there is hidden one who is sweeter yet, having in himself every delight of faith, humility, and kindness.[273] I myself can taste all three and, if you have a discriminating palate, I believe you too will taste the very same. And if we call to mind the water changed to wine, we shall not be lacking in wine either.

2. 14. Of the loaf which dripped blood

There is another loaf I think you should not be deprived of since it is from the same table. This loaf too was destined for the blessed man, but the fellow who had been charged with taking it to him broke his journey under a poor man's roof. At the sight of chil-

[273] Wis 16:20.

dren sitting round the hearth begging for bread (and there was no one to give it to them),[274] he pulled the loaf from his bag and got ready to cut it up. The loaf allowed itself to be cut, but, because it understood that this work of mercy did not square with obedience, indeed ran counter to it, it began to weep blood, so that even cut up it could not be eaten. One may well see this as akin to a sign of ancient power, as when the rivers of Egypt were turned to blood that the people might not drink of the waters.[275] As a result, and not without much fear and trembling, the loaf was put back in the bag.

Next morning, accompanied by his host who had both witnessed the miracle and been the author, or rather occasion, of the disobedience, our fellow related it all to the holy man. After listening to what had happened, the latter observed: "You see, my son, you shouldn't have gone against the order, even in a little thing." Then having taken the loaf, he blessed it with the sign of the cross, cleansing it from its blood: "There," he said, "now take it and give it to those children you got it ready for." Here was a faithful man, simple as an unleavened loaf on the Lord's table, and without any trace in him of the leaven of malice and evil.[276]

2. 15. Of the terrible death of the monk who was a thorn in his side[a]

This mildness of temper was once brought to a fall; and woe to that man through whom the falling came![277] There was an agreement with the monks of Montacute, whose house was not far off, to furnish him with food, but after a while their devotion towards him cooled, thanks to a certain cellarer, and they broke their covenant.[278] The holy man's servant who went to ask for his master's due was even received with slights and insults, the cellarer showing to him and through him contempt for the one who sent him. He would

[274] Lam 4:4.
[275] Ps 77:44.
[276] 1 Cor 5:8.
[277] Matt 18:7.
[278] Josh 7:11.

serve the lad with grumbling and short measure, often enough sending him home with nothing.

One day this cellarer, who chanced to be passing by, for some reason I do not know, called in on the man of God. The latter received him with a pleasant expression and had the table liberally spread with what he had to hand, as hospitality required. When the meal was over and the cellarer about to go on his way, the man of God, who thus far had held his peace, now cried out like a woman in travail.[279] "Up to now," he exclaimed, "you have crossed me and made my spirit bitter;[280] let God now judge between you and me."[281] The other, judged, went out condemned and carried his judgment with him, paying scant heed to his own temerity or to the sentence pronounced by heaven. Instead, adding obstinacy to the earlier injustice, he grew hugely inflated, and, taking pride in transgressing, came to sin beyond measure through contempt, until, when Wulfric's servant came to him again, he heaped the lad with invective and sent him back to his master empty-handed, carrying nothing but blasphemies and curses. The holy man flared up on hearing this and loosed a lethal word: "May God this day," he said, "take that man's food away who has taken mine from me!" And it happened that very day that the cellarer, on his mortal journey, was swept away in a sudden flood and, meeting a fearful end, fell into the hand of God.[282] **b**

Now this is slippery ground where I personally watch my feet, and I would advise you to do the same for fear of stumbling, as it is still dark. I say this to forestall any rush to premature judgment[283]—whether to predict this man's eternal death or the salvation of his soul when and if God should so decide—and arriving at an over-hasty verdict about a death which consists at present in the destruction of the body. It is, moreover, the height of blind presumption and a temptation passing human strength to seek

[279] Isa 42:14.
[280] Ps 105:33.
[281] Gen 16:5.
[282] Heb 10:31.
[283] 1 Cor 4:5.

rashly to determine matters which lie for now beyond our mortal day, and which, referred to the hearing of a higher court, are the preserve of God alone.

But when God's servant heard all this, he began to be eaten away with bitter self-reproach, persuaded that the breath of his lips[284] had killed the man. Battering the ears of God and his friends alike with his lamentations over him and pricked by repentance, he shouldered the blood guilt of the other's death. For the rest, when his closest friends reproached him in private about the business and asked why he had spoken so harsh a word, he replied: "That was what I had to do and what I needs must say." Let him receive it who can;[285] others must trust at least in the Gospel truth that it was better for this man to hasten to his destruction and be drowned in the sea[286] of that death with a heavy weight of judgment fastened on him. For thus he deterred the unspiritual[287] like himself who, having no understanding[288] (unless through an ordeal so dire as to exalt their judge, such as having a millstone hung round the neck) might otherwise by following his example be the downfall of a little one like these.[289][c] Perhaps, too, there was no better way for the cellarer to heal the soul of the holy man he had so gravely wounded, than by teaching him, already contrite over his fault, also to lament the death of an enemy, while arming him with the virtue of charity against any like occasion in the future. This I had from Brother William and he in turn from the holy man: but there are other very reliable witnesses, including a well-respected and religious woman called Muriel de Beauchamp.[d]

2. 16. Of a judgment on another defamer, his repentance and healing

It is true that he grew gentler after this and better at loving his enemies, but the Lord continued jealous on his behalf, even in the

[284] Isa 11:4.
[285] Matt 19:12.
[286] Matt 18:6.
[287] 1 Cor 2:14.
[288] Ps 31:9.
[289] Matt 18:6.

king's court and in respect of the king's close friend. The name of this friend was Drogo de Munci.[a] Originally from overseas, he was a great man in the household of King Henry. When he heard blessed Wulfric's name extolled at court and his doings reverently recounted by the courtiers, the wretch began to curse and scoff: "The king would do well to send to the cell of this charlatan and confiscate his money, for it cannot be that a man so many flock to has not got plenty stowed away." The blasphemous words were still on his lips when Satan, to whom he had been delivered that he might learn not to blaspheme, threw him to the ground, where he rolled foaming at the mouth, a mouth that was now twisted round to his ear. There was uproar as people crowded round, crying: "Ah!" and "Woe!" and "Alas, most noble lord!" for this was not any ordinary member of the household but one whose illustrious name rendered the judgment more awesome. All the witnesses stored in their hearts what they had seen and heard,[290] declaring that blessed Wulfric was truly a saint of God and that the hand of the Lord was on all who touched him.[291]

Those present at once reported the matter to the queen[b] and the queen herself informed the king, begging him daily and ever more insistently that he lose no time in going to so great a friend of God, who by his prayers and merits could confer great benefit both on himself and on his kingdom. So when reasons arose which called him to those parts, the king was glad to seize the occasion offered and bent his way to the man of God. There, setting aside all regal show, he spent a longish time in humble converse, commended himself urgently to the saint's prayers and then, at the queen's suggestion, put in a plea for the above-named knight, relating first his folly and then the punishment of that folly. Having heard him out, the holy man meekly replied: "For my part, I do not hold this sin against him."[292] Some were pressing him to lay his hand on the knight—for the king had brought him along, very weak and fearful to look at—and to these he said: "Myself, I am prepared

[290] Luke 2:51.
[291] Zech 2:8-9.
[292] Ps 31:2.

to do whatever I ought." So one of the bystanders took the saint's hand and placed it on the sick man's face, whereupon his mouth returned to its proper place and the man recovered his senses and spoke clearly, glorifying God and glorifying too his servant's gifts of healing. In regard to his own example he went so far as to testify in person and in the general hearing, saying: "Touch not God's anointed and do his prophets no harm."[293] The king and his followers marveled at this sign and went away strengthened by Wulfric's blessing and highly delighted with his presence. This story was told me by Brother William and by Muriel de Beauchamp, to whom the holy man had recounted it on separate occasions.

2. 17. Of his hospitality and almsgiving

Since it was suspicion over money that gave this knight occasion for slander, it should be acknowledged that much money was offered to the man of God, and of this the greater part was accepted. Indeed, for the rich to present themselves before him empty-handed with their petitions would not have been fitting; on the contrary, it is written: "And the daughters of Tyre will sue with gifts,"[294] and, "For the one sowing spiritual things it is not too much if he reaps material benefits."[295] These last were scrupulously dispensed by this devotee of hospitality and minister to Christ's poor, who placed with both hands what he had at the service of piety, while he himself kept within unvarying norms of simplicity and poverty. The parish church too he furnished lavishly with books and phylacteries[a] and precious vestments sent to him by the Lord, crowning with glory, in the matter of ornaments and riches, the beauty of the king's daughter.[296] As for Christ's poor men of Forde, he poured out on them the wealth of his simplicity, for he held them specially close in God's love and reverenced them as angels.

[293] Ps 104:15; 1 Chr 16:22.
[294] Ps 44:13.
[295] 1 Cor 9:11.
[296] Ps 44:14.

2. 18. Of praise for the Cistercians and some criticism too

Nor was it only the monks of Forde: he clasped all members of the Cistercian order to him in a close embrace, like sons of his own body, or rather of Jesus Christ's. He lauded the order to the skies and had no doubts in directing to it any who came to consult him about reforming their lives. This champion and herald of our order charged the Cistercians with displeasing God in one thing only: they exploited gifts, that is, properties, in their jurisdiction over-freely, paying more attention to what could be than to what should be done, and, in the case of those committed to their patronage, seemed insufficiently mindful of what was due to kindness. In all other ways, he said, they were like God's angels: in their self-denial in matters of food and clothing, in discipline, in charity, in every form of holiness they pleased him whose approbation they desired.

2. 19. Of the sacrifice of the altar consecrated without water

I will come now to visions and revelations of the Lord[297] in which God opened the eyes of his servant to what lay afar off, that he might interpret the divine will to humankind and announce the hidden secrets[298] of heaven to those to whom he was sent. Among those revelations I have thought right and proper to give the first and principal place to the sign worked for him at the altar, both because it says much about faith and also because it is seen to be the matter of the Church.

So it happened during the holy man's mass, when he had completed with due solemnity the rite of consecration and said the Lord's Prayer, that he was preparing himself to receive the sacrament when a doubt arose in him as to whether he had poured the water into the chalice. Searching his memory on this point and questioning the server who came in daily to assist him, he grew quite convinced that the water had not been added. At that he was

[297] 2 Cor 12:1.
[298] Isa 45:3.

pounced on by a fear that overpowered and all but engulfed him, for he had no idea what to do or where to turn for help. He began of course to question in his heart the validity of the sacrament: whether anything had been effected in the absence of the water, and if the water ought to be added even now and the prayer of consecration repeated from the beginning. In the end, so great were the faith and reverence of the man that the great storm[299] of anxiety weighing on him won the day. And so, to atone for his negligence in respect of the holy sacrifice, he proceeded to immolate his soul to God, along with the blood of bitterest sorrow and the pure water of penitence seemingly wrung from his heart into the chalice of the Lord. For a while he hung thus on the cross of anxiety and doubt with Christ, whom he had before him, and, totally intent on the Lord, with either hand he raised his soul to him,[300] experiencing in that most timely moment the power that pure faith has with God. Just like an arrow in the hand of a warrior,[301] the prayer of that just man, loosed with power, pierced every cloud to arrive in the heavens and, passing through, came trustingly into the presence of God; nor did it tarry even there, but felt free to enter the very ears of God. So this archer's right hand did not fail him at the last, nor did the arrow turn back, but prospered in the thing for which it was sent.[302] His prayer concluded, he looked in the chalice, and behold! a rose-red blood as of the immaculate Lamb, Jesus Christ, filled the cup to the rim. At this sight he was filled in very truth with overflowing joy and started to pour out his whole being in thanksgiving, and the darkness was as light to him.[303] Having received the sacrament of the Body of the Lord he drank the finest blood of the grape.[304] Thus the double consecration served to build up his faith, both as to how he should believe in accordance with truth and what he might hope for by grace of virtue.

[299] Ps 49:3.
[300] Ps 24:1.
[301] Ps 126:4.
[302] Isa 55:11.
[303] Ps 138:12.
[304] Deut 32:14.

2. 20. Of the conversion of Abbot Henry of Waverley which he foretold

The second place I thought should be given to matters touching the late revered Henry, who followed the lord abbot Gilbert as humble servant of the saints at Waverley.[a] I am very familiar with his story as I had it straight from his own lips, as though I had been chosen by God as a witness[305] fit to pass it on to you. But now I am going to tell the tale in his own person, to let it run more merrily and smoothly: so prepare yourselves to listen and believe.

"In the time of King Stephen," he began, "when men abused with growing lawlessness a providential period of peace, affronting God who had given it, there was sent, as you know, a sword into the kingdom of England which banished peace from the land, severed alliances, forged conspiracies, and led in the end to general mayhem. Like beasts of the forest that leave their lairs at nightfall,[306] lovers of war burst from their hideouts and scattered to rob and pillage across the land, and the thoughts of many hearts were revealed.[307] The enemies of peace prospered in their ways,[308] and wickedness, thinking it had found an opportune moment,[309] was active all night long in works of darkness.[310] In those days—which it helps to remember now to commend to the grace of God—I myself was one of that band who hated peace. I strove to ply my soldier's trade as circumstance allowed and succeeded better than many of my kind.[311][b] Yet such as I was, I still bethought myself from time to time of God,[312] and just as in the temptations that we now endure, I knew instinctively what was right but long lacked the will to do it.

"Then something arose to take me into Wessex, and it struck me that I might call in passing on the holy man of Haselbury, of whom many and marvelous things were told, and receive a bless-

[305] Acts 10:41.
[306] Ps 103:20, 22.
[307] Luke 2:35.
[308] Ps 36:7.
[309] 2 Macc 4:32.
[310] Rom 13:12.
[311] Gal 1:14.
[312] Jer 51:50.

ing from his lips. So I set out and came to Haselbury, but getting there too late in the day to see the man of God, I had to wait until morning. When day broke I attended the mass he celebrated, and on hearing him say a separate collect for a friend of his, I commented to myself: 'A lucky fellow indeed, to be honored with a collect by the holy man!' After the celebration, Brihtric, the priest of that church, came up to me, saying: Come to my master, he is asking for you. And I, filled with a high hope by this summons, followed Brihtric to the man of God. He greeted me directly with a smile as though he already knew me, and I returned his greeting reverently and proceeded to seat myself.[c] 'I said a collect for you at my mass today,' he said. I received this glad news with gestures of joy and started to pour out my thanks. Giving me a long look—and his look was intensely bright and penetrating—he burst into tears, saying: 'He'd be a happy man to whom it was given to do what you will do one day!' Exulting in wonderment at the suddenness of the salvation promised, I replied: 'Sir, I am a sinful man,[313] steeped indeed in sin, and living in sin to this day.' 'This I knew,' he said, 'but what you are to be I know as well.' Then rolling out my past life and interpreting my future as though he were reading and relating to me an unbroken story: 'That church,' he said, 'that you seized with violence, you must hand it back.' He spoke too of the success of my journey, and, regarding events which were to take place before my return in the region I was going to, he foretold them with richly detailed accuracy and in the order in which they were later proved to have happened.

"To be brief, after listening to him and drawing no little hope and edification from the gracious words which proceeded from his mouth,[314] I bade him at last farewell and went on my way rejoicing,[315] with the promise of my salvation folded in my heart. A little while later, having successfully dealt with the occasions of my journey and the affairs which had arisen since and which he had foretold me, I returned as I had promised to my messenger of

[313] Luke 5:8.
[314] Luke 4:22.
[315] Acts 8:39.

peace. For a time I was allowed to hang on his words, sucking in their milk, better by far than the wine[316] on which he had found me drunk; and when he had watered his new seedbed, I carried away the fruit of a second blessing.

"But alas for me, poor wretch! Too soon by far, and before Christ was formed in me[317] I let myself be torn away from him. How heavy the yoke of wickedness, how wretched the state of my servitude! I very soon managed to wipe these events from my mind, and just as a prisoner, recaptured after a furtive flitting, is held in closer custody and made to pay the price of his escape, so I too, fleeing from the face of the Lord and his saint, was caught in deeper darkness still. At length, as in the days of old, when after the coming of Moses to the people of Israel Pharaoh's hand weighed heavier upon them,[318] I too began to grumble privately against my Moses[319] and give utterance to my just complaint.[320] 'Where is the word of my prophet now,' I muttered, 'and where is the promise God made me through his mouth?' Nonetheless, because the word of the Lord could not fail,[321] in the fullness of time[322] as he had preordained it, he remembered his mercy and faithfulness[323] towards me and, arousing me to repentance, quickened his servant's word in me.[324] Because my weaknesses were greatly increased,[325] I fled hotfoot to make my profession in the humility of this order, that in its shadow I might hide from the face of God and from the glory of his majesty.[326] **d** Since then he himself has known of my progress and his eyes have seen what is unfinished in me;[327] but this is the track my feet have left[328] and this

[316] Song 1:1.
[317] Gal 4:19.
[318] Exod 7:14.
[319] Exod 15:24.
[320] 2 Sam 19:28.
[321] Tob 14:6; Rom 9:6.
[322] Gal 4:4.
[323] Ps 97:3.
[324] Isa 44:26.
[325] Ps 15:4.
[326] Isa 2:10.
[327] Ps 138:16.
[328] Job 13:27.

the order of the Lord's mercies bestowed on his poor servant to this very day. I understand no better by what order of God's judgments I was called to Tintern to serve as abbot when the novice I was had only just put on the monk; unless it be that he will not suffer me to rest but has me, after the pattern of my former ways, going to and fro on the earth and walking up and down on it,[329] groaning under servile burdens and in travail to this day.[330]

"Now that all was well with me I did not, you may be sure, forget my soothsayer, but was constantly setting his words beside the good outcomes in my life, until I said to myself: 'I will go and see the man of God, and congratulate him on his accuracy in my regard and the fact that not one of all his words has fallen to the ground.[331] What is more, if he promised me so many good things when I was still an enemy and a traitor, how many more will he not announce now that I am reconciled? And should there be miracles for me to work he surely wouldn't keep it to himself.' So it was that I secretly opened my heart to a certain poison of pride, for which God was already preparing without my knowledge a salutary antidote. Having seized on a convenient pretext, I set out on my journey to the man of God and on arrival greeted him and said: 'I, sir, am that man to whom you once foretold things which now by God's grace have been fulfilled in me: standing here before you is the fruit of your prophecy. I have come back to you to let you give thanks for me to God, who has been merciful to me and proved you truthful too.' Back came this medicinal word: 'Right, my son, keep your rule and you will be able to save your soul.' The let-down, I confess, was instant. My inflated ideas fell away and the wound opened by my pride was bound up. Suitably chastened by the reply I withdrew, and among the many mercies of the Lord, I pondered on this last as I repeated: 'It was good for me, Lord, to be humbled, so that I might learn your statutes.'"[332e]

[329] Job 1:7.
[330] Rom 8:22.
[331] 1 Sam 3:19.
[332] Ps 118:71.

2. 21. [Of Abbot Henry's way of life] [a]

Such was the tale the venerable Father Henry unrolled so pleasantly for the lord abbot of Forde and myself on the road to the Cistercian chapter,[b] carrying us along with him as, by means of this example so close to home, he made our hearts swell as much with praise for the grace of God, who has called those whom he first predestined,[333] as with faith in all that touches our Wulfric. As for the teller, all who knew him recognized in him a man of virtues, outstanding in humility, and so long-suffering as to be almost insensible of injury. To the industry and diligence he never mentioned his works bear witness,[334] for the monastery he found dispersed and gone to rack and ruin he rebuilt—modestly and simply as our rule requires—and having established it on a sound footing, left behind a memory crowned with praise. The unremitting and exhausting burden of work which this man discharged thereafter on behalf of his community left him unconquered in spirit, if sadly neglected in body, and could never prevent him chanting the psalter in its entirety by day and by night. In this he was seen to emulate his blessed master and prophet who used to sing it through once by day and once by night. Lastly, when celebrating at the altar, the grace of tears was given him so freely that he seemed as though intoxicated with the chalice, or rather he himself intoxicated the Lord Jesus [with his tears] and offered delights to kings[335]—certainly to those believed to have worshipped there before his King and his God.[c]

Should anyone push curiosity to the searching out of sins,[336] or folly to the passing of judgment on the weaknesses of another's servant[337] (a servant of God, be it said), it is no light sin that such a one commits against his own soul, given that in sinning against God's holy one, one sins against God. And seeing that he will himself be judged by the judgment he pronounces,[338] is it not wicked

[333] Rom 8:30.
[334] John 5:36.
[335] Gen 49:20.
[336] Ps 63:7.
[337] Rom 14:4.
[338] Matt 7:1.

and a monstrous weakness to uncover a holy father's nakedness,[339] when even failing to cover it when laid bare will be considered a wrong?[340] May I never be chosen to sit on the judgment seat in my order; may I not be found among those who seek out wickedness in the house of the righteous;[341] and lastly may I have no part with gluttons who bring their meat to the table[342] and gossip barefaced about the weaknesses of the holy.[d] May my lot lie rather with those who pattern themselves on Christ, tenderly holding the frail among them, who show the holy fathers due and caring honor, who have learned from Christ to bear one another's burdens[343e] and to wash one another's feet. He gave us an example that we might do the same,[344] for truly he has borne our infirmities[345] and he it is whose ministry of love extends to washing away the filth of the daughters of Sion and cleansing Jerusalem from the blood shed in her midst.[346] And indeed, to push the argument to its end, there is one only to whom we can say: "Lamb of God,[347] you who take away the sins of the world, have mercy on us." The one and only glory of God's only Son is, "This is my beloved Son in whom I am well pleased."[348] But we leave these matters to be discussed by others at some other time; ours to bring the story of our Wulfric to its close.

2. 22. Of some debts whose rapid resolution he foretold

The same abbot would tell a memorable tale which springs readily to my mind and which some perhaps need to hear. During his time as abbot of Tintern he found himself pressed by debt beyond his means, for in that house as in many houses of this order the modest income in no way covered the endless imperative outgoings.

[339] Ezek 22:10.
[340] Gen 9:20-27.
[341] Prov 24:15.
[342] Prov 23:20.
[343] Gal 6:2.
[344] John 13:14-15.
[345] Isa 53:4.
[346] Isa 4:4.
[347] John 1:29
[348] Matt 3:17.

Groaning with anxiety under these crushing bills, he had no rest for his spirit, nor would until he could disengage his hand from the bargains he had struck with his creditors. Eventually, with no one left to turn to, he remembered having good cause to know that there was a prophet in Israel[349] and that he might well have recourse to him to resolve his material needs. There followed a journey to the man of God and a conferring with him about the divers needs of the house the abbot served, in which the household's meager substance was made plain, along with the pressing weight of debts, the importunity of creditors, the anxiety of the debtor. It was with a sober expression and sustained gravity of voice that the holy man made this response: "Confess to me on what you spent these sums which have brought you such anxiety." "I have no recollection of much of the money being idly squandered," said the abbot, "it went only in honor of God and for the use of my house." Faced for a second time with the same question, he replied in similar vein; and when he perseveringly maintained his stance, the holy man gave this reply: "In the Lord's word I declare to you that within a short time whatever sums you spent in God's honor will be ready and coming to meet you." The abbot believed in the truth of his prophecy, having tested it over many years, and went on his way.

Arriving in Bristol for the crossing to Tintern, he ran unexpectedly into a man whom God had moved to give money to the poor and to religious houses and who sought the abbot's advice in this, as he wanted the sum he was duly offering to be rightly divided up under the other's direction. The abbot busied himself with making arrangements for each beneficiary, in the measure of his discretion and of the money to be distributed, but was too embarrassed to suggest his own house. His delicacy, however, did not go unrewarded, for when the man disbursing the money noticed, he asked immediately: "When are you going to mention your own house?" "This is for your benefit, not mine." "Write down for your house twenty-four marks,"[350] said the other. And the abbot added them to the account. It remains to be said that

[349] 2 Kgs 5:8.
[350] Luke 16:6-7.

the sum of the debt exceeded this sum, a fact that plainly led the abbot to consider whether he had spent the rest of the money on vain or superfluous things, or, if on the things of God, then with a less than pure intention.[a]

Those who are faint-hearted in similar circumstances, and with reference to what they have spent on God's behalf and according to his will, are advised to remember that it is God, not they, who is both debtor and creditor. The Lord is at hand,[351] to whom this account pertains; they should be anxious for nothing[352] as regards themselves. He is both faithful in cancelling what is owing to him and rich—should you doubt his willing what he is patently able to do. This should likewise be taken to heart by those who, in the hope of getting themselves an empty name (soon blown away), deal freely, not to say sacrilegiously, in what has been dedicated to God, and who use the substance of the poor[353] to trade in vanity. And then, as though the matter had been well managed, they end up dumping their debts on God, so that *he* may pay for what *they* have plundered; in other words they are far from salvation and so heedless of the Lord that even at this late stage they fail to repent of their expensive ambitions and return to the one who smites them.[354]

2. 23. Of Abbot Henry's reverence for the man of God

The same venerable father told another tale about the holy man which is eminently worth recalling. The matter in question, involving those men of surpassing merit, blessed Bernard and blessed Wulfric, was certainly well known to him, as it had evolved while he was serving as intermediary between the two. Having been conceived in Christ through Wulfric's gift of prophecy, Father Henry cherished God's saint with filial love and reverence. He listened devoutly to his doings and passed them on with an even greater devotion, principally to those who, by virtue of their own holiness,

[351] Phil 4:5.
[352] Phil 4:6.
[353] Sir 34:24.
[354] Isa 9:13.

had a particular veneration for holiness in others. Wherever he went he revolved the man's praises in his mouth as a horse champs at the bit, and he carried his name around with him like a troubadour his lute, purchasing for his Wulfric, as it were at a set price, the intimacy of holy men. When at last he obtained an audience with the supreme pontiff,[a] he duly produced his Wulfric, and the pope being as avid to hear as he to tell, even a long talk was not long enough. During this time there were great men standing outside the sacred audience chamber, pillars of the church wanting and waiting to enter, while causes of huge importance and the business of all the countries round about requiring the pope's attention were left in suspense. Inside, meanwhile, the lord pope and Father Henry had their heads together in blessed Wulfric's name; absorbed in the mystery of holiness they were eating the honeycomb with their honey and drinking their wine with their milk.[355] And Father Henry, as he told us later, was privately glorying in the fact that he had all the attention of the man whom the whole world was waiting on, and was seen to enjoy not only open access to such greatness but even a certain intimacy and fellowship.

Later, visiting blessed Bernard of Clairvaux, he unrolled the famous story yet again and preached the faith and splendor of angelic simplicity to this most holy and wise of men. Rejoicing mightily in the glory of God and his saint, blessed Bernard then humbly confessed to Father Henry an intemperance of his own and commissioned him to ask blessed Wulfric if he would obtain mercy for him from God in respect of it. Our going into the matter of this intemperance a little more deeply will not, we trust, weary the listener.

2. 24. Of the schism under Pope Innocent to whom blessed Bernard lent support

At the very outset of the papacy of the lord pope Innocent the church was rent in two and the roaring Pierleone[a] devoured many of its members.[356] And because the house was shaken from its

[355] Song 5:1.
[356] 1 Pet 5:8.

foundations, it began to fear imminent collapse, and the church, wounded in the head, feared naturally for the life of her whole body. Weeping and wailing she appealed to her sons for help, whereupon blessed Bernard, filled with grace and power,[357] hurried to the rescue, reverently and firmly taking the tottering mother in his arms.[358] For a time, the devoted son that he was set aside his holy and delightful leisure in order to succor his afflicted mother, believing he ought with his labors to purchase the peace of many, for he was one to whom it was truly given to say in all sincerity: "The king brought me into his wine-cellar,"[359] and "he set love in order in me."[360] And so this blessed soul, the bride of Jesus Christ, rose resolutely from that royal couch, and, not without some inner rending, tore herself for a time from the bridegroom's arms.**[b]**

He came forth then, accompanied as to a solemn festival, amid the plaudits of those who blessed him because he was coming in the name of the Lord and the admiration of those exclaiming: "Who is this coming up from the desert, overflowing with delights?"[361] The grace of the Lord attended his beloved and, poured generously on his lips,[362] flowed courteously from his mouth and dripped abundantly from his hands. Lastly, wherever the man was, there was light, wherever he walked grace was in the air, and the scent of his garments was like the scent of frankincense.[363] When he spoke and lifted his voice with power you might have said that it thundered,[364] and when he appeared and lit everything with his coming, that lightning had flashed from heaven.[365] Indeed the Lord's chosen arrow[366] went straight to the hearts of the king's enemies; not one escaped from his heat,[367] which consumed all things, took

[357] Acts 6:8.
[358] Luke 2:28.
[359] Song 1:3.
[360] Song 2:4.
[361] Song 8:5.
[362] Ps 44:3.
[363] Song 4:11.
[364] John 12:29.
[365] Luke 17:24.
[366] Isa 49:2.
[367] Ps 18:7.

all things captive, led all in triumph to do obeisance to Christ.[368] He pursued the wicked of Israel, and those who troubled the people of God he vanquished with the two-edged sword of his mouth;[369] and again, like the dove when the flood ceased, he brought back to the church the fruit of peace.[370] God was indeed in his saint, reconciling his church to himself,[371] and went before him destroying and scattering his enemies round about.

This is exactly how it was, and thus does the church take pleasure in its beloved son, whatever nonsense his rivals may put about, if there are any still alive whom God, his vindicator,[372] has neither humbled nor brought to ruin. And just as I in my turn, meeting this most excellent man on my road, kiss his feet, for it would not be right to pass by leaving him ungreeted, just so do I believe in my heart and confess with my lips that my service is both wanting and unworthy. For it is the bridegroom who has the bride,[373] and none but he can fittingly greet her, for while she was still with us, her soul found all day long its praise in him,[374] and his words were intimately known to her. So even if queens and concubines praise her,[375] and if her sons who rival today the stars of heaven[376] proclaim her most blessed, the voice of her beloved alone suffices to fill her with praise to overflowing.

2. 25. Of a fault of blessed Bernard's which the holy man expounded before it was told him and declared that it had been remitted

It was while the judgment of God was still pending and no one knew to which party heaven would give the victory, leaving the

[368] 2 Cor 10:5.
[369] Heb 4:12.
[370] Gen 8:10-11.
[371] 2 Cor 5:19.
[372] Isa 63:1.
[373] John 3:29.
[374] Ps 33:3; 43:9.
[375] Song 6:8.
[376] Deut 1:10.

population of Rome still wavering between the two sides,[377] that blessed Bernard lifted his voice in the midst of the church and addressed the people with a flow of eloquence. After spinning it out at some length, he let fall from his lips that heaven's will was this:[378] that the Church should turn to Innocent. Now, the abbot, being spiritual, scrutinized his every action lest the merest spot should discolor that face[379] so fair in the eyes of the heavenly bridegroom. Having sniffed in his discourse a whiff of presumption, he withdrew the arrogant words and tore his heart from them as though from a blasphemy. He then, zealot that he was, took himself to task with the freedom he habitually used when dealing with kings and princes and magnates, as one set by God over nations and kingdoms; one who, through the authority of the Holy Spirit which shone in him with a rare brightness, was to those princes as awesome and terrible as an army with banners.[380] And as in the house of the just man there were not differing weights,[381] so did he turn the same strictures on himself in a spirit of judgment and a spirit of burning,[382] and not presuming himself sufficient on his own to reconcile God to himself, he sent a messenger to our Wulfric to ask for a sacrifice of prayer to be offered for this sin of his.[a] So it was that Father Henry came to his father in God, greeted him in blessed Bernard's name, and explaining the case said: "Blessed Bernard sent me to ask you to pray to the Lord about a sin which puts him in great fear for his soul." The holy man snatched these words from his lips and would not let him continue: "Why did he want to lay claim to a knowledge hidden in God?" Then he added: "If he had said that he thought this was the will of heaven, he would have spoken rightly. All the same, God has accepted his penitence and from now on these words of his will not be imputed to him as a sin." Father Henry, left quaking by what was said, reckoned he had told the sage quite enough.

[377] 1 Kgs 18:21.
[378] 1 Macc 3:60.
[379] Song 1:5.
[380] Song 6:9.
[381] Prov 20:10, 23.
[382] Isa 4:4.

2. 26. Of the mutual embrace in which wisdom humbly accepted simplicity's bold rebuke

If what is salutary and gainful in my subject warrants my addressing you, then the virtues shown by our two saints, the high humility of the one, the splendid simplicity of the other, should not slip past unnoted. It was in truth fitting that, through the will of God, author of heavenly concord, wisdom and simplicity should meet[383] in the humility and charity of Christ, so that the wings of these living creatures might be joined together.[384] And it was especially fitting that they should, meeting to seal their bond in the kiss of peace,[385] fulfill all that righteousness demands,[386] the one increasing thereby, the other decreasing,[387] each through each, and yet advancing, abounding, growing by leaps and bounds. What then? Was this fault really so great that it could not be expiated where he was,[a] since blessed Bernard's abounding charity towards the whole church (for whose sake this word had imprudently leapt out of his eloquent discourse) sufficed to cover a multitude of sins,[388] and since, what is more, God does not spurn the humbled, contrite heart?[389] Is there then no balm in Gilead? Is there no physician there?[390] Consider and ponder who possess the sanctuary weight,[391] how the pillars of heaven tremble[392] at the nod of that eternal majesty, how great a love of justice is needed in true lovers of God, and, finally, what hatred of iniquity in those who thirst after justice.[393] O justice, sought far afield by your friend, the man of God,[b] how very far abroad are you from us who take no care for our wounds and are thus so far from a cure! Precious were you

[383] Ps 84:11.
[384] Ezek 1:9.
[385] Ps 84:11.
[386] Matt 3:15.
[387] John 3:30.
[388] 1 Pet 4:8.
[389] Ps 50:19.
[390] Jer 8:22.
[391] Lev 5:15 and Num 7 *passim*.
[392] Job 26:11.
[393] Matt 5:6.

to him for whom your price was beyond the farthest reaches,[394] great and glorious were you in his eyes and you ran to meet him like an honored mother.[395] O high humility of blessed Bernard, more precious to me than a thousand miracles, safest of spots where his feet stood planted, how will we do you worthy reverence, you who leveled that mountain of spices[396] down to the feet of this little one of God? But the simplicity of our Wulfric was exalted too that day, when that abode of wisdom, that holiness revered even by the citizens of heaven, bent down to the very soles of his feet. Master, you have grown in my eyes this day, inasmuch as you have been raised to the peak of this high mountain and made, in your simplicity, an angel of reconciliation and peace for so great a friend of God. Who will doubt that the coal you took from the altar of God, with the tongs of your simplicity[397] and in the charity of your heart, to cleanse our prophet's lips, was that glowing coal of reproof which lays waste?[398] But seeking pardon for this digression from those who walk with me, I am now obliged to bid farewell to blessed Bernard, not without keen regret, for my heart yearns after my father, the chariot of Israel, and its driver.[399] O sweet fragrance of Christ Jesus, fare you well now in the eternal kiss of your Solomon, draw us after you in the fragrance of your ointments,[400] and in your strength may there be peace[401] throughout God's church as in the days of old.

2. 27. Of Matilda, a recluse of Wareham, whose conversion, life, death, and future glory he foretold

The anchorite John, of Winterbourne in the county of Dorset, a man who has kept from youth to a holy way of life, tells the story I

[394] Prov 31:10.
[395] Sir 15:2.
[396] Song 8:14.
[397] Isa 6:6.
[398] Ps 119:4.
[399] 2 Kgs 2:12.
[400] Song 1:3.
[401] Ps 121:7.

am about to write and calls as witness to it truth in person,[a] whose presence in John's testimony we do not question as the anchorite lives with him in intimate friendship. Christina, too, the venerable recluse of Wareham, who has this truth in the safest of safekeeping, and of whom I more than once made careful inquiry, gave this story her full backing.

The holy man shouted for his lad one day and gave him these instructions: "My sister is just arriving; go out and call to her and bring her in to me." The lad went out and looked around but, seeing no one, went back to his master and told him so. "Be quick," said the man of God, "and run to meet her, for here comes my sister hurrying towards you!" Having gone back again, the lad met a woman coming through the graveyard and, greeting her, he led her to his master. When these two had exchanged courtesies, the holy man asked her her birthplace and the reason for her journey. She had been born in Wessex, she replied, and had been travelling in foreign parts. "You will be living nearer to hand," said the man of God, "your dwelling will be on this side of the sea. You will serve God fifteen years as an anchoress at Wareham, and the sixteenth year will see the end of your life. Then you will set out with joy to go to your Lord, for your dwelling-place in heaven has already been prepared.[402] But first you will work for two and a half years in that town as a mattress-maker, during which time you will, God aiding, build yourself a house to live in for the days remaining of your earthly journey.[403] As for where you are to live while your house is being built, the Lord has made provision for you here too and will give you grace in the eyes of one of the townsfolk. So take courage and get going,[404] for the Lord will be your helper in all you undertake." This was what the holy man announced with much grace and gaiety of spirit to that woman blessed of the Lord and in his name, and from that day on, thanks to these encouragements,[b] God's word of power sustained and built up the woman's faith.

[402] John 14:2.
[403] Eccl 7:1.
[404] 1 Esdr 10:4.

She meanwhile, adoring heaven's preemptive grace, gave thanks to God's saint and took to the road again, waiting confidently on the fulfillment of the divine promise and knowing the order, manner, time, and also place. So it was that, on coming to the town of Wareham, she met with God's graces one by one, as had been preordained and foretold to her. And eventually, when her house had been built in the set number of days and with the profits of the craft we spoke of, she entered into her long-desired solitude, where she lived in such favor with God and her neighbors as to prove that blessed Wulfric had been right to call her "sister"; that she even deserved that the king desire her beauty[405] when our sister was still a child and had as yet no breasts.[406c] Indeed it was she, of all the women he had seen, to whom this chaste man, who enjoyed the pure friendship of many, paid the highest tributes of praise, according her in his judgment the very palm, and he was a man who had in no small degree the discernment of spirits. The Lord alone is of course the true weigher of spirits, he who weighs the mountains in scales and the hills in a balance.[407]

2. 28. Of Matilda's patience

To give a memorable example of her virtues: it happened that her servant Gertrude, a maiden wise in every way[408] and fervently bent on all that is holy, developed a toothache, a pain which is held to pass all others, there being no pain like this one.[409] And so, finding no escape from this agony, the woman took refuge in the last resort of the desolate and poured out her distress in the ears of her mistress, hoping at least for some word of soothing solace. But the latter retorted: "Oh Gertrude, why do you complain so loudly and incessantly? Say rather, "Good for whoever suffers so with toothache that her jaw rots away from the pain and she drops down dead, without ever letting a moan or a groan escape her!'" So

[405] Ps 44:12.
[406] Song 8:8.
[407] Isa 40:12.
[408] Matt 25:1.
[409] Lam 1:12.

said Matilda (for that was her name) to Gertrude without elaborating, and, by suppressing the name, she reverently[a] concealed the secret of such extraordinary patience. She took a similar care of her modesty by maintaining that steady color in a serene countenance which delights the heavenly bridegroom, who, after the manner of an ardent lover, is the keenest observer of sacred beauty. That she was truly a woman of deep silence is plain: she abstained not only from grumbling when in pain but from any sort of muttering at all,[b] and having overcome these temptations, showed equal virtue in not parading her patience.

When this holy handmaid of the Lord arrived at the fourteenth year of her profession, she was visited by an ailment, or rather by several, which came running like messengers from the army of God, each on the heels of the last, to tell her that her days were numbered.[410] To Gertrude, offering sympathy and what practical help she might from outside the cell, she spoke as follows: "This year my sufferings have given me a warning and a sign, and next year they will impress it upon me more forcibly, and in the third to the limit." Thus in the sixteenth year of her conversion the Lord let her go in peace according to his word,[411] that he might show his beloved the glory of his kingdom and the countenance of his glory.

After Gertrude, fired with holy zeal, had succeeded her,[c] exploring one day a hole in the wall she saw what looked like a bone hidden there. On taking it out and examining it more closely she remembered the words of her mistress and recognized this for the bone of her patience—that strongest of bones—which, if hidden till now from the sight of men, was not hidden from him who made it in secret.[412] So while Matilda kept the strong woman[413] hidden from us, Gertrude, with God's guidance, found her, and from the treasures of her mistress brought forth the fine and desirable gemstone.[414] And if the dough offered as first fruits is holy, so

[410] Ps 101:24.
[411] Luke 2:29.
[412] Ps 138:15.
[413] Prov 31:10.
[414] Ps 18:11.

is the whole lump.[415] So if you want to know what Matilda was like, taste and see,[416] for she was like that all through: sweet, tranquil, exuding peace and patience.

With what praises shall we adorn one already arrayed in purple and crowned with bay, who has brought back from the mighty combat so glorious a triumph? Who is this who has gone up onto that high mountain[417] of virtue, who has climbed the palm tree and plucked[418] the sublime and soothing fruits of patience? Brightest red with the blood of martyrdom, she is worthy of the bridegroom's joyful greeting: "Your teeth are like a flock of shorn ewes."[419] For just as a sheep before its shearer is dumb and does not open its mouth,[420] so from between the teeth of this woman, when questioned and probed by pain, no grating is heard, no discordant sounds of complaining and temper escape: we hear only patience and peace. Weeping and grinding of teeth[421] belong to those in hell and their like, who complain when they are tormented and grind their teeth[422] at God's justice when it is visited on them, yet suffer more in their wretched state from their own impatience than from the torments inflicted. And truly grace and peace are the lot of God's elect, who, faithful in love, repose in him.[423] Their senses quieted and ordered, too, by the law of holy discipline, they hunger to get their perfectly disposed teeth (so to speak) into justice and relish its sweet fruits. To turn finally to the one who was the meekest man on earth:[424] it is written that his teeth stayed firm[425] because in all the afflictions with which the Lord tried or chastened Israel, as also throughout the murmurings with which the people angered both God and himself, he kept his meekness towards them and God unvanquished.

[415] Rom 11:16.
[416] Ps 33:9.
[417] Song 8:5; Isa 40:9.
[418] Song 7:8.
[419] Song 4:2.
[420] Isa 53:7.
[421] Matt 8:12.
[422] Ps 36:12.
[423] Wis.. 3:9.
[424] Moses. Num 12:3.
[425] Deut 34:7.

2. 29. How Matilda valiantly withstood the temptation of hunger

Now listen to something new on earth, how a woman put on the man,[426] and that, too, while she was still preparing herself for the religious life and building the cell in which she later lived. On a day when she stayed praying, as was her way, after the celebration of mass, she found herself attacked in church by sharp hunger pangs. She wondered at this inhabitual temptation, and what this hunger could want with her, there, then, and unwonted as it was. Well knowing where it came from, she braced herself and returned to prayer; holy hands were raised heavenward[427] with great insistence and faith.

What more's to say? The tempter once forced out, the temptation was blown aside. Ousted and baffled he might be but not as yet kept at bay: war broke out anew, the arrows of hunger were loosed again with dreaded aim, but Christ was no less present and Christ was again victorious in the woman. This debate was by no means friendly, nor one to be soon resolved, since thirst for God and bodily hunger are not compatible.

The continuing combat was interrupted by the dinner hour which called the woman home from church with her appetite now somewhat stilled. On the other hand, as she would not consider herself to be more than a woman with less than a total victory, she refused point-blank to taste any of the food she found prepared but, distributing it all for the love of God, consecrated the rest of the day to abstinence. Thus for Matilda it was too little to have won a nominal victory by not giving way to spiritual iniquity; in the fury of her zeal she dared to pursue the fleeing attacker, resolved to suppress the very goadings of temptation.

What shall I say in conclusion about that extraordinary fragrance, a scent as of nard distilled in the nostrils of those present, when her tomb was opened so that her blessed disciple Gertrude, who had

[426] Jer 31:22.
[427] 1 Tim 2:8.

successfully run her race to the end,[428] might be buried with her? Ralph, the priest of Wareham (a priest approved of God and men and renowned in those parts for clean living and holiness), told me, nay rather constantly assured me, lest my Christina should mislead me, being mistaken herself, that when he opened the grave—for he officiated in person at Gertrude's burial—he was miraculously refreshed by the sweetness of the fragrance that burst forth. And the board as well which had served to support that sacred body, as though changed by heaven into an aromatic wood, had thoroughly imbibed the sweetness of its sacred deposit and gave the impression of having been smeared or even steeped in honey.

But let us return to our Wulfric, although these matters should not be thought of as alien to his praises. For all these fruits are consecrated to Wulfric, all these things advance his reputation, add to his glory. Why did God send him this holy woman or venerable Father Henry or other people of the same merit, if not that they might in some way be justified through him and he himself glorified through them? And if we are at pains to point out this interchange, it is because he owed his own vocation altogether to God's grace, through what is believed to have been a prevenient angelic calling, enabling him to serve in a similar way as harbinger of peace and glory to others. But it was into vessels of mercy that he poured out these mercies, while to the vessel of wrath,[429] in a manner still to be revealed, he showed himself terrible—more precisely, he was not allowed to show himself at all but took measures to oust from his neighborhood one coming from afar. But if you don't mind, this tale and its truth will be held over for a new beginning. For the day as you see is drawing towards evening and I am most reluctant to keep you listening until after sundown,[430] anxious as I am to offer you, not tedium, but enjoyment.

Here ends the second book

428 2 Tim 4:7.
429 Rom 9:22, 23.
430 Eph 4:26.

Here begins the third book

3. 1. Of an instance of severity shown by blessed Wulfric

A rich woman held in high respect by holy men came to see the man of God. She was seated there talking with him of the salvation of her soul when he interrupted her by shouting so loudly for his boy that, in the shock of this sudden outburst, she feared her secrets were about to be divulged. The lad duly appeared and the man of God said to him: "Run quickly to the bridge outside the village and you will see a man on the opposite side walking with broken shoes on his bare feet and dressed in such and such a way. You will speak to him and warn him in the Lord's name not to cross that bridge or come near me, for I will have nothing at all to do with him. Hurry to meet him for he has already set foot on the bridge." Dashing off as fast as he could, the boy spotted on the far side of the bridge a man dressed as described, and by dint of shouting and waving, got him to wait where he was. He then joined the fellow and relayed to him what he had heard from the man of God, at which the other let out a great howl of distress and threw himself on the ground, writhing like a woman in labor. The boy who had given him this message felt for him acutely,[431] and, going back to his master, told him—not without his own voice breaking—of the groans too deep for words[432] that this man had given vent to. This upset in turn the woman, still on her stool, and she added her pleas to the boy's entreaties that the man of God might take pity on such extreme distress. But he, setting his face[433] and hardening it like adamant and flint,[434] said: "I will not spare and I will not take pity,"[435] and reinforcing the inexorable judgment: "I neither wish nor am able to take pity." The woman, dismayed at all this, was too frightened to plead the man's cause, and instead hurried home as

[431] 1 Kgs 3:26.
[432] Rom 8:26.
[433] Ezek 4:3.
[434] Ezek 3:9.
[435] Jer 13:14.

though fleeing from a great clap of thunder,[436] and as long as she lived she revolved in her heart the scene of this terrible judgment, and as she in turn related it to others she became herself a sign and a portent[437] for all who heard these things. If you wish to know, this was the wife of the powerful Alan de Phaleisa[a]—Margaret, her name was, and I had the story from herself.

We would do well to ponder with fear (if fear leaves anyone able to evaluate the wrath of God[438] in this case) the weight of the act by which the very approach was barred to this poor wretch and the bridge of mercy occupied in advance. And not even later did he find an occasion for repentance, although he sought it with tears,[439] being judged already and condemned beforehand. And the man of God kept his heart closed[440] throughout, so that this pitiful, nay, pitiable man, should in no way move him to pity.[b] Does this tale not reflect the judgment to come, when thrones will be set up for judgment[441] on foundations of immutable stability, and these, firmly united in their zeal for judgment with the one who sits on the throne, will rise up with him against the evildoers?[442] Then clearly there will be no crossing of the bridge,[c] when those who come too late seeking salvation will be met with heavy tidings,[443] a message full of wrath,[444] a word harsh and past bearing: "Away from me, I do not know you."[445] And finally, as they weep and wail, they will hear from the throne of the implacable judge: "What I have written, I have written."[446]

[436] Ps 103:7.
[437] Isa 20:3.
[438] Ps 89:12.
[439] Heb 12:17.
[440] 1 John 3:17; Ps 76:10.
[441] Ps 121:5; Matt 19:28.
[442] Ps 93:16.
[443] 1 Kgs 14:6.
[444] Isa 13:9.
[445] Matt 7:23.
[446] John 19:22.

3. 2. Of signs in which healing and prophecy went hand in hand

Blessed Wulfric showed a gentler face when he extended in advance of their arrival a sign of clemency to those coming to see him, and, to spare them longer weariness, went out to meet them with the double gift of prophecy and healing. Let me attach a few examples of this, the first recounted to me by one Odolina, a woman well pleasing to God and professed as an anchoress in the town of Crewkerne,[a] where she served with great devotion and discernment, closely bonded in the love of Christ with men of distinction[b] for her integrity and exceptional purity of conscience.

It happened that her grandmother, who had long been suffering from grievous abdominal pain and had a great desire to see the man of God in person, being supremely confident of obtaining healing, at length got her husband to agree to take her to him. On the first leg of their journey they arrived at Crewkerne, at no great distance from Haselbury, where they spent the night. In the morning when the woman was being heaved up into the saddle of the beast of burden—her infirmity meant she had no other way of mounting—the rough handling of the invalid caused the internal ulcer, at the root of this illness, to burst. Once the source of this putrid matter was ruptured, it flowed out freely and abundantly, and the woman, placed on the ground, brought up quantities of the lethal fluid. It was still her purpose to complete the journey begun, and receive full healing at the hand of the man of God, when his servant came to meet her with the words: "My master says: 'Don't put yourself out by going any farther, for you are wholly and entirely healed.'" So the woman went home jubilant and joyful, knowing for certain that the healing had been sent ahead to her by him who afterward announced it.

3. 3. Of a demoniac cured on the road

A certain demoniac born in the neighborhood of Gloucester was sent to the man of God with an escort of eight strong men, who had him roped round the body and were dragging him along, two to a rope—a horrendous and pitiful sight. It happened that during the usual overnight halt, as the others slept, a sleep of the Lord fell on this demoniac, who awoke in his right mind, took off the harness he found himself trammelled with and threw it aside. When the men responsible for him found him free, they set about tying him up again, knowing nothing of the shortcuts of divine compassion and their conjunction with his healing which they were seeking. But the demoniac protested, saying: "There's no longer any need for you to pull me along tied up. Look, I'll walk of my own accord to my master Wulfric. He appeared to me while I slept, and freed me from the power of the evil spirit and broke the cords round my wrists. And to help you believe, this is what the man looks like," and he described his face and his white hair and his clothes and everything about him. But as they didn't believe a word he said, they tied him back up with the ropes and persisted in pulling him along. They had got within a day's journey of Haselbury when the holy man's servant met them saying: "My master Wulfric says: 'What are you doing dragging bound a man whom God has already set free? Let him loose[447] and take him quietly home.'"

So merely taking the road to the holy man was reckoned as righteousness[448] enough to merit healing. And because he was both seer and physician, blessed Wulfric visited first in prophetic guise those he relieved with succor, and by expediting the practice of healing with the short-cut of foreknowledge, at one and the same time he eased anxiety and cured disease. All the above from Richard, priest of Corscombe,[a] a man well-thought-of and a lifelong friend of the holy man, who affirms having heard it from the servant in question.

3. 4. Of a lay-brother cured on the road

A lay-brother of ours,[a] while still a boy, was long and sorely troubled by an internal complaint and was taken by his family to the man of God. As he neared Haselbury he began to vomit as though he had been dosed with some potent draught from heaven, and in so doing threw up the cause of his trouble. He was taken regardless to the man of God and was standing before him when the latter said:

[447] John 11:44.
[448] Gen 15:6; Rom 4:3.

"Why are you bothering this boy when he's already cured?"[449] And looking at the lad, he added: "You were healed, son, there where you eased yourself by vomiting."

3. 5. Another tale of the same

The same youth, now grown older, had some business that took him to the man of God. Making his way on foot, he was pestered by dogs running after him and barking, so he picked up a sharp stone which presented itself, but instead of hurting a dog as he intended, he cut his own finger quite badly. Having reached the man of God in this state and disposed of his business, he was asked whether his hand hurt. Putting up a pretence, he replied that there was nothing wrong with it. "That's not true," said the other, "because the stone you were trying to hurt the dog near Winsham[a] with, you hurt yourself with instead: but give me your hand and you will be cured." He held out his bleeding hand for the holy man's blessing and was healed on the instant.

3. 6. Of a priest who fell ill on the road and was healed on invoking him

A certain priest set out to travel from the far north of England to the man of God. When he got to Glastonbury, which is about half a day's journey from Haselbury, he withdrew to empty his bowels, and while hurrying the natural process with a strong impulsion he happened to push out his own rectum. His faith, however, was in no way enfeebled; knowing whence he came and where he was going (that is, with what holy zeal he had set out and to how virtuous a man his steps were bent), invoking his own purpose and the other's venerable name, he called out again and again with great devotion: "Holy Wulfric, help me, if what I hear of you is true! It isn't right that while I am hurrying towards you, either illness or death should come to waylay me, when others who get to you find healing for every ill." While faith, supplied with argument by need, was setting up this clamor, behold! a heaven-sent hand placed

[449] 1 Macc 12:44.

itself courteously on the extruded part and gently pushed it back into its place. Nicholas, a canon of Christchurch,[a] affirms having had this story from the priest himself.

3. 7. How a woman brought to him by a revelation was told its meaning and received healing

Christina, the venerable recluse of Wareham, had, as I learnt from her own account, a mother by the name of Richelda—a mother in religion, that is, rather than her mother by blood. This woman had suffered a long time from an internal heaviness and languor, when a man of great age, his head of fine white hair inviting veneration, appeared to her in a dream, saying: "Go to the man of God at Haselbury and he will restore you to health and free you from the red-head[a] who is riding on your shoulders." On waking, she made arrangements for setting out, but the weight of her infirmity slowed her down even as she hastened towards her healing, so although the journey was short, it was many weary days before she knocked at last at the holy man's door. "Quick!" said he, calling to his boy, "Run to my sister!" So the visitor was let in, to be received with such open signs of pleasure and delight that she, not expecting so joyful a welcome from so great a man, asked wonderingly how he knew her. "You ask how I know my sister Richelda?" he replied. Now really astounded at being known by name, she said: "What is more, sir, I came to you through a revelation from God." Snatching the words from her lips, he answered: "I knew this too and that you have come to be freed from the red-head who has got you by the neck. "And," he went on, "do you know who this red-head is? This is the adversary who has used this burdensome infirmity to impede you until now from making the pilgrimage you had intended to Saint Edmund's shrine and other holy places. And nor am I unaware that this is the ninth day[b] since you had your revelation. But stay with me now and in a short time through God's grace you will recover health and strength." So it was that blessed Wulfric, filled to overflowing with the spirit of prophecy, was able like another Daniel to explain the dream and aptly expound its meaning.[450]

[450] Dan 4:15; 5:15.

3. 8. Of the healing of Samson of Lincoln

On one occasion when Samson of Lincoln,[a] a man of no small repute in his lifetime and uncle of the present Alfred, came and stayed a while at Haselbury (as he often did, being the lady of Haselbury's brother), he was taken ill with a fever. Sending to the man of God, he appealed for the succor of common kindness. To the bearer of the request the man of God made this reply: "He'll have one more shivering fit and then it will abate." Just as the man of God had said, after one more attack of fever the man was delivered, rendering those who heard about it curious to know why he was not relieved at once with the ease he was granted after another bout.

3. 9. Of the staff that was blessed, lost at sea, and amazingly recovered

This same man took a vow to go on pilgrimage to Jerusalem and brought his staff and bag for the journey to be blessed by the holy man, and with his blessing took to the road. But during the sea crossing, the staff was accidentally knocked from his hand and fell in the water. He was taking this misfortune exceedingly hard, for the staff was to him like a gage of holiness and he believed it protected him from all perils on the way, when a wave swept the staff unexpectedly back and yielded it up into his very hands. This outcome was attributed by the man of faith not to chance but to the power of God's saint. The same Samson told this in person to one of our brothers.

3. 10. Of the dumb man healed while he slept[a]

Roger de Nonant, a great man in the world's eyes, was lodging as a guest[b] not far from the holy man's cell and had brought a dumb man in his retinue, but without any view to his receiving the grace of healing. While his lord and companions stayed within, this fellow drifted aimlessly out-of-doors, where he was suddenly overcome by a heaven-sent somnolence and fell asleep in front of the holy man's door. Some paupers standing around outside the rich man's gate[451]

[451] Luke 16:20.

seemed to see a dove fly out of the lodging of the man of God and alight on the sleeper, then poke its beak now into his mouth and now his ears as though gently kissing them. The astonished watchers drew each other's attention to this novel sight, and running across like heedless children, appeared to frighten the dove away. But in truth it had already done its part and so returned to the one who had sent it. Whereupon the mute, awaking suddenly from this sweet sleep, found his tongue loosed[452] and his ears, which had been stopped before, opened by the same grace; and going back to his fellows, he said to his mistress who was looking for him: "Here I am." The lady, amazed, as were the others with her, asked him how he came to be speaking, and he told her that blessed Wulfric had stood by him while he slept and, laying his holy finger on his mouth, had opened it.[453]

Thus it was that a certain divine power was seen as keeping vigil on the very threshold of the holy man, so that salvation dwelt in his walls and praise in his gateways.[454] It is therefore not surprising if those I mentioned earlier as seeking healing met it coming to meet them on the way, since it offered itself spontaneously to those who were not looking for it and might even be said to have forced itself on the unaware. All this I had from Richard of Corscombe—as above—who affirms that he spoke with the same mute in the house of the man of God and from a number of other trustworthy men. Furthermore, there is no dissimilarity between the mute seeing blessed Wulfric appearing in a dream, and those paupers seeing the dove descending on the mute.[455] For blessed Wulfric was in truth a dove, not only because of the perfect and singular model of dovelike simplicity and innocence he offered but because he had the eyes of a dove:[456] eyes that were truly spiritual, with the power to penetrate to the secrets of God's mysteries,[457] and sharp enough to pierce the secrets of the human heart in the light that is God.

[452] Mark 7:33-35.
[453] Ezek 33:22.
[454] Isa 60:18.
[455] Matt 3:16.
[456] Song 1:14.
[457] Isa 45:3.

3. 11. Of the monk whom he convicted of certain thoughts

Finally there came to him a brother of ours whose name has not perished among us, nor slipped from the memory of God, as is our confident hope for him in the Lord. This monk, having gone through the courtesies of an exchange of greetings, seated himself and was asked before long by the man of God whom he had encountered on the road. A woman, he replied, had passed him going the other way. As the saint persisted, inquiring what kind of thoughts the monk had revolved in his heart about her, the latter blushed before the human face but was not as frightened as he should have been of the prophetic eyes: "I didn't think much about her at all," he said. Then the watchman of our sister's walls took away the mantle of evasion and the veil from his eyes:[458] "Actually," he said, "you thought such and such, and you yielded to impure feelings in a way improper to a monk." Convicted by the Holy Spirit, the other was now, if somewhat late, ready to fall in with his opponent,[459] or better, his witness and judge. And when, time passing, the love of truth had rendered the man ashamed of his shame, he would boast to us of how he had once been caught out, to the glory to God and his saint and also to help him keep better custody of his eyes and thoughts in the future. Thus did blessed Wulfric open up our thoughts to us and detect the depravity in our innermost recesses.[a]

3. 12. How he refused to show his face to men who had shown no kindness

On another occasion some men who were on their way to the man of God encountered others struggling to free a cart[a] which had got deeply sunk in the mud. The ones toiling away asked the passers-by to give them a hand, but they turned an indifferent or even contemptuous ear to this plea for human kindness and passed by on the other side.[460] So the man of God sent his boy to waylay

[458] Song 5:7.
[459] Matt 5:25.
[460] Luke 10:32.

them with this response to the greetings they had ready: "I shan't speak with you until you have given a hand to the men who are busy trying to free their cart, the ones you most unkindly refused to help just now." They turned back at once to the work to which God too was directing them, knowing in truth that the spirit of God rested on blessed Wulfric.[461] And they learned besides to be readier with their help in future, since, when acts of kindness present themselves on the road, everyone is a neighbor. People in Haselbury close to the man of God[b] testify to personal knowledge of this incident.

3. 13. Of the woman to whom he prophesied that she was pregnant

Again, there was woman of Chelborough,[a] a village not far from Haselbury, the maidservant of a man who lived there, who had undertaken the care and cherishing of the master's little son. She took him into her bed and would pet him tenderly, trusting to the safeguard of age to conceal this wanton using and abusing, but not long after the boy reached the age of nine or ten, or at any rate of puberty, she conceived. But when her womb began to swell, never dreaming this could indicate conception, she began to complain of her guts and to resort to medicinal herbs as a remedy for her sickness. But day by day the womb continued to swell, bent on avenging the violence done to age. And since the woman was still unwell and indeed getting steadily worse, despite ever larger doses of medicine, she rushed off to the mightiest physician of the day, namely, blessed Wulfric, and presented herself to him for healing. And he, knowing this kind of sickness without even feeling her pulse, said: "You have conceived, daughter, go and take good care of your womb." But not even the response of the famous prophet gave her an inkling of what lay inside her; instead with a woman's shamelessness she started to rail at the man of God and accuse him of lying and making fun of her. But the man of God held his peace throughout, looking for his words to be borne out in due time. The woman meanwhile went home and, when asked by her

[461] Isa 11:2.

friends what sort of response she had brought back from the man of God, without the least reverence for holiness she vented on the saint a stream of blasphemies and curses.

The day soon dawned which was to see judgment done between the prophet and the woman, when she, seized with labor pains, took herself to a place apart and there gave birth. Soon after the infant was delivered, the heartless mother, pricked by the goad of shame, attempted to smother it. But God, using the helping hand of another woman who sensed her intention, took care that the baby born of her was preserved, so that her secret doings as well as the man of God's words spoken through the Holy Spirit might be laid bare in the sight of this sun.[462] It was thus made obvious to everybody in the neighborhood that the father of this child was but a child himself. But God, disposing and bringing out of our disorder some kind of congruence, arranged that both father and son should be called Richard.

Some days later the woman, humbled under her burden of shame, accused herself and laid the charge at her own door.[463] Bundling up all her iniquities and loading her shoulders with those she had perpetrated, first against the boy, next against his parents, and lastly against the man of God, she returned to her physician and, showing him her wounds, experienced what he was able to do for them. So it was that blessed Wulfric, like some eye of the eternal judge, disclosed and brought to light both the works of darkness and the purposes of the heart;[464]and his clear and more than prophetic voice brought home the fear we should properly have of that solemn day in which there will be no cover for perdition. All this was told me by one of the brothers at Forde, who was living then in the house where the events took place, which he learned by stages from the woman's mistress.

3. 14. Of a chance remark which met with a jocular riposte

It happened that Brother William, the lay-brother hospitaller, had to go to Waverley, and one of our monks, namely Robert of Saint

[462] 2 Sam 12:11.
[463] Ps 49:21.
[464] Rom 13:12; 1 Cor 4:5.

Albans, was sent with him. And when Brother William bent his steps, or better, took a beeline to the man of God (for he would not have felt safe had he gone past without greeting him), his travelling companion said to him: "I'm surprised, considering I've often visited the man of God, that he has never invited me to eat with him." Smiling, Brother William answered him: "And I'll be surprised too if what you have just said doesn't rebound in your face today." Both men were given a jubilant welcome by the man of God on their arrival. A little later as they prepared to leave and were making their farewells: "Wait a bit," he said, "and you will eat with me." And with a charming smile to Brother William: "This man," he added, "has never taken a meal with me, and so today I must make up for what my courtesy has lacked in this respect." The monk, flushing a brighter red than if he had been caught stealing, was left tongue-tied. Whereupon the man of God took pity on the fellow and wiped away the glow of embarrassment by saying with the serenest of expressions: "If I haven't invited you to my table before it was not out of meanness or arrogance, but more from negligence and lack of thought."

Having received his blessing, the two took to the road again, urged by necessity or their own wish, and whiled away the miles with long and happy conversations about blessed Wulfric. When they got to Waverley and had done their business, Robert of Saint Albans stayed behind and Brother William returned to Forde, along with a monk of Waverley who was himself eager to see the man of God. Brother William having led this man to the object, so plainly desirable, of his desire, the holy man came out to them with all his natural graciousness and greeted his guests with formal courtesy not in word only but in his whole mien. While they were talking together Brother William took the opportunity to commend his companion to the holy man's intimacy and ventured to ask if he would not give one of the rings of his hauberk to him as a token of brotherly love. So, putting a hand to that part of the hauberk that covered his chest, he detached one of the rings with the greatest of ease and laid it in the hand of the monk lost in wonderment and awe at having hearsay changed into seeing before his very eyes. Thereupon Brother William, proceeding to strengthen the man's faith by a repetition of this sign, said: "Now would you please give another one to me." So the man of God, returning a hand to his treasure store, went to work again with the same economy of movement and reached out the extricated ring to Brother William, from whom I had the story.

3. 15. How he healed a man whose eyes had been put out

A man in the neighborhood of York had his eyes put out at the behest of the civil power. Not long after, he was told in a dream to go and present himself to Wulfric to be cured. Even the method of the cure was shown to him in advance. "You will be healed," he was told, "by the blessed man putting his thumb in the sockets of your eyes." So he made his way to the man of God, presented himself and the reason that brought him and demanded in return the promised application of the medicinal thumb. But the man of God resisted the fellow, as if he didn't know what he was asking or whom he was asking it of: "Man, you are mistaken," he said, "such signs are worked only by the great." But the other persistently threw back at him the authority of God who had sent him with a promise, adding that what God promised he was also able to do.[465] At this point Brihtric entered the contest as arbiter and turning to the man of God, said: "Is the faith of this thief, then, going to prove stronger than yours?" Whereupon Brihtric took the reluctant hand, and stretching it out, thumb first, pushed it firmly into the eye sockets. The eyeballs and pupils shot forward so suddenly as to eject the thumb, and light entered the eyes or, better, the eyes went out to meet the light. The venerable abbot of Malmesbury[a] says that he had this tale from the man of God and sent it noted down in writing; he also writes that he heard from the holy man in person that God had given back their sight to sixteen blind people by his hand.

The same abbot testifies to another sign which he affirms having seen with his own eyes. The man of God, by laying his hand on him, restored to immediate and perfect health his brother Laurence when he lay gravely ill, enabling him to set out that very day with

[465] Rom 4:21.

the abbot to travel to his properties. The abbot also writes that once, when a large crowd of people flocked in on the man of God, a sword left in the church porch was taken by a thief. The matter was reported to the saint, who ordered it to be kept quiet. When the throng had ebbed away with the passing day, the man of God sent his servant after the thief, who was found running this way and that in the churchyard, unable to find the gate.[466] The man of God sent to tell him to put the sword back in its place, which he lost no time in doing and recovered his sight.

3. 16. Of one who came late to mass

What follows was related by Osbern, the priest of Haselbury, who succeeded the late revered Brihtric in the charge of that church. While he was still a lad, he said, he used to go into the holy man's cell to serve when he celebrated mass. It happened one day, when the latter, having vested as usual, was about to begin the celebration and the boy took a taper to light the candle, that the man of God bade him stay his hand. He kicked his heels a while, albeit grumbling and put out, for being given over to the pursuits of boyhood he thought of nothing else, even there and then. When he pleaded that the usual hour was already past, the man of God said: "Wait, for someone is hurrying to this mass and we must wait until he comes." So he waited a bit longer, though he did not think much of the prophecies, till the holy man said to him: "Now run quickly! Here is the one we have been waiting for, coming towards you now." Out went Osbern and just as he was leaving the churchyard he ran into a man wearing the religious habit. "Here you are," he said. "We've waited for you all this time, and a very weary wait you've put us through." Thus in the spirit did the blessed man run reverently out in prayer to meet his visitor, so that he not only foresaw his coming but kept him company on the way, and can be said to have read the footprints of the walking man and counted his very steps.

[466] Gen 19:11.

3. 17. Of the woman whose death he intimated mystically

Living in the neighborhood of Totnes castle, in a village called Hurdestochia,[a] was a very religious woman, an example of piety and holiness to all her locality. She was one of blessed Wulfric's spoils of war, whom he had changed, it is said, by a prophecy of the Holy Spirit, from a priest's concubine into a friend of Jesus Christ, introducing into those parts a new and splendid light. And when this most fervent of women, whom God's grace had hastened to perfection, had seen out a long count of years, the Lord summoned her with the sound of the horn,[467] in the form of a severe and lingering prostration. She sent then to her only remedy on earth, blessed Wulfric, that he might save her from this sickness and put an end to her ills by sending her some of his holy water. The messenger bringing this request was met with the following reply: "Stay here tonight, and at first light I will give you an answer." Calling him back at daybreak, "Go," said the saint, "and hurry home, for your mistress is completely healed." And when he insistently demanded the holy water he had been sent for, the man of God said: "Go, she has no further need of it now." Failing to understand this saying,[468] for the holy man was speaking to him in parables,[469] he hurried back like someone bringing good news, and in truth the news surpassed his hope. On arriving home he heard that his mistress had passed from the world's day; and now at last he understood what was meant by "healed" and that this was the true health which no sickness can follow on or follow after.

All this was told me by one of our brothers who hails from thereabouts, a young man who gives much cause for hope, and with the firmness of his faith he prevailed over mine. But to make good any possible lack in it, I sent to the faithful in those parts, by some of whom I was introduced into the very truth of the matter. Thus did blessed Wulfric deserve to reap what he had earlier sown,[470] so that everything touching this blessed woman might rest with him—a woman

[467] 2 Sam 6:15.
[468] Luke 2:50.
[469] Matt 13:13.
[470] Matt 25:24.

he had once saved from eternal death, and now by his prayers had both loosed from this mortal body and sent onward into everlasting life.

3. 18. How he foretold the judgment of the Hiribelli

Neither did blessed Wulfric keep silent, although his prophecy was enigmatic, about the judgment visited on those whom ordinary folk call the Hiribelli,[a] brought by Duke Henry when he entered England in King Stephen's day to lay claim to the kingdom, which, with God's help, he later secured. While these men, whose sacrilegious hands reached everywhere, were plundering the poor, profaning the sacred, and indulging with unbridled license in all manner of wickedness, they went so far as to snatch booty from the house of the man of God. When someone came in to say that they had gone off with the horse that was used to fetch his wood and victuals, as well as some other of his belongings: "Let be," he said, "they won't be exulting for long, nor triumphing over me for what they have taken, and they won't get it back to Normandy either."

He sent messengers to the duke, notifying him of the price of the articles stolen, estimated at twelve shillings, and announcing besides that he would not reign in the lifetime of King Stephen. So when God had scourged England by means of these brigands and used them to accomplish the work[471] he had preordained, the wrath of the Lord was turned in the end against them and he himself broke the rod of his scourge to pieces. For when God took pity on England and peace was at last agreed, that impious horde was sent home along with the baggage of banditry it had amassed in England, and when it had put out to sea was shaken off like a locust,[472] and all, like some army of Pharaoh, went down like lead into the mighty waters.[473] It was now up to blessed Wulfric to sing to God, for the Lord had triumphed gloriously,[474] and the horse, if they still had it, which Wulfric had said they would not take to Normandy, was itself with

[471] John 17:4.
[472] Ps 108:23.
[473] Exod 15:10.
[474] Exod 15:1.

its rider thrown into the sea.[475] These things were told me by some of our older men and by Muriel also, wife of the puissant Robert de Beauchamp, a woman held in the highest respect and esteem.

3. 19. Of a dead man whose repose he made known

Richard the cantor, whom I spoke of earlier as having been blessed Wulfric's scribe, came to the man of God, anxious to consult him about the state of the soul of his father Segar, whom I also remember mentioning. He received this reply: "He has undergone great suffering, but now he is resting from his labors.[476] Indeed I saw the man in a vision stuck in the deepest mire, trying to get out but quite unable, until I rode up to him on horseback, set him on my own beast[477] and carried him joyfully away. So rest assured that this man is at peace." Richard was happy to hear this and went away giving thanks. Yet mindful with due devotion of his father's necessity, he was still unable to free himself from his original care and went back to the man of God with his earlier inquiry. The saint, seemingly indignant at having to repeat the definitive opinion once given, said: "Didn't I tell you that I set him on my horse?"

3. 20. Of the monk of Winchester whose death he announced

William fitzWalter, as the lord of that village was called, came one day to see the man of God and, after the customary knock at his window, spent a frustratingly long time waiting for him to emerge. When the holy man at last appeared, it was to say: "I know you were put out by my delay and your long wait. Please excuse me; I was busy and couldn't meet your wishes, or my own, any quicker." "Busy with what, master?" "One of our brother monks at Winchester left this life just now, and it came to me that I might ease his passing with my prayers. I was anxious to do this for him, and

[475] Exod 15:1.
[476] Rev 14:13.
[477] Luke 10:34.

this it was that kept me."The knight took care to elicit the name of the monk and the hour of his departing; he then sent with all haste to Winchester, wanting to know if things were really as said. So the messenger rode day and night and arrived at his destination just as a monk was being borne with due solemnity to the grave. He asked the name of the monk and the hour of his passing, ascertaining that it was indeed the one whose death the blessed man had seen and announced, and he reported the same to the lord who had sent him. While all this was going on, the man of God sent for the knight: "Is it true," he asked, "that you still don't trust me and have sent to Winchester for proof that I spoke the truth?" The knight, convicted then of prevarication, learned that absent and present were all one to God's saint and that even the heart's hidden depths were not hidden from him. This from his son Walter, a monk of Glastonbury.[a]

3. 21. Of the knight whose death he announced

Not dissimilar is the story of a knight called Durand de Mohun, who fell gravely ill and sent for William fitzWalter, this Durand being the brother of William's wife.[a] The messenger, failing to find William at Haselbury, pressed on through the night to another village of his called Piddle[b] in quest of him. The holy man, meanwhile, having a start on both the messenger and the man he was pursuing and being himself indebted to the knight's lineage, was chiefly concerned with ensuring the salvation of a soul, so calling to Osbern, who was still a boy, he said to him: "Go and tell your father to commend to God the soul of Durand de Mohun who has just died and to make haste to celebrate a mass for him." This from Osbern.

3. 22. Of the introduction of Canons Regular to Haselbury,[a] and his prediction of their subsequent departure

The same William, who was a devout and God-fearing man,[478] a state to which the familiar example and frequent discourse of the

[478] Acts 10:2.

man of God had gradually brought him, introduced to Haselbury the canons known as "regular," whom he enriched with many possessions and, being in those days a very powerful personage, settled them grandly and lavishly in buildings still standing today. Nevertheless, since he had the Lord's prophet to hand, he judged it good to consult him on the matter, so that the holy man might bless the work of his hands[479] and hallow the start of the undertaking with his favor and advice. What he heard was this: "You will make a start but will not bring it to fruition.[480] Those you are arranging to bring in will not prosper in this place. But truly, so that I am not seen as opposing my will to yours or to theirs, begin as you intended, letting your wish at least be tested by God and these alms bear fruit for you if not for them." The knight assented readily enough to this, though not to the point of abandoning his plans: in fact, once he had introduced the canons and handed a lot of property over to them, he gave himself wholeheartedly to watching over and fostering the foundation. Yet because in all truth the word of God cannot fail,[481] when they were planted they did not put down deep roots,[482] a tale I refrain from committing to writing lest I seem to be persecuting those expelled. This from the son of the same William, Walter of Glastonbury.

3. 23. How he prophesied that the queen's pride would be brought low[a]

It happened in the days of King Stephen that his wife came, if my memory serves me right,[b] to the castle of Corfe, and all the noblewomen from the country round came hurrying to pay her their customary respects. Among them was the wife of William fitzWalter, who approached the queen with due reverence, at pains to greet her with all deference and courtesy. But because the lady's husband, William, had not yet given his allegiance to King Stephen,

[479] Deut 28:8.
[480] Luke 14:30.
[481] Rom 9:6.
[482] Matt 13:6.

the queen declined to acknowledge her but with regal hauteur turned away. Thereupon the lady, put out of countenance in the eyes of the other women present, went back to Haselbury and poured out her embarrassment into the ears of the holy man, whose dear friend she was, being herself a sweet and holy woman. Having comforted her with quiet kindliness, he bided his time until, one day not far removed, the queen herself sought out the man of God. Mindful then of the insult he had been called upon to judge, he did not pay her overmuch attention but showed himself to her in his prophetic grandeur, saying: "It was you, was it not, who disdained to rise and greet a faithful and holy woman and shamed her and would not receive her with a kiss? Look, the days are coming[483] when you will allow that mouth of yours to bestow its favors on the poor and base-born, and far from spurning any mouth that offers itself, with the kiss of your mouth[484] you will kiss it in return." Those who remember what happened after—how King Stephen was taken and how the queen, anxious to get him freed, courted the common people by whose help the king's release is thought to have been hastened—will mark how the words of this prophecy were fulfilled. These things I had from the woman's son, Walter of Glastonbury.[c]

3. 24. How he saw in the spirit a woman make a mistake in her sewing

A length of linen was given to the man of God to have an alb made; and when Godida, the mother of Osbern the priest, had cut it as usual and was sewing it, she made the careless mistake of stitching one of the seams inside out. Calling to his servant the man of God said: "Go and tell Godida that she is not paying enough attention to what she is doing." On another occasion he sent his lad to pull out a man who had fallen in a pond. As for guests on the road, while they were still a long way off[485] he would have everything

[483] Luke 23:29.
[484] Song 1:1.
[485] Luke 15:20.

necessary got ready by his boy. But this particular servant of his was nonetheless always complaining that, no matter where he was sent, he could hide nothing of what he got up to on the road from the eyes of his master, who would set out before him on his return his every boyish prank and escapade as if the saint were the inseparable comrade and witness not only of his steps but of his very thoughts.

3. 25. How he shielded his servant who was dealing deceitfully[a]

It should not be passed over that this Elisha had another Gehazi and that the Gehazi in turn discovered another Elisha.[486] One of the holy man's servants, having got himself friends thanks to the reverence in which the saint was held, became seduced by money-making, and was not afraid to keep for himself the things the faithful destined for his master. And, what is more, he betrayed the poor men of Christ, for being a thief he had hiding places where he took things his master was sending to the monks.[487] All this the holy man, in emulation of Christ's meekness, covered up for quite a while, until there were complaints throughout the neighborhood, deeply resentful of this tarnish on the reputation of so holy a man; then he was compelled to cut the man off and send him away.

So when he was driven from the holy man's presence, this fellow walked off into exile, trusting to all the riches he had accumulated—numbering sheep and cattle as well as gold and silver and precious vestments—to keep himself and the whore to whom he cleaved. When reports of the abundant booty he had taken with him were broken later to the man of God, his words were: "Wait and see; ill-gotten gains return to nothing." And as those still alive can testify—faithful men and true—before ever that year was out he was condemned to such poverty that he had nowhere to lay his head;[488] indeed, publicly exposed to the shame of beggary, he hardly

[486] 2 Kgs 5:20-27.
[487] John 12:6.
[488] Cf. Matt 8:20.

found short breeches to cover his sinful flesh.[489] This was related by the venerable woman Muriel and by the priests Osbern and Segar.

3. 26. How food destined for him and secreted began crawling with maggots

A devout woman named Joan, the wife of the powerful Durand de Mohun[a] and sister of the lord of Haselbury, sent two servants to the man of God, laden with gifts conveying a threefold blessing in the form of bread, pasties, and two flasks of wine. As they drew near the holy man's lodging they agreed between them to keep back for their own use a portion of each of these commodities, and this they did, leaving their share with a poor man on the way. When he heard them knocking at his door, the man of God called to his boy: "Go," he said, "and take from the hands of those men what they are carrying, but don't let them come in to me. And forbid them on pain of death from eating any of what they have stolen and laid aside for themselves." The boy went out and in the words of his master accused them of theft, warning them to look to their salvation. Retracing their steps with troubled consciences they found the wine they had left swarming with the tadpoles of venomous frogs. Similarly what they had left of bread and pasties was crawling with maggots and loathsome to look at. Beating their breasts, they hurried to tell God's saint of these things and their rotting and poisonous state. As they confessed their fault and asked for pardon, the holy man forgave them readily, and taking the things from their hands he blessed them, and with the blessing made them whole, after which he gave the two pressing instructions to take them back to the poor man they had left them with. "Otherwise," he said, "if you touch any of this you will bear your own blood-guilt."

The venerable recluse of Newton,[b] Aldida by name, attested to this story, having learned it not only from public report but heard it many a time from the aforementioned Joan.

[489] Exod 28:42.

3. 27. Of a prophet's joke

A knight of the village of Mudford, one William fitzTerric,[a] being a familiar of the holy man, was attentive to his needs and solicitous with gifts. Throwing his net one day into a nearby stream (which he said had long yielded no catch), he caught four huge fish of the sort commonly known as pike. He had no hesitation in ascribing this to the holiness of the man of God, and keeping one fish for himself, he selected three for him. The man of God accepted them and expressed his thanks to the servant, adding with a smile: "Your master hasn't portioned them out fairly; take one of these three back to him and the shares will then be equal." William fitzTerric's son, William, and wife, Beatrice, attest to all the above.

3. 28. Of the pilgrimage to Jerusalem for which he foretold a sorry ending

Alfred of Lincoln, great in the eyes of men, but happier far in having a deeply religious spirit which renders him great in the sight of the Lord, was sitting at the holy man's window. A discussion arose about the notorious and lamentable expedition against the Saracens in Jerusalem which a number of nations embarked on in the time of Pope Eugenius—would that its tale were not told in Gath nor published in the streets of Ascalon,[490] or indeed in our own ears save insofar as it allows us to give glory to God for his judgments, to God who abandoned the false pilgrims, who sheared the scalps of the proud[491] and brought to shame the lordly of the earth[492] because they did not seek the Lord in truth but defiled the road of their pilgrimage with their idols.[493] At the time when the man of God and his visitor were conversing about these matters, the enterprise was still in preparation, and armed and unarmed were alike boasting.[494] "Don't get worked up about this business," said the

[490] 2 Sam 1:20.
[491] Isa 3:17.
[492] Isa 23:9.
[493] Ezek 36:18.
[494] 1 Kgs 20:11.

holy man, "in a short time it will all come to nothing." As it might be from a lofty watchtower the blessed man, laughing at the sons of Ephrem bending and shooting with the bow,[495] foresaw the end and foretold the confounding of pride.[a] This from the same Alfred.

3. 29. How in a dream he saw himself free three priests from hanging, and in the morning delivered them from spiritual death through confession

Once when the man of God, tired out from the night office, was ambushed by sleep, he saw in a dream what looked like three youths[a] hanging above his altar on ropes drawn so tight that they were on the point of suffocating. One of them turned to the blessed man, saying: "Master! Master Wulfric! Why so slow in jumping up to save us?" And when the holy man objected that he could not see how to do it, he was told: "Climb up here on the altar and give a helping hand to men about to die." And it seemed to him that he yielded at once to the suppliant and saved them from death and hanging with his outstretched hand. Later that day, as he was turning this vision over in his mind, three downcast and penitent priests presented themselves, seeking from him and receiving forgiveness of sins and a norm for healthier thinking and holier living. Why these three, until then assisting unhallowed at the holy mysteries, were seen hanging above the altar, takes little fathoming. Walter of Glastonbury told me this and the holy man told him; the following tale I had from the same Walter.

3. 30. Of a mocking clerk

The prior of Gloucester[a] set out for religious reasons to visit the man of God and took with him as companion for the journey one Robert of Cirencester, a clerk of little consequence in those days but who was to grow in substance and repute. This man, no follower of his devout associate in either spirit or behavior, spent the journey devising how he could poke fun at the holy man's

[495] Ps 77:9.

simplicity. So after they reached their goal and the prior had come back fully refreshed from the intimate conversation with the man of God for which he had been thirsting, the tempter stayed behind and began to lay little snares in the form of questions, keeping his eyes on the other's lips in the hope of entangling him in his talk.[496] But in vain is the net cast in the sight of the birds.[497] The holy man, indubitably forewarned by the Holy Spirit, brushed these subtleties aside like so many spider-threads. Having tested the mouth, the clerk then set about tempting the saint's heart through avarice, and, holding out two pennies,[b] offered them to him. "Put them there," said the saint; "there are those coming who will take them." Abashed, he went away at that, and while he and the prior were staying overnight in the village,[c] two poor women came up to them begging for alms. The clerk repulsed them haughtily: "Go to the man of God," he said, "it's his business to give alms, the more so as he is loaded with money." Showing him two pennies, the women said: "That's just where we've been, and look, we took these from his window." The clerk, having inspected and recognized them, did redden, but not enough to signify true repentance. Then as he was chewing his meat, he suffered a fluttering at the heart and an acute pain in his vitals, which indicated plainly if belatedly to him and all who saw it that the Lord's hand was at work, vindicating his servant. So at his own request he was taken back to the man of God and humbly confessed his folly, receiving healing and absolution in return. He was cautioned too to learn to reverence God in his servants from on, for he who spurns them, spurns the one indwelling there.[498] The saint told him much about his future state and that he would rise from present inconsequence to a reputation of more substantial worth.

In later years this clerk, appointed procurator of the monastery of Glastonbury and with substantial revenues at his disposal, rehearsed this story regularly to a number of the monks, among them the venerable Walter, who passed it on to me. The man added,

[496] Matt 22:15.
[497] Prov 1:17.
[498] Luke 10:16.

too, that every single thing the holy man had predicted for him had come about, save one which still remained to be fulfilled and caused him not a little anxiety. On being asked privately what it was, he answered: "The man of God foretold that before my death I would provoke the blessed Virgin and be punished for it in my last days with five years of blindness." In the end it came to be common knowledge that he was stricken with blindness for just that length of time, dying a few days before the term. So it was that the holy man in his simplicity eluded the deceiver's wiles, and in his charity returned good for ill and gave prophetic warning of what was to come.

3. 31. Of the Woman Who Admitted Her Sins and Received Much in Return

Two very rich women had come to see the man of God, the one being Bence, the mother, still living, of Alfred of Lincoln, while the other, Agnes, was sister to the countess of Gloucester.[a] When Bence commended herself insistently to his prayers, the man of God nodded and pledged himself to pray for her as long as he lived. But when Agnes then made the same request with similar urgency, he first sat a while in silence, and when she pressed him more urgently still, said: "I shall pray, should I be given leave." Beaten back as it were, the lady battered still harder, but he too persevered in speaking his truth,[499] before going to the altar as usual to celebrate mass.[b] On his return, Agnes enquired if he had prayed for her. "I did not," he replied, "because when I started to do so I was prevented." As she persisted in seeking the reasons for this rebuff: "You have not observed the feast days in your grand halls," he said, "nor given God's saints their due of honor. And thus far you yourself have lived in God's sight a less than holy life." At that, before God who scrutinizes the heart[500] and before his saint, she threw herself on the ground and wailed: "It is true, that is the way it has been, but from now on with God's help I will live a stricter life." Speaking with him then

[499] 2 Cor 6:7.
[500] Wis 1:6; Ps 7:10.

in greater privacy,[c] she renewed herself through confession and absolution of her sins and clothed herself in the firm purpose of a holier way of life. Whereupon as though she were already garbed in white the holy man gave her kind words of comfort: "Have no fear, from now on I shall pray for you faithfully; hold resolutely to your purpose though, knowing even now that your days on earth are few in number."[501] The woman went home and took care to spend better the brief span left to her and to make up with fitting fruits of penitence for the waste of the days gone by.

3. 32. Of the death of King Henry which he foretold

King Henry I of England was organizing an expedition overseas, and common talk brought the news to the man of God, who commented: "He will go, but he will not come back: or if he does, it will be neither safe nor sound." These words were reported to the king,[502] who took them badly, and sent to ask him if he were indeed the author. "If I said it," said the holy man, "I have no regrets, for I did not speak it of myself."[503] The king departed as he had arranged. Sometime later the man of God sent for the lord of the village and said: "The king died yesterday. Consider what you will do." The knight was dumbfounded and enjoined him to silence. "It is easy enough for me to be silent, but everyone will be talking of it soon." He went on to prophesy that the king would receive mercy from the Lord,[504] because he had fought for peace and justice during his life and had built the abbey of Reading with royal munificence.[a]

3. 33. Of the reign and capture of King Stephen as foretold by him[a]

One visitor to the man of God was Count Stephen, who later reigned over England and already then, being kin to the king, had

[501] Job 14:5.
[502] 1 Kgs 2:29.
[503] John 12:49.
[504] 2 Macc 9:13.

extensive landholdings in this country. He was accompanied by his brother, Henry, bishop of Winchester, a man supremely grand. Looking straight at the count, the holy man said: "Long live the king!"[505] The other two gazed at one another, wondering whether he was misled by fallible human opinion. "It is to you, Stephen," the holy man insisted, "that I am saying 'Long live the king.' God has delivered the kingdom of England into your hand; for your part, strive your utmost after peace and justice and take care to honor and defend the church of God." Accordingly, when the kingdom had come to Stephen as God purposed, and peace, what with others trying to wrest it from him, had been driven from England amid disorder which the holy man had also prophesied, the lord of the village came one day and asked the man of God how he fared. "Well," he replied, "except that I feel sorry for our friend." "Which friend is that?" "King Stephen will be given tomorrow into the hands of his enemies and taken captive." The knight groaned: "What then, master? Will he not be freed?" "Indeed he will be freed, and the one who took him prisoner will later drink of the same cup." King Stephen subsequently came to the holy man, and after many rebukes and much salutary admonishment, the latter promised him among other things that he would reign lifelong. And not to be omitted is that he pressed the king to do penance for a particular sin which he even named to him, adding that until he repented there was no possibility of his throne being made firm or peace established. Hearing this, the king began to weep profusely and, having confessed the sin, presented his cheek to the prophet to be struck and spat upon.

3. 34. Of the Judgment that Fell on a Detractor

Two men came to see the man of God, the one to keep the other company and as a chore rather than in pursuit of truth, as later became clear. Certainly, while his fellow was doing what he had come for, namely, commending himself earnestly to the prayers of the

[505] 2 Sam 16:16.

man of God and drinking in his words like a parched land thirsting for rain,[506] the companion, recoiling from this self-betterment, let himself be worried and devoured by a devilish disgust and animosity. He seethed till he couldn't hold it in, and the poisonous slander he had conceived finally burst out in gross abuse: "How long are you going to talk with that fool, that country bumpkin? I'm not waiting for you any longer." With this he rushed out, or rather was suddenly and fearfully seized by the evil spirit to whom he had yielded himself, and went on his way to perdition with the fury of the Lord in his wake, which caught him in due turn. The man of God, meanwhile, paying scant attention to the wretch's raving, continued to indulge his avid listener who at length, his thirst satisfied, made use of a break to say: "I am afraid of losing my associate who has such a start on me, so with your blessing I'll hurry after him." "He is not far off," replied the man of God, "you will catch him up quickly." Following hard on the heels of his companion, he had gone about half a mile westwards from the holy man's cell when he spotted his comrade some way ahead lying slain in his own blood. Profoundly shocked, he went back at once to the man of God, revolving in his awestruck mind both the judgment of blasphemy and the prophetic word he had not noticed at the time. But the man of God said only: "Didn't I tell you that he was not far off and you would catch him up quickly?"

3. 35. Of the foretelling of a rich man's death

Two great men of Wessex, Earl Baldwin[a] and Stephen de Mandeville,[b] had gone on a journey for reasons of devotion and were away a long time, exposed as they were on the road to hardships, dangers, and ambush. When death—God willing—had taken Stephen and the earl was struggling home, a rumor spread across England that Stephen was on his way back and the earl had died. But that lover of truth, God's prophet, was not to be deceived by rumor. He affirmed the contrary and said that, as Stephen had made in truth a pious end in the paths of justice, great grace was laid up

[506] Joel 1:20.

for him,[507] wherefore he himself took care to celebrate the solemn office of human kindness for the dead man.[c] This I had from the woman Muriel whom I named earlier.

3. 36. How the arrival of the lord of Haselbury was foretold

The steward of Haselbury, about to take the road to his lord who was staying elsewhere at the time, called on the man of God. Fearful of falling among robbers,[508] so general was the unrest, he was commending himself urgently to his prayers when the saint said: "There's no need for you to go to him, because in the morning he is coming here." The steward said he doubted this as he had had no advice of his arrival, but the other replied: "I have no doubts at all; he is getting his horses foddered this very minute. After this, when he has waited a while, he will ride through the night and get here tomorrow at daybreak. So be sure to arrange for food to be got ready which you can set before him when he arrives, for it will be a dog-tired and famished man you will receive." This was asserted so firmly that the steward, not daring to resist the Holy Spirit, confidently awaited his lord's arrival and received him with due provision. Thus was it given the blessed man to prophesy not merely in spiritual matters but also in those pertaining to the body and to arrange, through an exchange of complaisance, for the physical comfort of the man who ministered to his own material needs. This I had from Brother William the hospitaller.

3. 37. Of a certain slanderer

A sick man of Cirencester, hearing of the miracles the Lord was performing through his saint, sent to beg him for something which would restore him to health, and the holy man sent him some water he had blessed. When the man tasted it, finding it salty and cloudy in appearance, he promptly spat it out and even swore in blasphemous

[507] 2 Macc 12:45.
[508] Luke 10:36.

terms that what the man of God had sent was his own urine. But the illness, getting worse, punished his unbridled tongue—though not enough to humble his heart as he deserved, as was proved when a further request sent to the man of God was left without effect. This finally brought home to him that what he had done and said in regard to the earlier blessing had been no different from speaking the words into Wulfric's ears, and had pronounced him unworthy of a blessing he might again revile. We had this from one of our brothers who came from those parts.

3. 38. Of Walter of Glastonbury

Since I have often called on Walter of Glastonbury to bear witness to the truth, it is time that I myself bore summary testimony to my witness so that you may judge and measure his fitness for the part. He owed his intimacy with the man of God partly to his father and mother, and partly to future matters touching himself which the holy man, by the grace of God, already at the time foresaw and foretold. These last were the more important, as we shall see.

It happened that in the days of King Stephen his father left the lad in London, in the house of one of the citizens, as surety in some money matter. When the boredom and restriction of this captivity (freely entered upon, yet with a sinking and uneasy heart) made it ever more irksome and harder to endure, he sent to blessed Wulfric to ask him for his prayers, confidently expecting a quick release to follow. The holy man gave him the following answer: he must wait a little while longer, for the day of his liberation had not yet come. When it did come, he said, he would be freed without difficulty or delay. Cast down, indeed dismayed by this reply, the lad focused all his expectations on the fulfillment of the prophecy, but after several years of captivity he was reckoning this "little while" extremely long. "What does he mean by a little while?"[509] he muttered to himself. Then, shortly before the longed-for day, the holy

[509] John 16:17.

man sent someone to whisper welcome words of comfort[510] in his ear, saying: "Keep your spirits up: you've been freed!" So just as the man of God had said, when the moment favored most he burst from his fetters and presented his family and friends with a red-letter day at his homecoming.

His was the charm of an innate simplicity, which both endeared him to the man of God and made him a fitting confidant to whom the saint opened his inner life during their frequent converse. It happened one day that some would-be oracular words were bandied about in the holy man's presence as to which of the sons of William fitzWalter would do best in life. The man of God gave his voice to Walter: "He is the one," he said, "who will be the best provided for of all the brothers."**[a]** Walter took this on the human level, as designating him already as his father's heir, and, pride being always on the ascendant in human nature, he began to place inordinate hope in these words: he conceived new plans and ambitions, behaved more arrogantly, and adopted a more self-indulgent way of life. His mother noticed this, and bewailing her son as no better than dead, she appealed for help to the holy man. "Don't cry," he said to her, "these things will not detain your son for long." His reply came to the ears of the young man, who understood it to mean that his death was imminent, and, as is the way with boys when it starts to rain, put an end to playing.

At that point it entered his mind to renounce the world and he began to discuss this with the man of God. But the idea that had surfaced sluggishly was discussed without urgency, and with an excess of prudence hardly befitting religious vows he dragged out the ponderous proceedings over a long period. Eventually the holy man said to him: "What you have been talking about will be implemented much earlier than you yourself were intending and come to pass more quickly than you hope."

To sum up, at the request of the lord Henry, bishop of Winchester, for reasons arising that it would take too long to relate, he took the habit in the monastery of Glastonbury.**[b]** There he has lived ever

[510] Zech 1:13.

since without drawing a murmur of criticism—held indeed in high favor—and there he flourishes still in ripe old age, ready to give an account of the deeds of blessed Wulfric to all who ask, at an opportune time[511] of course, and preserved by both profession and age from any suspicion of untruth. For the upshot is that a good and simple man is ashamed to lie, and in a monk it is utterly unbecoming. What is more, it is deceitful, wicked, and abominable for a witness to the truth, brought forward to give testimony to that truth, to side with falsehood and uphold a lie. Lastly, to see a white-haired ancient joke and play the fool is unpleasant enough, but for one already on the threshold of eternity to busy himself with childish tales[c] is not merely unattractive, it must be seen as downright offensive.

3. 39. That the signs worked by the man of God are past counting

Where do we draw a line? If the significance and power of his signs already weighed me down, I am completely overwhelmed by their number. Yet the matter rests squarely on my shoulders; it is too late for me now to withdraw. I not only engage myself to set out the works of this most blessed man, beloved of God, in a fitting manner but also to unroll them in sufficient number. As I have shown in very truth, the whole world is full of the glory[512] of his signs if anyone can and will, out of pious curiosity, take the trouble to hunt them down and dig them out of the places where they lurk. They constituted the strenuous exercise of this man, his daily toil as he battled here below to do or say something new or wonderful. If you consider the tongue, it was the Holy Spirit's deputy; if the hands, they were rounded gold, set with jewels of Tarshish.[513] Well might we marvel, much and in every way,[514] to see this place now deserted and so glorious a man still lying there like any common son of toil, had not he himself foretold these very things in the Spirit.

[511] Ps 31:6.
[512] Isa 6:3.
[513] Song 5:14.
[514] Rom 3:2.

3. 40. How he foretold the desolation and future exaltation of that place

He did indeed foretell the abasement of that place once glorious and revered, but he prophesied too that it would be raised up again a little while later. So take comfort in the meantime, beloved Haselbury, set firm in joyful hope, for your salvation will come soon;[515] and if to the one who yearns the wait seems never-ending, yet in a little while you will be visited.[516] Today it is not without tender pain at heart that can I say or you can hear that your roads mourn[517] and none come to the feast, but knowing whom you have believed,[518] and must believe because he did not fail you in a single word, wait a short time till the day of your visitation comes. Then you will see that this providential waiting was the Lord's preparation for tomorrow's day, the festal day: it is the dying of the grain of wheat[519] in preparation for something like resurrection glory: but enough of this.

3. 41. Of the signs which preceded his death

It is time now to speak of the blessed man's death. Long before the event, he had foreknowledge of it, as the Holy Spirit infused this in the living words he used to utter in the saint's ear, and signified it clearly too by outward signs. For when a year remained of his life, or maybe even more, and he was sitting one day in his cell, his hauberk, by divine agency, came apart at the shoulders and slid suddenly down to his knees. His heart fell with it, and catching the falling mail with his quick hands he called to his boy and with his help hitched the shirt back onto his shoulders, fastening it with strong laces. Then suddenly blisters started breaking out all over his body, and the flesh till recently rendered iron-hard by God's Spirit was now found, of itself, to be but flesh. Thus both mail and flesh

[515] Isa 56:1.
[516] John 16:16.
[517] Lam 1:4.
[518] 1 Tim 1:12.
[519] John 12:24.

conveyed the same message, heralding the completion of his years of knightly service. Therefore the flesh, already told by the Spirit that it might rest from its labors,[520] showed itself justly indignant at having its burden reimposed. And although, despite his great victories, he was the humblest of men, he had to be humbled still further, so that this repository of glory might be made perfect in humility and ever kept so.

Thus it was that the man of God sent for his closest and most trusted friends, namely, Brother William the hospitaller, Henry of Corscombe,[a] Osbern the priest, and others high in his regard, and when he had told them these happenings one by one, he consulted them as to what should be done. The matter should be referred to the bishop was their advice, so Osbern the priest was sent and brought back these instructions: he was to take off the hauberk and not wear it any longer but keep it by him wrapped in a cloth. So the man of God took from his sacred shoulders this servant and helpmeet in his feats of arms, and laying it aside in a linen cloth, from that day on, like a veteran, he awaited in peace the hour of his releasing. One of our brothers,[b] speaking with him more intimately, said that he hoped, God willing, to be found worthy to attend his deathbed. "If that is what you wish," said the holy man, "it will be very easy. I shall send to you shortly before that day and you will hurry over, and your abbot too, should he so decide." Asked privily how death would come to him, he replied that he would not be thrust out of this life on the point of some great pain, but as his vitality dwindled and ebbed he would make the crossing quietly on a flood tide. And speaking with the late revered Robert, bishop of Bath, of his passing, he said: "When you hear that I have departed this life, see that you lose no time in coming to officiate at the commending of my soul and the committal of my body." This was no humble entreaty, nor the anxiety of a self-important man to procure the ministrations of great men at his funeral; frank and free in his simplicity he enjoined even on the bishop what he foresaw in the Spirit ought and would need to be done.

[520] Rev 14:13.

In the meantime, with what longing sighs he, her son and citizen, had called on the Jerusalem he was so soon to see, with what glad shouts he hailed her, now that he was on the point of entering her glory and partaking in the feast, none is fit to think about, let alone describe. One thing is quite certain: hovering in happy expectation with wings already spread for flight and swelling heart, he had already darted out to greet joy on the way. For us there is no doubt that he had run to meet Christ coming from the wedding feast to fetch him to it[521] and been blessed with foretastes of ineffable joy. For if from day to day his outer man was decaying and, wearing out like a garment,[522] was hastening to yield what was its own to death,[523] so day upon day the inner self was as surely being renewed[524] and hastening too in turn towards its own, which, thanks to a life of holy and enduring poverty, was undoubtedly even then the kingdom of heaven. And so, urged daily on towards his end by those last days of his, now nearly spent, the blessed man sent for Osbern the priest to come and speak with him one to one.

3. 42. How he foretold the future dispute over his body

"Osbern," he said, "the hour of my calling is at hand; on the fifth day—that is, Saturday—as it draws towards evening, I must be ready." Osbern groaned at this and the saint saw his face fall: "Do not distress yourself," he said, "nor take these words too much to heart. I am going to the Lord whom I have served, and the day that now approaches is the day I have long desired. Let your concern be rather for this: to bury my body in this place as soon as I am dead. Otherwise you will find yourself in trouble, and the false allegations of men backing their claims to my body with armed force will bring turmoil upon you; I am telling you this in advance. However, I trust to my Lord that they will not prevail and that it will not be given them to take it hence. I was called to this place by God, here

[521] Luke 12:36; see Matt 25:10.
[522] Ps 101:27.
[523] Phil 2:21.
[524] 2 Cor 4:16.

have I labored, and here he wills that I should take my rest." When he had spoken these words, he made a pure and humble confession of his sins—for life cannot be lived without sinning—and having received absolution from the priest he was fortified by rite with the other sacraments of the church. After this he took to his bed and consented to rest his limbs, weak from debility and age.

Quickly the sad news spread to the neighboring faithful. Learning that their father was ill and that the physician of all the world had taken to his bed,[a] they came flocking to weep over him and to receive his dying blessing. Mindful too of keeping truth with Brother William and of the love with which he loved his dear friend to the end,[525] he sent for him as he had promised, that the monk might once more see his Wulfric as he was leaving our day and exchange on earth a last farewell. Brother William hastened over and inherited a blessing from that holy hand; indeed, rejoicing in the abundance of blessings he had profited from in the past, he took care to add that day to the load, knowing that in a little while he would not see him anymore because he was going to the Father.[526]

So this brightest of suns, which had lit the world until then with word and example, both knew and made known to others the hour of its setting. And lest death should take him unawares or disquiet him with the horror of its coming, Christ did not suffer it to come like some thief or brigand to his little one; seen from afar, it walked before him, and when it did come, if not agreeable, it was certainly less harsh. Thus it was that Wulfric, child of Christ deservedly loved, full of years and virtue, at the day and hour of his predicting, with joined hands pointing heavenward, passed from our light to light eternal. It then happened that Osbern the priest, who had received the saint's instruction about hastening his burial, judged that to steal from this world a man of such glory without the dues of solemn funeral rites would be disrespectful to God and beyond his authority. He held back for a time, and not, assuredly, against God's will, so that the holy man's prediction about the future

[525] John 13:1.
[526] John 14:19, 28.

wrangle over his body might be fulfilled, and because this is indeed the place which the Lord made ready for his saint's repose .[527]

3. 43. Of the struggle for the blessed man's body which the monks of Montacute began in vain

Along came the monks of Montacute, with a strong force of soldiers and others retained for the purpose, demanding the holy man's body as of right, on the grounds that he was their brother and had obtained his daily pittance from them and had given them his body for burial, or so they said. For their part, Osbern and those who sided with him agreed it was a fact that the man of God had been the monks' brother, as he had of other holy men, as far as participation in spiritual benefits went, and nor could they deny the daily provision of victuals. But that he had chosen to be buried at Montacute, of that they said they had no knowledge whatever; quite the reverse: they knew with perfect certainty that he had dedicated this place to himself and himself to this place. As the argument continued in this vein, the monks, opting for force over reason in their undertaking, were preparing to lay hands on the sacred body exposed as was customary to public view. Whereupon Osbern, hemmed in so tight a corner, thought up with heaven's help an even straiter way out. Slipping from the church, he locked the door behind him, leaving the intruders shut in and shut up, and set about actively summoning help from every quarter.

Meanwhile, those inside were far from idle, but were working frantically to break through the wall where the holy man's window had been,[a] and make a way out for themselves and the sacred treasure they were vainly slavering after. Outside, the villagers were trying to keep this route blocked and straining every nerve to frustrate their adversaries' efforts. Once the wall had been broken through, the Montacute lot, handling the sacred clay without any reverence, endeavored to push it out to some of their own party who had scrambled out to catch it. The villagers, equally impassioned, strove

[527] Deut 12:5.

with might and main to push the venerable body exposed to view back inside again. Since men cannot vie so violently without loss of peace and innocence, blood was shed and wounds were inflicted, but—God battling for his saint—not mortal ones.

At the height of this manly uproar, back came Osbern with a strong force gathered from Crewkerne and other places he had sent to—for having had forewarning of this dispute he had taken appropriate measures. Unlocking the church, he made his entry and, with a show of his newfound strength, demoralized the opposition, broke up the fighting, and deflated their presumption. He then spoke to the monks in conciliatory terms and convinced them with sensible argument that it would be best for both sides to consult the bishop on the matter and wait on his decision for a solution. Shamefaced and sad at heart, the monks went back, leaving unfinished business in their wake. However, it is puerile and ill-advised to scoff at the deluded, particularly when their zeal may be attributed to religious motives and their pious ambitions have been frustrated not by human agency but by divine decree.[b]

Upon this, the bishop, learning of the holy man's passing, came as the latter had himself predicted and was taken in to him, and there in the cell which had witnessed such signs and wonders, and with the reverence called for by such holiness, the bishop buried the sacred and precious treasure. And, lest pleasurable memories of disorder should disturb in some degree the weaker minds, he calmed everything down with some well-chosen words, reminding the people of how, long ago in the early days, the whole city of Jerusalem was thrown into turmoil on Saint Paul's account.[528]

3. 44. How the holy body was twice translated

Notwithstanding that the solemn rite had been celebrated in due form, Osbern the priest, fearful that thieves might dig up his treasure and steal it, came secretly and moved it into the church, burying it on the north side of the altar, where he levelled the surface

[528] Acts 21:30-36.

of the grave till it was flush with the surrounding area, lest any unevenness give rise to suspicion. When later, with the passing of time, he caught people whispering and realized he had been found out, he looked round for a still safer cache and finally hid his secret in the western end of the church in a spot known only to God and himself, using, without a doubt, the lowliness of this inferior position as a sign. Blessed Wulfric fell asleep in the year of Our Lord 1154, on the 20th day of February, in the first year of King Henry II, and in the everlasting reign of Our Lord Jesus Christ, to whom with the Father and the Holy Spirit be all glory and honor, world without end, Amen.

3. 45. Of a revelation, thought to have been angelic

It happened one day after the passing of blessed Wulfric, when Osbern the priest was sitting in the church, that a man in pilgrim's garb appeared quite suddenly, a man with strikingly fine features and a head of white hair inviting reverence. After laying his offering of prayer before the Lord,[529] he turned to the priest: "Good man," he said, "if you have anything left that belonged to blessed Wulfric, beloved of God, I beg you in the Lord's name not to refuse it me but let me have it as a token of his holiness." Osbern replied that he had nothing apart from objects consecrated to sacred use, which he was not free to give away. "That is not so," said the other, "there, in that chest belonging to you, you have the dish and spoon he used to eat with. Get up and give me these." The priest jumped to his feet, and, having caught in the man's voice as he spoke some sound beyond the human, made haste not so much to grant a request as to obey an order. Opening his coffer he took out the dish and spoon and handed them to the waiting pilgrim. But no sooner had he closed and relocked the coffer than he began to repent and tax himself with over-hastiness in having been so feebly generous in a matter of such import towards an unknown man. So he ran after him hotfoot, ready to buy back what he had given away.

[529] Ps 118:108.

After he and others had searched high and low for this man and found no trace of him, Osbern became persuaded by the way the man appeared without warning and left without notice, or even by the angelic aura of his countenance and—more commanding of belief—the authority of his words and the secret knowledge he revealed, that this was a more than human being. And perhaps the visitor wanted to teach the sons of men with what devotion blessed Wulfric ought to be embraced, seeing that those belongings of his which we hold cheap are not to be disprized, being both devoutly sought out and eagerly seized on by the denizens of heaven. Walter of Glastonbury declares that he had this from Osbern himself.

3. 46. Of another revelation and a woman healed

The woman bidden by revelation (as was told earlier in the *Life*)[a] to send the blessed man a piece of silk for covering a Psalter kept to this day in Haselbury church had enjoined on herself at the time the pious practice of visiting the saint once a year. As long as he lived she faithfully paid him this annual due at the right season, but once he had fallen asleep she considered herself released from the obligation. It then happened that she fell ill, and the man of God appeared to her in her sleep, saying: "Why have you neglected to visit your friend this year? Is it because you think him dead who is living in the glory of God? Get up as quickly as you can and go to the place of his rest.[530] Healing will not come to you in any place but that." Starting up from her sleep, she set out as soon as she could on the long road from Kent to Haselbury; there she found the healing promised and venerated her healer and dearly beloved friend. Thereafter she held him lifelong and did not let him go,[531] reviving with the holy kiss exchanged at his holy tomb the faith of their former charity and the original covenant between them, keeping both to the end. This too came from Walter.

[530] Acts 7:49.
[531] Song 3:4.

3. 47. Of another revelation and a man healed

There is a woman hereabouts at a place called Hurcott,[a] a most godly widow: indeed, to give her her full due of praise, assuming the testimony borne her by the faithful to be true, she is second to none round here in faith, piety, and devotion. I did not hear personally from her lips what I am about to relate; instead, as she lives quite close to us, I sent three of our most trusted brothers to her one by one, lest someone should harbor the thought that death had unstrung blessed Wulfric's hand and weakened his power.

This woman had a husband called Wudeman, a faithful and God-fearing man in every way, who fifteen years ago and at least fifteen after the holy man's death, suffered for nearly a year from the serious illness to which doctors give the name of lientery. For whatever food he took was promptly ejected from his ailing gut, along with blood, and in the same raw and undigested state. He had paid out large sums for nothing to doctors who despaired of him; not really for nothing, though, but to allow the extent of blessed Wulfric's power to measure how far, where sickness was great, grace was still greater,[532] and thus hold a mirror up to glory. So at a time when dragging infirmity had drained this man of all substance and he shrank to see no outcome but death, Liviva, as his wife is called, dreamed she was standing in the church at Haselbury, praying. And suddenly a dignified man with a head of white hair was there with her and said: "Do you want your husband to be healed?" "I do indeed, sir, if it be God's will." "Then go," he said, "to the north end of the altar and gather up dust from the man of God's grave. You will give some of this to your husband to drink in water and he will be cured." On waking she related the vision to her husband, but he, very wary of illusion from having been taught that dreams are not to be trusted, dissuaded his wife from meddling in such matters and thereby retarded his own cure.

Then the woman saw herself a second time set down in dream in the same church, and to the north of the altar stood a splendid tomb draped with a rich cloth. She approached with reverence,

[532] Rom 5:20.

preparing to kneel at its foot. But the one lying in the tomb seemed to stretch out his feet towards her, striving angrily to push and kick her away with his shoes, as if indignant that she had not yet obeyed the divine command. And as the woman stood there, quaking and dumbfounded, of a sudden the man appeared as before and began to ask sternly why she had thus far neglected heaven's bidding and her husband's healing. He then pointed out to her the exact place of the grave from which she was to take the dust. This was the woman's dream. When she woke up, fearful this time not of being blamed for negligence but accused of apparent contempt, and also of being guilty of her husband's death, she arranged to take with her as companion for the journey a certain John, whom they surnamed Falconer,[b] and after consulting the village priest she left for Haselbury. There she told her visions to Osbern the priest and to the lady,[c] who was still living then, filling them with such joy as poured itself out in an abundance of tears. Then making her unguided way to the level surface of the burial place, she scooped up a handful of dust and went back home, where she mixed some with water and gave it to the sick man to drink. The power of this drink was so vital and efficacious that the man, only half alive, or more properly half dead, rose on the third day from virtual death[533] and walked the short distance to the church where he offered to God in his tabernacle and to his saint a sacrifice of thanksgiving.[534] As the unhoped-for recovery of a man locally so well known could not be hidden and the manner of it was promptly trumpeted everywhere, those who had something wrong with them came to the woman, who cured several more with the rest of that dust. So the whole church of God came to know that blessed Wulfric is in the glory of God the Father[535] and is ready if anyone calls on him; indeed, before he is even invoked, he says: "Look, here I am."[536]

Here ends the Life of Blessed Wulfric, anchorite.

[533] Luke 24:46.
[534] Ps 26:6.
[535] Phil 2:11.
[536] Isa 52:6.

[Of the bone which was wonderfully divided][a]

The prior of Dunstable once related to me, Hamo, a monk of Saint Mary of Woburn, when I had chanced to say something about holy Wulfric, that John, the sacristan of Saint Bartholomew's church in London, had heard from the prior of that house, a worthy and devout man, the following story. "I once visited Wulfric, the man of God, at Haselbury," he said, "being anxious to see and speak with him and commend myself to his prayers. When I had been given a most gracious welcome and enjoyed an intimate conversation with him, the holy man strengthened the bonds of love binding me to him by showing me the ornaments he had himself provided for the church, as also the many relics of the saints he had in his possession. Among these tokens of the saints was a bone which was thus inscribed: 'Bone of Saint Augustine, bishop of Hippo.' Gazing at it as I held it, and deeply moved, I said to the man of God: 'I beg you, good Father, for Christ's love to give me a little piece of this bone. For we have professed the Rule of Saint Augustine, and having obtained from him the name of canon and this rule of life, we beg that our church may be enriched, thanks to you, with relics of his.' 'I will gladly give what you ask,' the holy man replied, 'if I know it will be pleasing to God and the saint,' adding in his holy simplicity: 'Let us prostrate ourselves before the Lord in prayer, that he may make known to us his pleasure in the matter, for he does the will of those who fear him and answers their prayers.' So having prostrated ourselves in prayer and then stood up again, we found that bone in two parts, as equal as if it had been sawn through the middle with a file. Both rejoicing in the Lord, we gave thanks to him and his saint, and there came to me thus one part of that bone, the holy man being content with the remainder."

Here ends the Life of Saint Wulfric, anchorite of Haselbury.

NOTES

Prologue 1

a) E is the only ms. to have *prologus* in the title, the others preferring *epistola*.
b) Bishop of Exeter 1161–84. See introduction, 3, 4, 11, 12, 14–17.
c) *ad Dei gloriam . . . conscribendam*, the reading of C, preferred to *ascribendam*, as given in E.
d) Baldwin of Forde, bishop of Worcester 1180–85, see introduction, 3–5, 11–13, 15–17.
e) Reginald fitzJocelin, bishop of Bath 1174–91, following an eight-year interregnum. See introduction, 16.

Prologue 2

a) To be, as it were, chewed over. The monk, intent on his *lectio divina*, read the words aloud to himself and then spent time ruminating on their content.
b) Probably Robert II, abbot of Forde, 1180–90. See introduction, 5, 14, 16, 17.
c) Thomas Becket, archbishop of Canterbury 1162–70, canonized 1173. The *Life* has *beatissimus Thomas recens scilicet purpura et de ipsis canalibus nuper extracta*. The Vulgate text behind it (Song 7:5) is obscure to the point of incomprehensibility, but that John interpreted *purpura regis vincta canalibus* as canals or channels running with purple dew is plain from his later commentary on the verse (*On the Song of Songs, V*, 203).
d) William fitzHerbert, elected archbishop of York in 1141. Deposed in 1147 by Eugenius III and restored in 1153, he died within weeks and was canonized in 1226. His election in 1141 was contested and his tenure of the archbishopric was opposed by the Cistercians on behalf of Henry Murdoc, abbot of Fountains and Eugenius's choice to replace him. Saint Bernard led a relentless campaign against him. It is thus interesting that John gives him the title *beatus* on the strength of local veneration and the many reports of miracles worked at his tomb.

e) Godric of Finchale, b. ca. 1165, d. 1170, pedlar, sailor, merchant, and finally hermit in co. Durham, where he lived for many years by the river Wear. John had surely read his *Life* by Reginald of Durham in one of its three recensions—even the third was written before 1173. There were strong Cistercian links here too, all positive. Ælred of Rievaulx visited Godric on several occasions, and visits by other white monks are also noted. It was Saint Ælred who pressed Reginald to write the *Life*, after enjoining on him to visit Godric (Reginald of Durham, *Libellus*, 19 and 269).

BOOK 1

1. 1.

a) Now Compton Martin.
b) An illustration of the "clash between two cultures: the spiritual ambience of the ascetic holy man and the unregenerate earthly huntsman" (Golding, "The Hermit," 110–13). John, as a Cistercian, makes no secret of his disapproval of hunting. In his view it was not an occupation for a priest or, for that matter, any committed follower of Christ, and indeed "by the mid-twelfth century there was a powerful body of opinion that held that clerics at any rate should not hunt" (Golding, "The Hermit," 113). Interestingly, Reginald fitzJocelin, the bishop of Bath who figures in the first Prologue, held hunting rights throughout Somerset (Bell, 138), which would hardly have made for sympathy between him and John, and may be one reason why, after Bartholomew's death, all reference to him disappears from the *Life*.
c) Henry I introduced ca. 1108 measures to reform the English coinage, consisting then of the silver penny. Halfpennies were normally created by cutting pennies in two; to end the practice, the king had round halfpennies minted, but the numbers issued in his reign seem to have been small. In 1124 he proceeded against false moneyers with ruthless zeal. Memories of any or all of this activity may be reflected in the tale of the new money, *novus nummus*, to which has been attached a symbolic significance rooted in Scripture.
d) One of the Wiltshire Deverills. Four lie in a line between Warminster and Mere, and a fifth a few miles to the east.
e) William fitzWalter, see introduction, 19–21.
f) John notes the absence of episcopal involvement at Wulfric's enclosure, his surprise reflecting the extension of diocesan control over recluses in the course of the twelfth century (Warren, *Anchorites*, 56–57). Godfrey, chaplain to Adela of Louvain, the second wife of Henry I, had been bishop of Bath for two years in 1125 (*Fasti Ecclesiae Anglicanae 1066–1300*, 7, ed. D. E. Greenway [London: Institute of Historical Research, 2001]). He may well have been much at

court. The bishop was, nonetheless, "by virtue of his office, the guardian of every solitary in his diocese" (R. M. Clay, *The Hermits and Anchorites of England* [London: Methuen, 1914] 93), and we find Godfrey's successor, Robert of Lewes, taking a continuing and beneficent interest in Wulfric from the time of his appointment in 1135 until the recluse's death and burial some twenty years later.

1. 2.

a) *Iudeorum*, "of the Jews"; presumably a reference to pharisaic practices condemned in the Gospels.

1. 3.

a) There are numerous echoes between this passage and Ps 101, notably the use of the verbs *arere, arefacere, deficere.*
b) *bersisa*: Bell suggests this was a kind of barley water (Bell, 143). "We" renders the latin *nostri*, our brothers, our order. A drink probably local to England, its name given a Latin form to allow of its use in community.
c) Neither the translator nor such experts as have been consulted have been able to make sense of the last clause of this chapter. I offer the Latin to any readers who may wish to try their hand: *ne Wulfrici vel simplicitas vel emulatio quarum utraque seductioni proxima est et ipse potentissimus in utraque ea que perfectorum est solidus cibus discretione vacasse credatur.*

1. 4.

a) "by weight and measure": the connection with sleep is not immediately evident, but the scriptural reference came readily to a society in which revenues, both rents and taxes, were commonly paid in kind and sparingly weighed out. The word *pensio*, a due, tax, perquisite, is used in a similar metaphorical sense elsewhere (2. 13; 3. 46).
b) The first mention of Robert of Lewes, appointed bishop of Bath in 1135 (see introduction, 13, 14, 35–6). His later interventions seem to have been equally sensible (3. 41 and 3. 43).

1. 5.

a) Wulfric's passing from the hair shirt to the coat of mail signified a more extreme, and therefore higher, form of penance. The difference between the two was not of essence but degree, hence "noble both, but the second emphatically nobler." The use of the vocabulary of warfare to symbolize spiritual struggle goes back to Scripture and particularly to Saint Paul (as here, Rom 6:13 and, particularly, Eph 6:10-17). Saint Benedict saw anchorites and hermits as specially trained and armed for solitary combat (RB 1.3-5). Mail shirts are known to have been worn from the eighth century onward, initially in Italy, and the custom spread northward to France and England (see Bell's extensive note, 143–44). The garment denoted the warrior (only a knight could afford one) and just as the knight was in the forefront of the struggle for social order—as well as disorder—so the anchorite was in the vanguard of God in battling against the powers of evil and the temptations of his own flesh. A representation of knights fighting was not thought out of place even in the Saint Albans Psalter made for the recluse Christina of Markyate (J. J. G. Alexander, "Ideological Representation of Military Combat in Anglo-Norman Art," *Anglo-Norman Studies* 15 [Woodbridge: Boydell, 1993] 1–24).

b) *in vas quoddam frigida aqua infusum descendebat.* Presumably he sat in it. The tub may have stayed in the cell, the water being brought in a pail by the servant through the church door and carried out the same way.
Christi puerulus, "Christ's little slave-boy." The terms *puer, parvulus, puerulus,* when used of Wulfric, present a problem I have resolved in varying ways. The two last are diminutives of undoubted tenderness, expressing his relation to Christ, of whom he is both child and servant. I was put in mind here of Ps 122:2, where the eyes of slaves are on the hand of their master (see also 1. 10 and 3. 40).

1. 6.

a) *dura ut inferus emulatio.* The word *aemulatio* represents, in its good sense, zeal, in its bad, jealousy. It is found in the Vulgate in both senses: in Saint Paul chiefly as zeal, though not always. The Old Testament has the substantive *aemulator* (compare Deut 2:4), usually translated as "a jealous God," but a footnote to the verse in the New Jerusalem Bible has: "God's 'jealousy' is the extravagance of his love." How John understood it here is impossible to say, but since he uses it often of Wulfric with the sense of "zeal" (see 1.3), I have rendered it "passion." The same sentence has *expetiit*, a clear reference to Christ's words to Peter: *Simon, Simon, ecce Satanas expetivit vos* (Luke 22:31).
b) *exquisitus* has the double meaning of "choice" and "chosen."

1. 7.

a) *puro nomine*, an echo of RB 63.11, where the use of the plain name within the monastery is forbidden. Another example of the freedoms accorded to hermit and anchorite, who turned social norms on their head, addressing a servant as "son," a king as "Stephen."
b) In 1136 Stephen was active in Wessex, putting down a rebellion, and could have called on Wulfric, who had already promised him the crown on an earlier visit.

However, as the anchorite takes issue with him in this chapter for his leniency, the episode should probably be placed after the king's captivity in 1141, when Wulfric rebuked him at length (3. 33). Speaking truth to kings was a privilege of the holy. Wulfric's view that Stephen was ineffectual is identical with that of Orderic Vitalis. Both use the word *gladium*, Orderic adding *iustitiae*—the sword of justice proper to sovereigns: "He could easily have stamped out the flames of terrible evil that were being kindled . . . if . . . he had struck down with the sword of justice . . . the pestilential strength of those who desired rapine and slaughter and the devastation of their country" (*The Ecclesiastical History of Orderic Vitalis*, ed. and trans. Marjorie Chibnall, 6 vols. [Oxford: Clarendon Press, 1969–80] vol. 6, 535).

David Crouch sees Stephen as a markedly religious man, citing not only his visits to Wulfric, which included private confession (3. 33), but his patronage of the new and reformed orders, in particular the monastic house founded at Savigny, on the confines of Normandy and Brittany, by the hermit Vital de Mortain, which in 1147, along with its thirty-three daughter houses, became affiliated to Cîteaux (David Crouch, *The Reign of King Stephen* [Harlow: Longman, 2002] 314–19).

1. 9.

a) This story is also found in Henry of Huntingdon's *Historia Anglorum*, written in Wulfric's lifetime and more than forty years before John's *Vita*. Given that this earlier version of the tale was circulating within ten years of Wulfric's enclosure, it seems useful to include it here. John admits to having heard varying accounts but describes the differences as "merely circumstantial" (1.10). It is possible that he had read the *Historia*, which Henry of Huntingdon updated at intervals until 1154. In the last recension Henry changed the verb for "lived," *degere* (first sentence), from present to past tense (*Historia Anglorum*, 696, n. 156), which suggests that he had already heard of Wulfric's death that February. Both writers insist on their concern for reliability in their sources.

> In the county which is called Dorset, at a town which is called Haselbury, there lived a servant of God, by name Wulfric, by profession a priest, by way of life a hermit [*anachorita*]. He always wore a hauberk next to his flesh to subdue his turbulent passions, and begged a new one from his earthly lord, since his own was almost worn out and torn in pieces by his sweat. He put on the new one, but was enraged with its length, because it might be seen below his garment. So he snatched up the shears and cut the soldered iron rings at the bottom and in the openings of the sleeves, as if it were linen cloth. The servant of God

> applied the shears a second time, in case there was any unevenness, cutting it through without delay or difference. Seeing this, his lord was filled with immeasurable joy and sank down at the holy man's feet. The man of the Lord was embarrassed, pulled him upright, and swore him not to tell anyone what he had seen. But it could not be kept secret. For many religious rejoiced to have rings from the holy hauberk, and the famous story has travelled everywhere through all parts of the kingdom. I would not have included this miracle in this cautious and carefully researched work, except that Pope Saint Gregory gives the narrative of Saint Benedict and other saints, recording some from what he had heard from a fellow religious and from other extremely reliable witnesses. The story of Wulfric, however, is attested by those who have seen parts of the hauberk, or visited his delightful presence, or heard his desirable speech, or have freely sought out the religious life and become religious themselves, and it also spread among all the people and is commonly known everywhere. (*Historia Anglorum*, 697)

Profuse sweating, not mentioned by John, who knows of only one hauberk, would certainly result in corrosion and the final disintegration of the garment; Godric of Finchale is said to have worn out three hauberks in this way in the space of fifty years (Reginald, *Libellus*, 28.77–78). According to John, Wulfric's lasted until a year or so before his death (3. 41), or roughly twice the time of Godric's. (All details pertaining to chain mail in general and Wulfric's hauberk in particular have been referred to Thom Richardson, F. S. A., Keeper of Armour and Oriental Collections at the Royal Armouries, to whom I am much indebted for help and advice.)

1. 10.

a) The links of Wulfric's hauberk would have been either all riveted, or, more probably, given the date, half welded closed and half riveted. "Un-riveting them, though it happened by accident when mail was damaged, is very difficult to do, even with the proper tools (pliers), and cannot be done by hand unless the links are actually broken. Likewise if the welded links are considered, these can only be released by opening the riveted links joining them, or using wire-cutters on them" (Thom Richardson, as above).

b) See introduction, 24–25.

c) See introduction, 23–24.

d) See introduction, 21–23.

1. 11.

a) The theologian known as Robert Pullen. A Devon man once thought to have taught in the Oxford schools from 1133–38, though it now seems more likely to have been Exeter (see introduction, n. 2). During the Anarchy he moved to Rome, where he was made cardinal and, as John correctly states, chancellor. He was clearly among Wulfric's earliest visitors, proof that men of learning already considered the recluse of Haselbury worth a journey or a detour. Although history has him as Pullen, John describes him as *Robertus quidem cognomento Pullus*, one Robert known as—or nicknamed—the Fowl, and some apt or comical reference presumably lay behind it. John uses a similar turn of phrase twice more, each time with reference to a servant (see notes to 2. 6 and 3. 47) who has clearly been given a nickname by his master or mistress (*quem Ostrucerium cognominabant*, 3. 47), whereas here the origin of the name is unknown to John.

1. 12.

a) Much turns on the interpretation of the phrase *retro statui iussit*: he told him to stand "behind" or "at the back." Bell has the demoniac placed behind the altar facing the priest in order to hear "'the words of power,' which are the words of consecration effecting the change in the elements, and also that he be compelled to look on the Blessed Sacrament, *a facie sacrorum*" (Bell, 147). This understanding implies an altar set far enough forward to enable a man to stand between altar and wall. There is no suggestion in the story that Wulfric was celebrating mass anywhere but in his cell. Whether he ever celebrated in the church except on the feast of Saint Michael (2. 8) is open to debate (see note to 2. 20), but either in the cell or in the chancel of the small church, the altar would almost certainly have stood against or been fixed to the east wall. As regards the cell, we know only that there was a step in front of Wulfric's altar (2. 5), which was therefore raised above the floor level. Furthermore, the demoniac was *adductus*, brought by others, firmly if not forcibly, and would surely not have been left facing the celebrant with the consecrated elements within his grasp. It seems that the demoniac and necessary attendants were admitted to the cell and told to stand at the back while Wulfric celebrated. In the confines of the cell the words of consecration and the elevation of the host would have been clearly heard and seen.

1. 14.

a) See introduction, 55.

b) Almost certainly Robert of Lewes. For the language issue, see introduction, 35–36.

1. 15.

a) See introduction, 56.

b) Bampton in Devon, just over the Devon-Somerset border. The castle was built in the reign of William I, and was taken by Stephen during the rebellion of 1136 (see 1. 8b, and 3. 35a).

1. 16.

a) The lord of the manor, who built the church and dowered it with land to provide for the needs of the priest, suited his own convenience. He wanted the church close to his residence, but he also wanted to keep the land adjacent to his hall in his own hand. The priest's land, like the villagers', lay farther off. For the proximity of church and manor, see 3. 10.

b) See RB 63.17, with its reference to Rom 12:10.

1. 17.

a) The word used here is not in fact *homagium*, the feudal "homage," but *hominium*, given by Du Cange (*Glossarium ad scriptores mediae et infimae Latinitatis* [Graz: Akademische Druck- u. Verlagsanstalt, 1954]) as expressing an act of subjection or dependence.

b) *in cuius manu dicebatur resquiecere salus*; an allusion to Gen 47:25, when the people of Egypt came to Joseph, saying: *Salus noster in manu tua est*, "our life is in your hand," illustrating the different and overlapping senses of *salus*.

c) An example of a eucharistic miracle frequently met with in hagiographical writings of the period: the bread and wine, once consecrated, take on the appearance of flesh and blood. In this case the change was apparent only to the penitent, a grace given to confirm his faith in the real presence. In Wulfric's eyes, the inward disposition of the penitent is the true touchstone.

1. 18.

a) A story found first in Gregory of Tours' *Miracles of Saint Martin*, 1. 5. Saint Ambrose, celebrating mass one Sunday at Milan, was seen to be apparently asleep. Two hours later someone woke him, saying: "Will the lord bishop order the lector to read the lesson, for the people are very weary of waiting." The saint excused himself, explaining that he had been officiating at the funeral of his brother Martin—later discovered to have been taking place at Tours at just that time.

1. 19.

a) That is to say throughout the Psalter, from the beginning of Psalm 1 to the end of Psalm 150.

1. 20.

a) *necessarium quiddam . . . quod vulgo stapellam dicimus*—"a necessary which in common parlance we call a staple." John always underlines, apologetically, any deviance from classical practice. Necessity being the mother of invention, English monks have forged a new word based on the OE *stapol* to replace a Latin one lost from lack of use.

b) Like Brihtric, a married priest, and one with sufficient means to educate four sons. Nothing connects him specifically with Haselbury; he could well have been fetched from a neighboring village.

1. 21.

a) "bested"—lit. "outlasted," one of the meanings given for *expetitius est.* The use of the verb is a clear reference to Luke 22:31: *Simon, Simon, ecce Satanas expetivit vos ut cribraret sicut triticum.*

1. 23.

a) The night of the Easter Vigil, which sees the renewal of baptismal vows for which Wulfric was preparing himself. The quotation from Ps 138, immediately following, forms part of the Exultet after the blessing of the Paschal candle.

1. 24.

a) *ad eum ingrediens*: presumably to the inner cell, via the church. Since any contact that required physical presence had to breach the privacy of the cell, the woman would have entered it, exceptionally, through the church door, later followed by the monk, who was clearly a habitual visitor and probably Brother William.

1. 26.

a) An echo of RB 5.7-9.

1. 27.

a) The reading of E is *accidit*, "it happened," but I have preferred that of C, *attulit*; it makes better sense and echoes *deferret*, "she should take," in the previous sentence.

1. 29.

a) He was also one of the four sons of the priest Segar (1. 20; 3. 19).

1. 30.

a) *cappa*, "a species of overcoat worn by male persons and especially clerics" (Bell, 152, citing various authorities, including Du Cange), a hood (*Medieval Latin Word-List from British and Irish Sources*). Clearly, a substantial garment protecting from the cold.
b) Wulfric's mouse is the only wild animal to appear in the *Life*. Unlike hermits, anchorites did not live close to nature. And this was no tame mouse sharing Wulfric's bread and cheese; it was a pesky nuisance; nonetheless it became an object of compassion and the recluse's attitude is sharply contrasted with the practical views of the parish priest. Saint Thomas of Cantilupe, less inhibited than Wulfric, had no hesitation in resuscitating a pet dormouse, accidentally trodden underfoot. (Valerie I. J. Flint, "The Saint and the Operation of the Law: Reflections on the Miracles of Saint Thomas Cantilupe," *Belief and Culture*, 343, n. 3.)

BOOK 2

2. 2.

a) *communicans cohabitantibus sibi*: presumably the priests, and possibly his servant. It is difficult to see who could be described as "dwelling with" an anchorite.

2. 3.

a) *Divina institutione formatus . . . audenter dicebat*: compare the words from the canon of the mass introducing the Our Father: *Praeceptis salutaribus moniti et divina institutione formati, audemus dicere.*

2. 4.

a) Chapter heading largely illegible in E, missing in C, supplied from F and H.
b) *peractoque denuo servitutis sue penso*, another echo of the words of RB 49.5: *solito pensu servitutis nostrae.*

2. 5.

a) *dulcoris*, supplied from mss. F and H. E and C repeat *odoris*, clearly in error.

2. 6.

a) *puerum suum quem Taillefer nominabat.* This is a strange piece of information to include, forty years after the event, in a story where the servant in question was a mere bystander. A second example—a servant, a nickname, readily explicable—is found in 3. 47. There are many servants in the *Life*, some with significant roles and all anonymous save these two. The name itself, given in French, is no less curious but easier to explore, if not explain. Taillefer was the name of the "jongleur" said to have ridden in the Norman vanguard at Hastings, juggling with his sword and drawing first blood when attacked. He was known, Latinized as *Incisor ferri*, to a Norman bishop composing a poem in honor of the Conqueror within four years of the battle, if date and attribution are correct (*The "Carmen de Hastingae proelio" of Guy, bishop of Amiens*, ed. and trans. Frank Barlow [Oxford: Clarendon Press, 1999] 24–25). He figures in Geoffroy Gaimar's *Estoire des Engleis* (ed. Alexander Bell [Oxford: Basil Blackwell, 1960], vv. 5265–302) and in Henry of Huntingdon's *Historia Anglorum* (392–93), both written in Wulfric's lifetime (as well as in Wace's later *Roman de Rou*, where he sings of Charlemagne and Roland "and the vassals who died at Roncevaux"). It is hard to see these written sources in Latin and Norman French providing a nickname for a priest's servant in an English village. The whole point of a nickname is to serve as a common reference within a group, from a family outward. John got the meaning, or the joke, or he would not have repeated it. Perhaps we should be looking rather to an oral tradition spreading out from the lord's hall, through his retainers and into the English population. In that case the name Taillefer, with attendant associations, would have to percolate barriers of class, language, and culture, possibly acquiring new meanings in the process. The juggler, the "hewer of iron," was a mascot of the conquerors; did he remain a man of valor to the descendants of the losers, or might his name be appropriated sarcastically? Osbern, who gave it as a nickname to his servant, was the son of a man who spoke no French and resented those who did. If it came to him as part of an oral culture, it is an eloquent example of the osmotic power of storytelling and singing.

2. 8.

a) Michaelmas, September 29th.
b) *cipho stagneo*—incontrovertibly a cup and not "a bucket of generous proportions" (Bell, 153). Given that the whole village partook, we may assume that Wulfric dipped the cup in a ewer or pail. The term reappears in 2. 12, where a mother offers her sick daughter water in a *cipho stagneo*. In the last sentence of the present chapter the word *poculum* is used—again, a cup, or, metaphorically, the content.
c) *conversi*—the usual term for lay-brothers, but here "the faithful," "the lay congregation," referred to elsewhere in the passage as *ecclesia*.

2. 9.

a) This chapter turns on the words *salus*, *fons*, *potus*, *haurire*, pointing to Isa 12:2-3; John 4:6-7; 1 Cor 10:4; Apoc 21:6. The story being one of physical illness, the healing sense of *salus* must have primacy, but all the scriptural echoes are of salvation.

b) *mulier in poculo hilaritatis hausit hilaritatem salutis.* John at his most inventive.

2. 10.

a) *Justitia*, "Peter the Venerable of Cluny expressly mentions vessels of wine 'which they call *justitias*' [Lib. 1, ep. 30]. The word was well known among Cistercians: in the early Customs the abbot is allowed to take two monks to eat with him when there are no guests, and it is the duty of his cook to take to them their *scyphos et justitias* and return them afterwards" (*Monuments primitifs de la règle cistercienne*, Guignard, p. 228, etc.), Bell, 154.

2. 11.

a) Bence, widow of Robert de Lincolnia or of Lincoln (d. ca. 1138). John twice says she is still alive (2. 11 and 3. 31) but does not appear to have spoken with her. On the other hand, he gives her son Alfred (d. 1199) as the source for one story (3. 28) and her brother-in-law Samson as the indirect source for another (3. 9). The family was clearly well known at Forde. They were supporters of the empress Matilda and also patrons of Montacute; H. Mayr-Harting refers to Alfred as a man "rising to be amongst the royal *familiares* and administrators of the next generation" ("Functions," 346. For genealogy and background, see Bell, 154–55).

2. 12.

a) Abbotsbury, situated on the coast ten miles west of Weymouth and some fifteen miles south of Haselbury; it had from Saxon times until the Reformation a large Benedictine abbey.

b) *ultro*: the use of this word makes it clear that John had in mind the Virgin birth. It would have come to him from, or taken him to, the freeing of Peter in Acts 12:10: *venerunt ad portam ferream . . . quae ultro aperta est eis*, which led, again by association, to *porta* in Marian imagery—*salve radix, salve porta, ex qua mundo lux est orta.* I am grateful to Father Hilary Costello, OCSO, for pointing me to the reference.

2. 13.

a) There are three Chinnocks, West, East, and Middle, lying north and northeast, within a few miles of Haselbury. The nearest, West Chinnock, is within easy walking distance. The name *de Cinnoc* was too well distributed for this particular William to be identified (Bell, 155).

b) *singulis, ut vulgo loquar, furnaturis*—another example of John's sensitivity about his Latin.

2. 15.

a) This chapter is rich in points of interest and not without difficulties, and the more general aspects have already been considered (introduction, 43, 57–58, 73).

b) An instance of cursing under provocation, which was probably known to John, is Ælred's uncharacteristic prayer that the vituperative abbot of a daughter house "might speedily suffer an end to his malice." The abbot returned home unrepentant and died a week later in agony (Vita A 37; Powicke, *Life*, 44–45). Walter Daniel presented this as a miracle, though later, in the "Letter to Maurice," he backtracked on the issue of cause and effect (Powicke, *Life*, 68). More pertinent to the story as a whole is Chapter 31 of the Rule of Saint Benedict on the person and role of the cellarer. The length of this chapter underlines its importance and it is relevant in its entirety to John's description of the cellarer of Montacute. He would have had it all in mind, and in the forefront the lines: "Above all, let him be humble. If goods are not available to meet a request, he will offer a kind word in reply." Conclusive is the ending, with the reference in both texts to Matt 18:4-7: "He will provide the brothers their allotted amount of food without any pride or delay, lest they be led astray. For he must remember what the Scripture says that person deserves *who leads one of the little ones astray*" (RB 31.13, 16). Various English translations of the Vulgate terms *scandalum* and *scandalizare* are current: I have used what fitted most smoothly into the context.

c) This sentence has proved a stumbling block to the translator and such experts as have kindly looked at it. Here is the original, as given in the Eton manuscript, for those who may wish to improve on the rendering:
Sic quippe homines animales [1 Cor 2:14] *similes eius quibus non est intellectus* [Ps 31:9] *nisi a vexatione gravi ad exaltationem iudicis sui velut ad suspensionem mole asinarie deterruit, ne exemplo eius scandalizarent unum de pusillis huiusmodi* [Matt 18:6].
The translator's confidence is not increased by manuscript variants: E has *iudicis*; the other three mss. are in agreement in giving *iudicii*. I have kept to *iudicis* under the impression that John is balancing, rather as on a seesaw, the weight of the punishment and the sublimity of the judge (i.e., Christ), the first raising the mind to the second.

d) Muriel, wife of Robert II de Beauchamp, who died shortly before 1196 (Bell, 156–57). John, who considered her a good witness, had five tales in all from her (2. 16; 3. 18; 3. 25; 3. 35).

2. 16.

a) A member of a Norman family established in East Anglia since the Conquest who figures as a witness on several of Henry I's charters (H. Mayr-Harting, "The Functions," 342, n. 36). Drogo de Munci's allegations of Wulfric's wealth were probably a bit premature, if we fix the date for Henry I's visit to the anchorite some time in 1130 or 1132, the most likely years. (For the king's itinerary, see C. Warren Hollister, *Henry I*, ed. A. Clark Frost [Newhaven: Yale UP, 2001].) For an overview of Wulfric's material resources, see introduction, 40–42.

b) Adelicia of Louvain, second wife of Henry I.

2. 17.

a) *phylacteriis*—a word with a wide range of reference, here probably objects connected with the saints. We know that Wulfric possessed a considerable collection of relics (see above, 217).

2. 20.

a) For Henry of Waverley, see introduction, 25–28.

b) John sees turmoil, disorder, and war as divine judgments visited on humankind (see also 3. 18), a slant favored by monastic authors, including the Cluniac bishop Robert of Lewes, if he was indeed the author of the *Gesta Stephani* (Frances Ramsey, "Robert of Lewes," 251). Henry of Waverley's view of his role is echoed by contemporary chroniclers: "there were many castles all over England, each defending its own district, or rather plundering it. The knights from the castles carried off both herds and flocks, sparing neither churches nor graveyards" (William of Malmesbury, *Historia novella*, ed. and trans. K. R. Potter [London: Nelson, 1955] 40, par. 483, quoted in Bradbury, *Stephen and Matilda*, 76).

c) This is the only occasion apart from Michaelmas (2. 8) where Wulfric is shown celebrating mass in the church. Had Henry of Waverley been following mass from the outer cell, he would have had first to knock on the shutter and introduce himself. As it is he has no contact with the anchorite until Brihtric approaches the knight after mass and leads him to Wulfric (*Brictricum secutus sum, venitque ad hominem Dei*). Even then there is no mention of the cell; it seems likely that he was taken out of the church and round the side to the *vestibulum*. There, like any other visitor, he exchanges greetings and proceeds to seat himself. On every other occasion it is fairly clear that Wulfric was celebrating at his own altar, either in private with an acolyte (2. 19)—usually Osbern (3. 16)—or joined on occasion by a visitor (1. 12; 1. 17; 3. 16; 3. 31) who was either admitted to the cell for a special reason, or watched through the window.

d) Sudden conversions of knights *in media res* as the result of a crisis of conscience were by no means rare (C. Harper-Bill, "Piety of the Anglo-Norman Knightly Class," 71–74).
e) Quoted in RB 7.54, under the seventh degree of humility.

2. 21.

a) There is no chapter heading here in any of the mss. There is, however, a clearly formed capital, marking a break in the text, and the consequent space into which the chapter heading would normally be squeezed. Dr. Day has provided for his forthcoming edition the heading *De moribus Abbatis Henrici*, which I have adopted with his permission.
b) See introduction, 13, n. 22.
c) Presumably a reference to visiting sovereigns, who may well have comprised Henry I, who facilitated the founding of Rievaulx in 1131, Stephen, and Henry II. The abbey was convenient to London, Windsor, and the Channel ports.
d) It seems that there was some criticism of Abbot Henry at Waverley after his death, possibly to do with what his community may have seen as "excesses." The Rule of Saint Benedict lays down a week for the chanting of the whole Psalter and points to the example of the Fathers, who strenuously fulfilled this obligation daily, as to an unattainable ideal (RB 18.23-25). The monks of Waverley may have found it hard to live with an abbot who was holier than they, or perhaps they felt that other things got neglected. This much is speculation, but both Eadmer and Walter Daniel found that detractors and skeptics picked away at the reputations of even the holiest of abbots.
e) *qui didicerunt a Christo alter alterius onera portare*—omitted in error by the scribe of E, added from C.

2. 22.

a) Father Henry insisted that he hadn't squandered *much*, and Wulfric's ambivalent prophecy confirmed this, insofar as the sum he was given was less than the abbey's debts. Most abbots came from the knightly class where liberality was seen as an essential virtue. Unfortunately, its practice required a large and regular income, and nobles lacking this advantage tended to recoup what they spent to maintain their reputation by pillage of one sort or another, frequently from religious houses, less well defended than the property of other feudal lords. Henry of Waverley had done his pillaging, but retained the knight's open-handedness, spending now—mostly—on behalf of his God.

2. 23.

a) Eugenius III.

2. 24.

a) Cardinal Pierleone, the grandson of a Jewish convert baptized by Leo IX. The father went by the name of Petrus Leonis, the form used by John, which allows the allusion to the devil prowling around like a roaring lion, seeking whom he may devour (1 Pet 5:8). The death in February 1130 of Honorius II was followed by the election of two rival popes: Innocent II and Pierleone, who took the name Anacletus II and whose influence and authority predominated in Italy. Pope Innocent took refuge in France, where Saint Bernard was instrumental in obtaining his recognition by all the great powers. Pope and abbot returned to Italy together in 1132, where Bernard continued to win back support for Innocent. The schism nonetheless continued and in 1137 Bernard returned to Italy, intervening successfully between the emperor Lothair III and Roger of Sicily, convincing the latter of the rights of Innocent. He also silenced the final supporters who sustained the schism. It is hard to tell whether John is referring to the first or second visit: the chapters read rather as though two interventions had been telescoped into a single triumph.
b) There is an unmarked passing here from "he" to "she," from Bernard the man to the *sponsa Christi*. Christ is the bridegroom, Bernard the bride throughout this passage.

2. 25.

a) Depending on whether Saint Bernard pronounced his rash words in 1132 or in 1137 (probably the former), he must have carried this "sin" on his conscience for some fifteen years before unloading it onto Father Henry. It is as abbot of Tintern that the latter travelled to Rome after attending the General Chapter at Cîteaux, returning to England via Clairvaux, and thus around 1150, after his own election and before the deaths of Pope Eugenius and Saint Bernard in 1153 and that of Wulfric in 1154.

2. 26.

a) *in finibus illis*: "in those parts," probably Clairvaux.
b) It is clear from the context that the expression *vir Dei*, otherwise used exclusively of Wulfric, refers here to Bernard.

2. 27.

a) *ipsam veritatem*, Christ himself (John 14:6).
b) E has *propriis exhortationibus*, while C has *his exhortationibus*; the latter seems the better reading and I have followed it.
c) A quotation from the Song of Songs interpreted as referring to the immature soul: Matilda, when she calls on Wulfric, is still a beginner in the spiritual life.

John later expounded this text in his Commentary (*Super extremam partem cantici canticorum sermones*, S 111; *Sermons on the Song of Songs, VII*, CF47 [Kalamazoo: Cistercian Publications, 1984] 131–41).

2. 28.

a) *reverenter*: through self-effacement, out of reverence for God, the source of all grace.
b) *mussitatione*: another echo of the Rule of Saint Benedict, RB 38.5, to which Bell draws attention (Bell, 145).
c) The anchoress was frequently succeeded by her servant, who was considered to have a "right of inheritance" to the cell (Warren, *Anchorites*, 26, n. 18).

BOOK 3

3.1

a) Alan de Faleisa: his name appears on two charters in the Montacute cartulary (Bell, 161).
b) *ut miser homo immo homo miseriarum nullatenus esset ei miserabilis*, is the reading of three of the four mss., including E and C, the most reliable. The replacement, in Bell's edition, of *miserabilis* with *immiserabilis* renders the sentence, and hence the story, incomprehensible.
c) A passage rich in scriptural references which may need unpacking. "Those who sit on the thrones" are the apostles (Ps 121:5), the thrones of judgment set for the house of David, seen later as a prophecy fulfilled in Christ's promise to the apostles that they will sit on thrones judging the twelve tribes of Israel (Matt 19:28; Luke 22:30). The one who sits on the throne is Christ (Matt 19:28 and 25:31) speaking the words of Pilate (John 19:22). "There will be no crossing of the bridge" is an allusion to the parable of Lazarus and Dives, "between us and you a great chasm has been fixed, in order that those who would pass from here to you may not be able, and none may cross from there to us" (Luke 16:26).

3. 2.

a) The site of an anchoress's cell in the churchyard at Crewkerne was being pointed out as late as the 17th century (Bell, 161).
b) *magnis viris*: presumably clerics; John usually uses *potens* to qualify knights and barons.

3. 3.

a) The village of Corscombe lies some 5 miles southeast of Haselbury. Richard of Corscombe is given as the source also of 3. 10 and may well, through a scribal error, lie behind the Henry of Corscombe given as one of the small group of friends summoned by Wulfric before his death (3. 41 and note a).

3. 4.

a) The text has simply *Quidam ex nostris*, "one of ours," making it almost certain that the chapter headings were added at Forde, perhaps under John's supervision, since only at Forde would the identity and therefore status of the man have been known.

3. 5.

a) Winsham, a Somerset village lying between Crewkerne and Chard.

3. 6.

a) Baldwin de Redvers (see note to 3. 35), in 1150, replaced the secular canons of Christchurch priory with Augustinians. Nicholas, who seems to have passed the story directly to John, was probably one of these.

3. 7.

a) *a rufo puero, qui collo tuo incubat, liberabit.* Not a boy named Rufus, the meaning conveyed by the introduction of a capital R to *rufus* (Bell, 93); simply "the red-headed." The word was frequently attached where appropriate as a *cognomen*: William II, known as William Rufus, is the obvious example; a more amusing one is that of the two brothers known respectively as Alan Rufus and Alan Niger, Alan the Red and Alan the Black, or Dark (Southern, *Anselm and his biographer*, 185–88). More pertinent to this case is the fact that the devil was frequently portrayed in the Middle Ages as red-headed, and the incubus is named by Wulfric as the adversary. The lethargy which affected Richelda and prevented her from making her pilgrimage to Bury Saint Edmunds, site of the shrine of Saint Edmund, king and martyr, was a consequence or projection of an unrecognized diabolical possession.
b) *dies nonus*, the ninth and last day of a novena of prayer made, frequently to one of the saints, for the recovery of health.

3. 8.

a) See note to 2. 11. Bell believes Samson of Lincoln to have been in fact brother-in-law to William fitzWalter's wife (Bell, 163, 165).

3. 10.

a) See introduction, 56.

b) Roger de Nonant, lord of Totnes from ca. 1140–ca. 1177, married to Adelicia, d. of Baldwin de Redvers. He was presumably staying at the manor house.

3. 11.

a) All four mss. inexplicably have *Beatus Wulfricus factus est nobis introductionem* (or some variant spelling) *cogitationum nostrorum*, which is clearly wrong. Day offers *fecit* in place of *factus est*, which makes more sense. The sentence ends with *et in angulis nostris repperit pravitatem*. Bell has *angelis*, but this is plainly a slip; the reading is not borne out by any of the mss.

3. 12.

a) *bigam, quam corrupte quadrigam dici usus obtinuit*: lit. a two-horse cart "which usage has incorrectly caused to be called a *quadriga*," the latter being a four-horse cart or chariot, or more usually a team of four horses. In John's day *quadriga* was no doubt the usual word for cart or wagon among monks and clerics who spoke Latin as a quasi-vernacular. Having made his linguistic point, John proceeds to put *quadriga* in Wulfric's mouth as the word he would have used had he spoken Latin to a group of villagers: a nice touch.

b) *quidam de Haselbergia ex viri Dei domesticis*: normally a person's family or household, hardly relevant in the case of a recluse. Perhaps his servant, the priest, the sacristan.

3. 13.

a) Probably East and West Chelborough, near Tollerford, Dorset (Bell, 163).

3. 15.

a) John refers to his correspondent simply as "the venerable abbot of Malmesbury," thereby implying that he is still in office. Moreover, he speaks of him in the present tense: *perhibet, scribit*, so we should look for the abbot in place ca. 1180, one who knew Wulfric as a young man, perhaps before entering the religious life, as he refers to the healing of his brother Laurence. This is surely a blood brother, not a monk of Malmesbury (Bell, xxxvii), for he is not merely the abbot's brother (*Laurentio fratri predicti abbatis*); the abbot is his brother (*cum fratre suo iter ad propria susciperet*). The only abbot to fit the bill is Osbert Foliot, 1176–82, a former prior of Gloucester and hence a local man who could easily have had contact with Wulfric as well as a brother with lands in the neighborhood. His six years as abbot gave ample opportunity for acquaintance with John at the very time the latter was assembling his material ("House of Benedictine Monks: Abbey of Malmesbury," *A History of the County of Wiltshire*, Volume 3, R. B. Pugh and Elizabeth Crittall, eds., Victoria

County History [Woodbridge: Boydell and Brewer] 1956, 210–31, and British History Online). The abbot's final story about the thief who is unable to leave the churchyard is similar to one recounted by Eadmer about a clerk who made off with Anselm's chrismatory and couldn't find the way out of Harrow. In both cases the thief is pardoned on restoring the object (Eadmer, *Life*, 67–68).

3. 17.

a) This village has not been identified.

3. 18.

a) Also written Hiribecci, Guirebecs; a name originally applied by Orderic Vitalis to Angevin troops harrying Normandy (*The Ecclesiastical History*, ed. Chibnall, vol. 6, 466, 468), and subsequently to these same troops who accompanied the young Henry of Anjou at his first unsuccessful attempt on England in 1149. Henry, however, came twice with mercenaries he could not pay, and it was on the second occasion, in 1153, that many were drowned on the return passage (Bradbury, *Stephen*, 157). There may well have been some conflation. In Orderic's chronicle (*The Ecclesiastical History*, ed. Chibnall, vol. 6, 472), as in the *Life*, the Angevins plundered the peasants and desecrated churches; for this God punished them with dysentery. They were not quick learners.

3. 20.

a) This chapter with its odd beginning, which presents William fitzWalter to the reader as it were for the first time, seems to have been written earlier and then placed, when John came to compose the *Life*, among the prophetic *exempla* of Book 3. This may also account in some way for the yet odder ending, where all four mss. have *Hec filius eius Willelmus monachus Glastonie*, instead of, as we should expect, and as is found in 3. 22, *Hec filius eius(dem Willelmi) Walterus Glastoniensis*. Then in 3. 23 we find, still more strangely, *Hec filius eiusdem mulieris Willelmus Glastoniensis*, where the woman in question is incontrovertibly the lady of Haselbury. The fact that these readings are common to all mss. points back to John's own copy, or one made from it. A moment of inattention? An abbreviation incorrectly expanded by a scribe? William fitzWalter did have a son called William, probably the eldest. He held the fee after his father's death (Bell, xlv), was not a monk of Glastonbury, and figures nowhere in the *Life*. Both chapters 3. 20 and 3. 23 recount (as does also 3. 22, correctly attributed to Walter of Glastonbury) fitzWalter family stories, all of which came to John from Walter, his principal witness, probably over a period of years. I have restored them both to him. Keith Day, in his edition of ms. C, has corrected the attribution only in 3. 23, where doubt is impossible; but one scribal error strongly supports the argument for the second.

3. 21.

a) Durand de Mohun, here called the brother of William fitzWalter's wife, was married to Joan, described elsewhere as the sister of William fitzWalter (3. 26), suggesting that both brother and sister married Mohuns. The head of the family, William II de Mohun, whose steward Durand was, held Dunster castle against King Stephen during the rebellion of 1138–39. Durand de Mohun is known to have been dead by 1142 at the latest; this locks in with the fact that Osbern appears as a boy in the story (Bell, 165; Bearman, *Dictionary of National Biography* [Oxford: OUP, 1986, updated 2004], available online).
b) Probably Pidere or Pidele Walterton, the modern Puddletown (Bell, xliii–xliv), some 20 miles southeast of Haselbury, easily covered on horseback in a night.

3. 22.

a) The bishop of Bath, which might seem surprising in a Cluniac, was particularly keen on establishing Augustinian canons in his diocese (Ramsey, "Robert of Lewes," 259) and may have sown the seed in William fitzWalter's mind. Nothing is known about this short-lived foundation, but its existence seems confirmed by the brief narrative of the monk of Woburn, Hamo, appended to the *Life* in ms. F (see above p. 217).

3. 23.

a) The events in this chapter took place certainly before 1141, when King Stephen was taken prisoner at the battle of Lincoln, as Wulfric foretells here, and almost certainly before 1139 when Baldwin de Redvers (see note to 3. 35) returned from exile to seize Corfe castle on behalf of the empress Matilda. Already in 1137 the king had ousted Baldwin from Exeter after a siege and banished him from England. It seems likely that the queen's visit to Corfe took place during this unsettled interim period when Corfe, at least, was in royal hands. John's statement that William fitzWalter had not yet given allegiance to the king slots into this timescale: the Wessex magnates did not favor Stephen, and the named families in the *Life*—the Lincolns, Nonants, and de Mohuns—some of whom were intermarried with the fitzWalters and all of whom held lands in the neighborhood, were without exception supporters of the empress. That William fitzWalter, although he seems to have played no active part in the rebellion, was known to be not the king's man is thus unsurprising. Wulfric's prophecy, if spoken as narrated, turned out to be remarkably exact. David Crouch suggests a date between the king's coronation in 1135 and the fall of Exeter in 1136, but this seems unnecessarily early and puts a strain on the prophecy by advancing it to a period where there was not as yet overt opposition to Stephen's rule (*The Reign of King Stephen*, 316, n. 74).

b) *si recte memini*: John must have written this down sometime after being told the story, which tends to confirm that he did not at the outset have a clear program or a defined method.

c) See note to 3. 20.

3. 25.

a) This episode seems to have taken place when Wulfric's reputation was at its height, leading to a large number of gifts in money and kind. Opportunities for interception by the servant were not lacking, both when the gifts were brought and when, as often happened, they were passed on to others. Dishonest servants were not unusual, which, given their conditions, does not surprise. Godric also had problems with servants (Ridyard, "Functions . . . Revisited," 245), and he, like Robert of Knaresborough, had several at once, but both of these were hermits with small holdings (Reginald, *Libellus de vita*, 195; Golding, "The Hermit," 100).

3. 26.

a) See note to 3. 21.

b) Sturminster Newton, a Dorset town in the Blackmore Vale.

3. 27.

a) William fitzTerric would appear to have been a subtenant of William fitzWalter (Bell, 167–68). Mudford is 3 miles from Yeovil, so the fitzTerrics were near neighbors of Wulfric.

3. 28.

a) The Second Crusade, called by Pope Eugenius and preached by Saint Bernard in 1146. Saint Bernard himself came to regret having espoused the cause, while John condemns it wholeheartedly. Saint Gilbert of Sempringham took a similar view of the no less ill-fated Fourth Crusade, though a less detached one: "Father Gilbert, hearing that Henry II had been signed with the cross, groaned and in an expressive Latin phrase delivered himself of these words: 'It has pleased God to end all things'" (*The Book of Saint Gilbert*, 106–7).

3. 29.

a) *tres pueros*. The meaning is not obvious: boys, youths, servants? There is nothing to prove the priests were in fact young, and the word, with its connotations of immaturity and class, was probably chosen as a measure of their fall from grace.

3. 30.

a) Probably Humfrey, first prior of the Augustinian canons at Gloucester, established in 1153, around the time at which William fitzWalter introduced them at Haselbury (Bell, 168–69).

b) *duos denarios*, two pennies. The silver penny represented roughly a day's wage for a working man, throwing interesting light on what a mean-spirited cleric considered likely to tempt a recluse, and what the same recluse was happy to leave as alms for the indigent.

c) Wulfric's visitors must have often found themselves in need of overnight lodging. Could their numbers have supported an inn, or did they seek hospitality according to class, the rich with the lord, the poor with their like (2. 14)? Montacute was not far away, but these two clerics chose to stay where they were, *in villa eadem*.

3. 31.

a) Neither Mabel fitzHamon, wife of Robert, earl of Gloucester, d. 1147, nor the wife of William, his heir, Hawise de Beaumont, appears to have had a sister called Agnes.

b) An example of mass celebrated by the recluse at his private altar, while one or more visitors follow the mass from the outer cell.

c) It is interesting that privacy is only ensured for sacramental confession. Companions seem to have entered the outer cell together, approaching the window one at a time (see also 3. 30 and 3. 34).

3. 32.

a) Henry I founded the abbey of Reading, dedicated to the Virgin Mary and Saint John the Evangelist, in 1121. His body was buried there when it was brought back from France after his death in 1135.

3. 33.

a) We have an exact date for this conversation as Stephen was taken at the battle of Lincoln on February 3rd, 1141. Since Wulfric refers to the king as a friend, both of himself and of William fitzWalter, it can be assumed that William had changed his allegiance, or at least confirmed his fealty to Stephen, since the queen's visit to Corfe castle. Probably a case of needs must.
The *Life* notes two visits by Stephen to Wulfric: one as count and one as king. This one, the second, is shown as taking place after his captivity, and would

seem to be the one already narrated at 1. 7, but with the added detail of the secret sin. John may have heard about the visit at different times and from two sources.

3. 35.

a) Baldwin de Redvers (d. 1155) was a declared supporter of the empress Matilda and the Angevin interest. Exiled by Stephen after a first rebellion in 1136, in 1139 he led the Angevin invasion of England, landing at Wareham and capturing Corfe castle. Matilda made him earl of Devon in 1141. It is probable that he went on the second crusade (1147–49), and it may be this expedition that John is referring to. Baldwin de Redvers founded a Cistercian house at Quarr, on the Isle of Wight, where he was later buried. A number of his supporters, including Stephen de Mandeville, held manors round Crewkerne, itself held by Baldwin (Robert Bearman, "Baldwin de Redvers," 29, fig. 1). The de Redvers and de Nonant families were tied by marriage (Bearman, "Baldwin de Redvers," 41); John has Roger de Nonant staying with William fitzWalter (3. 10).

b) Stephen de Mandeville was an active ally of Baldwin de Redvers. Wulfric was kinder to his memory than the author of the *Gesta Stephani*, who finds little to recommend him: he "stirred up a great amount of strife in the kingdom" and "to the king's supporters, whenever they came into his neighbourhood, he caused infinite trouble" (*Gesta Stephani*, 112).

c) A requiem mass.

3. 38.

a) "his brothers": William, Henry, and John (Bell, 141).

b) Henry of Blois, brother of King Stephen and bishop of Winchester, was abbot of Glastonbury from 1126 (Ramsey, "Robert of Lewes," 251). The intervention of this very powerful man suggests some kind of political *quid pro quo*.

c) "Childish tales"—E has *pluribus fabulis*, "with many tales"; the reading of C, *puerilibus*, is clearly preferable.

3. 41.

a) There is no earlier mention of Henry of Corscombe. To introduce at this late stage and solemn juncture an unknown character as one of Wulfric's closest and most trusted friends, and sandwich him between Brother William and Osbern, makes no sense. The priest Richard of Corscombe, described as a lifelong friend of Wulfric and known also to John (3. 3; 3. 10), is a much more likely candidate for the privileged role of counselor to the saint. He was still alive ca. 1180, as John refers to him as *bone opinionis* (3. 3) as opposed to *bone memorie*, and he could well have served as a source. An early scribal error seems the best explanation.

b) Brother William (see 3. 42).

3. 42.

a) *quia infirmaretur pater ipsorum et quia medicus universe terre lectulo acubuisset.* The association of the words *pater* and *medicus* would have come naturally to John in this context, as they were traditionally used to describe the priest-confessor. Basil the Great refers to the monastic confessor as *pater et medicus* (Reg. brev. 99; PG 31:1151), and Saint Benedict wishes the abbot to act as a *sapiens medicus* (RB 27.2). Wulfric had healed many physical ills, but for John, and especially at this juncture, he was above all the father and physician of the soul. (Background and references in Helen Forshaw, *The Pastoral Ministry of the Priest-Confessor in the Early Middle Ages, 600–1100*, unpublished thesis, London University, 1975, 284.)

3. 43.

a) The anchorite's shuttered window had apparently been blocked up after his death, while the door to the outer room was left latched or open.

b) Some thirty years after John wrote his dramatic account of these events, there occurred with wonderful irony an almost exact repetition, which has the Cistercians as the "villains." "Shortly before his death, which probably occurred in 1218, Robert [of Knaresborough] prophesied that monks from the Cistercian abbey of Fountains would come, bearing a white habit to receive him as an *ad succurendum* entrant to the community. All happened as he had foretold; on his death a group from Fountains turned up to seize the body, bearing a monastic habit in which to wrap the corpse for burial. Fortunately, however, the inhabitants of Knaresborough heard of the proposed raid and a force of armed men turned the monks back" (Golding, "The Hermit," 101).

3. 46.

a) 1. 27. "Muriel," in Bell's edition, is a misreading; both E and C have *mulier* here, as also in the earlier story. There is no connection with Muriel de Beauchamp.

3. 47.

a) Probably Hurcott in White Lackington, "nine miles west-north-west of Haselbury in the direct line" (Bell, 172).

b) *Ostrucerium*, see under *austrucaria: ostriciarius, ostricer* in *Medieval Latin Word-List from British and Irish Sources*, ed. J. H. Baxter and Charles Johnson, (London: OUP, 1934, rep. 1947). Another of the nicknames noted by John, presumably to assist in the identification of witnesses.

c) The wife of William fitzWalter, still alive in 1170.

[Of the bone which was wonderfully divided]

a) This piece is peculiar to the Faustina Cotton ms., which was written ca. 1200 by a Cistercian monk named Hamo, of Saint Mary's Abbey, Woburn, founded in 1145. He added to the *Life* a story which he had heard from the prior of Dunstable, a story relating to the prior of Saint Bartholomew's, Smithfield, who had visited Wulfric at Haselbury. Both priories belonged to the Augustinian canons; Saint Bartholomew's was founded in 1123, and Dunstable, a direct foundation by Henry I, in 1132. The identity of the priors in question cannot be established with any certainty, and the sacristan John, the only individual named, was a simple intermediary, passing an anecdote he had heard from a deceased prior to a living one.

WITNESSES WHO KNEW BOTH WULFRIC AND JOHN

Witnesses Described as "Still Alive Today" or Who Are Referred to in the Present Tense:

Abbot of Malmesbury, probably Osbert Foliot, who died in 1182 (3. 15).

Alfred of Lincoln (2. 11; 3. 27; 3. 28).

Beatrix fitzWalter (2. 9).

Bence, mother of Alfred of Lincoln (2. 11; 3. 31).

Christina of Wareham (2. 27; 2. 29; 3. 7).

John, anchorite of Winterbourne (2. 27).

Liviva, living at Hurcott (3. 47).

Muriel de Beauchamp; her husband died shortly before 1196, she probably earlier, but John refers to her in the present tense (2. 15; 2. 16; 3. 18; 3. 25; 3. 35).

Ralph, priest of Wareham (2. 29).

Richard, priest of Corscombe (3. 3; 3. 10).

Walter of Glastonbury (*passim*).

William, lay-brother hospitaller (*passim*).

William fitzTerric's wife and son (3. 27).

Four others spoke in person with John, but were probably dead by the time he wrote the final draft between 1180 and 1184:

Margaret of Phaleisa (3. 1).

Richard the scribe (1. 28; 1. 29; 3. 19).

Osbern (see introduction, 28–32).

Odolina, anchoress of Crewkerne (3. 2).

There were also a number of unnamed monks and lay-brothers of Forde (see particularly 1. 19; 3. 4; 3. 5) as well as certain members of the fitzWalter household from 1124–25 (1. 1).

TABLE OF CROSS-REFERENCES TO BELL'S EDITION

Present Text	Chapter Headings	Bell's Edition	
Bk. Ch.		**Ch.**	**P.**
1. 1	De uocatione eius et conuersione	1.	13
1. 2	De gratia interioris hominis	2.	15
1. 3	De initiis conuersationis eius et abstinentie rigore	3.	17
1. 4	De uigiliis eius et lecto	4.	18
1. 5	De asperitate uestis et balnearum	5.	18
1. 6	De morsu diaboli in serpente	6.	19
1. 7	De gratia et libertate eius in colloquendo	7.	20
1. 8	De emulatione taciturnitatis	8.	21
1. 9	De lorice incisione	9.	22
1. 10	De anulorum lorice absolutione	10.	23
1. 11	De somnio signorum prenostico	11.	24
1. 12	De demoniaco sanato et auctoritate loquendi uirtutes proprias	12.	26
1. 13	De radicata altius humilitate in eo	13.	27
1. 14	De muto sanato et altercatione Brictrici	14.	28
1. 15	Item de alio muto sanato	15.	29
1. 16	De laude Brictrici	16.	30
1. 17	De quodam qui diabolo hominium fecerat mirabiliter reparato	17.	31
1. 18	De excessu mentis in oratione	18.	35
1. 19	De stabilitate cordis in Psalmis	19.	36
1. 20	De uisitatione quadam celesti	20.	37
1. 21	De uisibili impugnatione demonum	21.	39
1. 22	De molestiis quibus eum uexauit hostis in corpore	22.	41

1. 23	De confessione publica illusionis nocturne	23.	42
1. 24	De pace carnis ad spiritum	24.	43
1. 25	De subita calefactione aque frigide in cellula eius	25.	44
1. 26	De opertorio per reuelationem ei delato	26.	44
1. 27	De opertorio libri per reuelationem allato	27.	45
1. 28	De neglentia scriptoris sui prophetice castigata	28.	45
1. 29	De monachi insompnietate curata	29.	45
1. 30	De mure qui leui quadam maledictione interiit	30.	46
2. 1	De uigiliis eius	31.	47
2. 2	De lucerne extincte reaccensione	32.	48
2. 3	Repetitio signi eiusdem	33.	49
2. 4	De candela qui ardebat et non consumebatur	34.	50
2. 5	De lucis celestis inter orandum apparitione	35.	52
2. 6	De simili item consolatione	36.	53
2. 7	De aqua conuersa in uinum	37.	54
2. 8	Item signum idem sed non aliquatenus idem	38.	55
2. 9	Item tertio	39.	56
2. 10	De pane et uino celitus ei delatis	40.	56
2. 11	De pane miraculose multiplicato	41.	57
2. 12	De uirgine quadam in sompnis ab eo sanata	42.	58
2. 13	De pane furtiuo in lapidis duriciam commutato	43.	59
2. 14	De pane sanguinem manante	44.	60
2. 15	De monacho ei molesto terribiliter mortuo	45.	61
2. 16	De blasphemi alterius iudicio et penitentis curatione	46.	63
2. 17	De elemosinis eius et hospitalitate	47.	65
2. 18	De laude simul et uituperatione Cisterciensium ex parte	48.	66
2. 19	De sacrificio altaris sine aqua consecrato	49.	66
2. 20	De conuersione abbatis Henrici de Wauerleia ab eo prophetata	50.	68
2. 21	[Hec uir uenerabilis Henricus . . .]		
2. 22	De quibusdam debitis quorum celerem solutionem predixit	51.	74

2. 23	De reuerentia abbatis Henrici ad uirum Dei	52.	75
2. 24	De scismate in diebus Innocentii pape cui beatus Bernardus succurrit	53.	77
2. 25	De quodam lapsu beati Bernardi quem uir sanctus priusquam ei referretur exposuit et dimissum esse nuntiauit	54.	78
2. 26	De congruentia sapientie se humiliantis et simplicitatis libere castigantis	55.	79
2. 27	De Matilde inclusa de Waram cuius conuersionem et conuersationem et uite finem et gloriam preparatam uir Dei prophetauit	56.	81
2. 28	De patientia Matildis	57.	83
2. 29	De temptatione famis cui Matildis fortiter restitit	58.	85
3. 1	De seueritate beati Wulfrici in causa quadam	59.	88
3. 2	De signis in quibus curatio et prophetia simul fuit	60.	90
3. 3	De demoniacho quodam in uia sanato	61.	91
3. 4	De quodam conuerso in uia sanato	62.	92
3. 5	Item de eodem	63.	92
3. 6	De presbitero quodam in uia egrotante et ad eius inuocationem sanato	64.	92
3. 7	De muliere per reuelationem ueniente ad eum cui tandem reuelationem dixit et salutem contulit	65.	93
3. 8	De Samsone de Lincolnia quem sanauit	66.	94
3. 9	De baculo a uiro sancto benedicto in mare lapso et mirabiliter restituto	67.	94
3. 10	De muto per sompnum mirabiliter sanato	68.	95
3. 11	De monacho quem conuicit de quibusdam cogitationibus	69.	96
3. 12	De quibusdam quibus aspectum suum negauit pro quadam negligentia	70.	97
3. 13	De muliere cui prophetauit quia concepisset	71.	97
3. 14	De monacho cui quedam que dixerat iocose replicauit	72.	99
3. 15	De quodam oculis effossis sanato	73.	101
3. 16	De quodam quem expectauit ad missam	74.	102
3. 17	De muliere cuius obitum mistice significauit	75.	103

3. 18	De iudicio Hiribellorum quod predixit	76.	104
3. 19	De defuncto quodam cuius requiem denuntiauit	77.	105
3. 20	De monacho Wintoniensi cuius obitum denuntiauit	78.	106
3. 21	De militis obitu quem denuntiauit	79.	106
3. 22	De canonicis regularibus Haselbergiam introductis, item expellendos predixit	80.	107
3. 23	Quod regine superbiam humiliatum iri prophetauit	81.	108
3. 24	Quod mulierem suentem errare in spiritu uidit	82.	109
3. 25	Quomodo in puerum suum dolose agendo uindicauit	83.	109
3. 26	Quod quedam cibaria ei missa et furtim reseruata uermibus scaturire ceperunt	84.	110
3. 27	De quadam prophetica iocatione	85.	111
3. 28	De Ierosolimitana peregrinatione cuius exitum sinistrum predixit	86.	112
3. 29	De tribus presbiteris quos per sompnum uiderat se a suspendio liberare et mane per confessionem a morte anime liberauit	87.	113
3. 30	De clerico quodam illusore	88.	113
3. 31	De muliere cui peccata sua prodens plurimum contulit	89.	115
3. 32	De morte regis Henrici quam prophetauit	90.	116
3. 33	De regno et captiuatione regis Stephani que prophetauuit	91.	117
3. 34	De blasphemi cuiusdam iudicio	92.	118
3. 35	De prophetatione mortis divitis cuiusdam	93.	119
3. 36	De prophetatione adventus domini Haselbergie	94.	119
3. 37	De blasphemo quodam	95.	120
3. 38	De Waltero Glastoniensi	96.	120
3. 39	Quod innumerabilia sint signa viri Dei	97.	122
3. 40	Quod loci illius destitutionem et postea exaltationem prophetauit	98.	123
3. 41	De presagiis precedentibus obitum eius	99.	124
3. 42	Quod altercationem futuram pro corpore suo prophetauit	100.	126

APPENDIX: "WULFRIC AND THE GREEDY BOY"[1]

This tale, heard by the folklorist Ruth Tongue as a child in the early years of the twentieth century and with an unverifiable history behind it, has some facets, unlike the few others that have crept out of the past, which seem to point to an oral tradition stretching back over a number of years, possibly of generations. This is not to say that the essence of the story did not originate in the *Life* but that its present form shows signs of an independent evolution in a rural setting. Its affinities are not with the anecdotes seized on by the chroniclers—such as the cutting of the hauberk—which, having lost their points of reference in contemporary culture, were no longer susceptible of development, but with the potency of the "everyday" to point a moral and to change behavior, though not, at least in John's terms, to convert a life.

This is a story about the generosity of the simple—a poor widow, who gives her mite to the saint in the form of bread, only to get it back several times over—and the dishonesty of a boy, a *puer*, whose greed leads him to steal from them both. In the *Life* the thieving *puer* is a servant; in the folktale he is the widow's son. The tale is a variant of two themes in the *Life*: the dishonest servant, who steals bread he is prevented from enjoying, and the multiplication of loaves, which here get eaten by the greedy boy, only to reappear intact on the widow's table and the holy man's shelf. Other elements in the tale will be familiar from the *Life*: Wulfric sending bread to hungry children and his kindness to the poor; the thief's contempt for the saint which turns quickly into terror; the way the homily or moral evolves from the story. This last trait is even more marked in the folktale,

[1] I am grateful to Dr. Caroline Oates of The Folklore Society for help and information on this section.

where the saint says nothing openly to the boy, who is neither led nor persuaded but thoroughly frightened into better behavior.

It is this, more than the appearance of potatoes as the new staple and the glimpsed village life of a later era, which distinguishes most sharply the nineteenth-century ambience from that of the twelfth. Although much use is made of the word "saint," there is in the tale no reference to God or to any aspect of religious belief or practice. Nor can the sly Dicky be said to suffer at any stage from pangs of conscience. Where conscience made cowards of medieval servants—and no doubt their masters and mistresses too—Dicky quakes with terror before the "uncanny." In Wulfric's day supernatural power was vested in God and, in the popular mind to a more frightening degree, in the devil. By the nineteenth century, this awe-filled fear has been replaced by an unfocused terror of "ghoulies and ghosties," and Wulfric, an otherwise amiable sage, is shown as exercising a power akin to white witchcraft, which makes Dicky's hair "stand on end," and for which no explanation is offered.

Saint Wulfric and the Greedy Boy[2]

There was a poor widow with a large family and they all worked hard, even the little ones, and folk were very kind. There was always an egg or two and a sack of teddies, or a cabbage, or a bit of bacon put by to help them out. Then the farmers found work and their food for the biggest lads, and they ought to have managed, but they all went on looking so thin as a yard of pump-water except Dicky—and he grew fat. One day the poor widow crept to Saint Wulfric's cell. She'd brought him a thin little flat oat-loaf, made from the scrapings of the meal chest. Saint Wulfric took it, and the three little trots that had come with their mother burst into tears as they saw it go.

[2] Katharine Briggs, *British Folk-Tales and Legends* (London: Katharine Briggs Trust Fund, Routledge Classics, 2002) 303–5, used with permission. "Recorded from Ruth L. Tongue, September 29, 1963, who heard the story as a child at Hazelbury Plunkett in Somerset. Note: Miss Tongue was told this story by an old retired clergyman of eighty-three. He had heard it from his great-grandmother, who was seventy-three, and she had heard it from her great-grandmother. At a rough estimate, the line of tradition stretches back to 1681 Teddies are potatoes; a 'dew-bit' is an early-morning snack; 'drashel' is a threshold." Briggs, 305

The saint looked down at their poor little pinched faces and whispered gently: "Go down to the spring for me, and see what the birds have left me." So off they toddled—half the size of the pail the baby was—but he would go. And back they staggered with it only half full, their poor little sticks of arms and legs couldn't lift more—but the baby's face was rosy with joy over a big loaf with fresh butter and a crock of cream they'd found there.

"Now, sit down and eat them," said the saint. "My birds must have known you were coming. But I've a use for your mother's oat-cake." Down they sat in the sunshine, and down the good food went—and after that it was easy for the grateful widow to tell her troubles.

"'Tis our Dicky, zur; he do get his vittles all down to Varmer Mellish, where he be bird-boy, and they do give he a-plenty. But never were such a boy to eat, Missus Mellish say, and they be hearty trenchermen down there. But when he do come whoame a-night he do gollop up all in the house if I don't stop him. Then he do sneaky round when all's asleep and there's nought for breakfusses. *And* he do get his dew-bit at farm, no fear! All my others, they do bring a few bits of vittles whoame for me and they little trots, but if Dicky be about 'tis all goed down his throat while they be getting two bites in—and him so fat as a pig!"

"Tell him I want to see him," said the saint. So, after they'd picked the saint a bunch of primroses and he'd blessed them, she took the little trots home. They even ran a bit. Next day a fat, sulky lad came to the cell. "I want you to take any bread you see on my shelf down to your mother," said the saint. "Be very quiet, for it's time I was at my prayers."

Dicky glanced at the shelf and saw his mother's oat-cake. He'd searched for it all night! And she'd given it to an old man who knelt on a cold stone floor—the old fool! Here he looked at the shelf again and there were two large white cottage loaves beside the oat-cake. Dicky grabbed them in terror and ran for it, scared out of his wits. He was so fat he soon lost his breath, and sat down on the turf—and the loaves smelt delicious. Nobody would know what had happened to them. The silly old saint was busy praying and his mother wouldn't expect any food. Down Dicky's red lane went all three loaves, yes, oat-cake and all, and my young raskill strolls off home. He wasn't feeling at all happy inside and there were no end of queer pains so he didn't go indoors, but sat down on the drashel. Out came his mother smiling and handed him a big crust of white bread covered with butter. "There, Dicky," she said. "You shall have a taste for being such a good, kind boy, bringing in they three loaves from the saint. Lovely bread 'tis, like us ate yesteddy, I did wish you others could taste." But Dicky's hair was standing on end. "Three?" he gasped. "A girt big oat-cake and two white loaves all a-buttered," she said. "I did find they on table where you did a-put them." With that Dicky took off in terror and never stopped till he got back to the saint's cell. Saint Wulfric was still kneeling, and there on the shelf above him were a poor thin little oat-cake and two cottage loaves. Dicky stood there and shook with fear. Then Saint Wulfric stood up. "You must be hungry after your climb," he said. "Finish your bread and butter." Dicky dare not refuse, but, oh, how terrible it was. It left him with such a taste in his mouth that he didn't eat for days—until he was as thin as the baby had been. After that he never made fun of saints or took more than his share. He even brought his mother home *three* eggs one evening!

BIBLIOGRAPHY

Primary Sources

Ælred of Rievaulx, *Rule of Life for a Recluse*, trans. Mary Paul Macpherson, in *Treatises and Pastoral Prayer*, CF2 (Kalamazoo: Cistercian Publications, 1971).

Baldwin of Ford, *Spiritual Tractates*, vol. 1, ed. David N. Bell, CF38 (Kalamazoo: Cistercian Publications, 1986).

Baldwin of Forde, *The Commendation of Faith*, trans. Jane Patricia Freeland and David N. Bell, CF59 (Kalamazoo: Cistercian Publications, 2000).

Bernard of Clairvaux, *Vita s. Malachiae, Sancti Bernardi Opera* 3, ed. Jean Leclercq, C. H. Talbot, Henri Rochais (Rome: Editiones Cistercienses, 1963).

Briggs, Katharine, *British Folk-Tales and Legends*, 2nd ed. (London: Routledge Classics, 2002).

English Episcopal Acta, ed. B.R. Kemp (London: British Academy, 1999).

Fasti Ecclesiae Angelicanae 1066–1300, vol. 7, by John Le Neve, ed. Diana Greenway (London: Institute of Historical Research, 2001).

Foreville, Raymonde, and Keir, Gillian, eds., *The Book of Saint Gilbert* (Oxford: Clarendon Press, 1987).

Gaimar, Geoffrei, *L'estoire des Engleis*, ed. Alexander Bell (Oxford: Basil Blackwell, 1960).

Gerard, Thomas, *The Particular Description of the County of Somerset, Drawn Up by Thomas Gerard of Trent, 1633*, ed. E. H. Bates (Somerset Record Society, 15, 1900).

Gesta Stephani, ed. and trans. K. R. Potter (Oxford: Clarendon Press, 1976).

Henry of Huntingdon, *Historia Anglorum, The History of the English People*, ed. and trans. Diana Greenway (Oxford: Clarendon Press, 1996).

John of Forde, *The Life of Wulfric of Haselbury, by John, Abbot of Ford*, ed. Maurice Bell (Somerset Record Society, 47, 1933).

———. *Sermons on the Song of Songs*, 7 vols., trans. Wendy Beckett, introduction by Hilary Costello, CF29, 39, 43, 44, 45, 46, 47 (Kalamazoo: Cistercian Publications, 1977–84).

———. *Sermons sur le Cantique*, trans. Pierre-Yves Émery (Paris: Éditions du Cerf, 1999–).

ORDERIC VITALIS, *The Ecclesiastical History of Orderic Vitalis*, ed. and trans. Marjorie Chibnall, vol. 6 (Oxford: Clarendon Press, 1978).

POOLE, Charles Henry, *The Customs, Superstitions and Legends of the County of Somerset* (London: 1877, 2nd ed. St. Peter Port: The Toucan Press, 1970).

RB 1980: The Rule of St Benedict in Latin and English with Notes, ed. Timothy Fry, OSB (Collegeville: Liturgical Press, 1981).

REGINALD OF DURHAM, *Libellus de vita et miraculis s. Godrici, Heremitae de Finchale*, ed. J. Stevenson (London: Surtees Society, 1847).

ROGER OF WENDOVER, *Flores historiarum*, 1, ed. H. G. Hewlett (Rolls Series, 1887).

SOUTHERN, R.W., ed. and trans., *The Life of St Anselm by Eadmer* (London: Nelson, 1962).

TALBOT, C. H., ed. and trans., *The Life of Christina of Markyate, a Twelfth-Century Recluse* (Oxford: Clarendon Press, 1959).

TONGUE, Ruth L., *Somerset Folklore*, ed. Katharine M. Briggs (London: UCL, for the Folklore Society, 1965).

WALTER DANIEL, *The Life of Ailred of Rievaulx*, ed. F. M. Powicke (London: Nelson, 1950).

WILLIAM OF MALMESBURY, *Historia novella*, ed. and trans. K. R. Potter (London: Nelson, 1955).

SECONDARY WORKS

ALEXANDER, D., "Hermits and Hairshirts: the Social Meanings of Saintly Clothing in the *Vitae* of Godric of Finchale and Wulfric of Haselbury," *Journal of Medieval History* 28 (2002): 205–26.

ALEXANDER, J. J. G., "Ideological Representation of Military Combat in Anglo-Norman Art," *Anglo-Norman Studies* 15 (Woodbridge: Boydell, 1993).

BARLOW, Frank, ed. and trans., *Carmen de Hastingae proelio of Guy, bishop of Amiens* (Oxford: Clarendon Press, 1999).

BEARMAN, Robert, "Baldwin de Redvers: Some Aspects of a Baronial Career in the Reign of King Stephen," *Anglo-Norman Studies* 18 (Woodbridge: Boydell, 1996): 19–46, and under Baldwin de Redvers, *Oxford Dictionary of National Biography* (Oxford: OUP, 2004), and online.

BLAIR, John, ed., *Minsters and Parish Churches: The Local Church in Transition, 950–1200* (Oxford: Oxford University Committee for Archaeology, 1988).

BRADBURY, Jim, *Stephen and Matilda: the Civil War of 1139–53* (Stroud: Alan Sutton, 1996).

BROOKE, C. N. L., "Gregorian Reform in Action: Clerical Marriage in England, 1050–1200," *Cambridge Historical Journal* 12 (1956): 1–21.

CHIBNALL, Marjorie, *The World of Orderic Vitalis, Norman Monks and Norman Knights* (Woodbridge: Boydell, 1984).

CLANCHY, Michael T., *From Memory to Written Record: England 1066–1307*, 2nd edition (Oxford: Basil Blackwell, 1993).

CLAY, Rotha Mary, *The Hermits and Anchorites of England* (London: Methuen, 1914).

COSTELLO, Hilary, "John of Ford and the Quest for Wisdom," *Cîteaux, Commentarii Cistercienses* 23 (1972): 141–59.

CROUCH, David, *The Reign of King Stephen* (Harlow: Longman, 2002).

DAVIS, R. H. C. "The Authorship of the *Gesta Stephani*," *English Historical Review* 77 (1962): 209–32.

DAY, Keith, "John of Forde's Life of Wulfric of Haselbury and the Identity of 'the Lord Abbot *pie memorie*,'" *Cîteaux, Commentarii Cistercienses* 49 (1998): 221–32.

DUTTON, Marsha, "John of Forde's *De Vita Beati Wulfrici Anachoretae Haselbergiae:* A Model for Cistercian Contemplative Life," *A Gathering of Friends. The Learning and Spirituality of John of Forde*, ed. Hilary Costello, Christopher Holdsworth, CS161 (Kalamazoo: Cistercian Publications, 1996), 65–92.

FANOUS, Simon, and LEYSER, Henrietta, eds., *Christina of Markyate, a Twelfth-Century Holy Woman* (London: Routledge, 2005).

FARMER, D. H., *Saints and Saints' Lives. Essays in Honour of D. H. Farmer* (Reading: University of Reading Library, 1990).

FINUCANE, R. C., "The Use and Abuse of Medieval Miracles," *History* 60 (1975): 1–10.

FLINT, Valerie I. J., "The Saint and the Operation of the Law: Reflections on the Miracles of St Thomas Cantilupe," *Belief and Culture in the Middle Ages: Studies Presented to Henry Mayr-Harting*, eds. Richard Gameson and Henrietta Leyser (Oxford: OUP, 2001) 342–57.

GOLDING, Brian, *Gilbert of Sempringham and the Gilbertine Order c. 1130–c. 1300* (Oxford: Clarendon Press, 1995).

———. "The Hermit and the Hunter," *The Cloister and the World. Essays in Medieval History in Honour of Barbara Harvey*, eds. John Blair and Brian Golding (Oxford: Clarendon Press, 1996) 95–117.

HARPER-BILL, Christopher, "Piety of the Anglo-Norman Knightly Class," *Proceedings of the Battle Conference*, ed. R. Allen Brown (Woodbridge: Boydell, 1980) 63–77.

HOLDSWORTH, Christopher, *Learning and Literature of English Cistercians 1167–1214, with Special Reference to John of Ford* (Cambridge University, PhD thesis, 1959).

———. "John of Ford and English Cistercian Writing 1167–1214," *Transactions of the Royal Historical Society*, 5th Series, 11 (1961): 117–36.

———. "Hermits and the Powers of the Frontier," *Saints and Saints' Lives, Essays in Honour of D. H. Farmer* (Reading Medieval Studies XVI, University of Reading, 1990) 55–76.

———. "John of Forde 1191–1991," *A Gathering of Friends. The Learning and Spirituality of John of Forde*, ed. Hilary Costello, Christopher Holdsworth, CS161 (Kalamazoo: Cistercian Publications, 1996) 17–42.

———. "Baldwin of Forde," *Oxford Dictionary of National Biography* (Oxford: OUP, 2004), and online.

HOLLISTER, C. Warren, ed. and completed by A. Clark Frost, *Henry I* (Newhaven/London: Yale UP, 2001).

HUGHES-EDWARDS, Mari, "Anchoritism: The English Tradition," *Anchoritic Traditions of Medieval Europe* (Woodbridge: Boydell, 2010), 131–52.

JONES, E. A., "Hermits and Anchorites in Historical Context," *Approaching Medieval English Anchoritic and Mystical Texts*, ed. Dee Dyas, Valerie Edden, and Roger Ellis (Cambridge: D. S. Brewer, 2005).

KEMP, E. W., *Canonization and Authority in the Western Church* (London: OUP, 1948).

KNOWLES, D., BROOKE, C. N. L., LONDON, V. C. M., *The Heads of Religious Houses, England and Wales, I, 940–1216*, 2nd ed. (Cambridge: CUP, 2001).

LEGGE, M. Dominica, "Anglo-Norman as a Spoken Language," *Proceedings of the Battle Conference*, ed. R. Allen Brown (Woodbridge: Boydell, 1980) 108–17.

———. *Anglo-Norman in the Cloisters: the Influence of the Orders upon Anglo-Norman Literature* (Edinburgh: Edinburgh UP, 1950).

LEYSER, Henrietta, *Hermits and the New Monasticism* (London: Macmillan, 1984).

L'HERMITE-LECLERCQ, P., "Anchoritism in Medieval France," *Anchoritic Traditions of Medieval Europe* (Woodbridge: Boydell, 2010) 112–30.

MATARASSO, Pauline, "John of Forde as Portrait Painter," *A Gathering of Friends. The Learning and Spirituality of John of Forde*, ed. Hilary Costello, Christopher Holdsworth, CS161 (Kalamazoo: Cistercian Publications, 1996) 43–64.

MAYR-HARTING, Henry, "Functions of a Twelfth-Century Recluse," *History* 60 (1975): 337–52.

MCAVOY, Liz Herbert, ed., *Anchoritic Traditions of Medieval Europe* (Woodbridge: Boydell, 2010).

MCGINN, Bernard, *The Growth of Mysticism* (New York: Crossroad, 1999).

MOREY, Adrian, *Bartholomew of Exeter, Bishop and Canonist: A Study in the Twelfth Century* (Cambridge: CUP, 1937).

MURRAY, Alexander, *Reason and Society in the Middle Ages* (Oxford: Clarendon Press, 1978).

POOLE, R. Lane, "Robert Pullen and Nicholas Breakspear," *Essays in Mediaeval History Presented to T. F. Tout*, ed. A. G. Little and F. M. Powicke (Manchester: 1925), 61–70.

POWICKE, F. M., ed. and trans., *The Life of Ailred of Rievaulx by Walter Daniel* (London: Nelson, 1950).

PUGH, R. B. and Elisabeth Crittall, eds., *A History of the County of Wiltshire* 3, "House of Benedictine Monks: Abbey of Malmesbury," Victoria County History (Woodbridge: Boydell and Brewer, 1956, and online) 210–31.

RAMSEY, Frances, "Robert of Lewes, Bishop of Bath, 1136–1166: A Cluniac Bishop in His Diocese," *Belief and Culture in the Middle Ages: Studies Presented to Henry Mayr-Harting*, ed. Richard Gameson and Henrietta Leyser (Oxford: OUP, 2001) 251–63.

RIDYARD, Susan J. "Functions of a Twelfth-Century Recluse Revisited: The Case of Godric of Finchale," *Belief and Culture in the Middle Ages: Studies Presented to Henry Mayr-Harting*, ed. Richard Gameson and Henrietta Leyser (Oxford: OUP, 2001) 236–50.

SHORT, Ian, "On Bilingualism in Anglo-Norman England," *Romance Philology* 33 (1979–80): 467–79.

———. "Patrons and Polyglots: French literature in 12th-century England," *Anglo-Norman Studies* 14 (Woodbridge: Boydell, 1992): 229–49.

———. "*Tam Angli quam Franci*: Self-definition in Anglo-Norman England," *Anglo-Norman Studies* 18 (Woodbridge: Boydell, 1996): 153–75.

———. "Language and Literature," *Companion to the Anglo-Norman World*, ed. C. Harper-Bill and E. Van Houts (Woodbridge: Boydell & Brewer, 2003) 191–213.

SOUTHERN, R. W., *St Anselm and His Biographer: a Study of Monastic Life and Thought, 1059–c. 1130* (Cambridge: CUP, 1963).

TONGUE, Ruth L., ed. Katharine M. Briggs, *Somerset Folklore* (London: UCL, for The Folklore Society, 1965).

TUDOR, Victoria, "Reginald of Durham and Saint Godric of Finchale: Learning and Religion on a Personal Level, *Religion and Humanism, Studies in Church History*, English Historical Review (Oxford: Blackwell, 1981) 37–48.

VAN HOUTS, Elisabeth, "Historical Writing," *A Companion to the Anglo-Norman World*, ed. C. Harper-Bill and E. van Houts (Woodbridge: Boydell & Brewer, 2003), 103–21.

WANSBROUGH, Henry, *The Use and Abuse of the Bible: A Brief History of Biblical Interpretation* (London: Continuum, 2010).

WARD, Benedicta, *Miracles and the Medieval Mind. Theory, Record and Event, 1000–1215* (London: Scolar Press, 1982).

WARREN, Ann K., *Anchorites and their Patrons in Medieval England* (Berkeley: University of California, 1985).

WOOD, Susan, *The Proprietary Church in the Medieval West* (Oxford: OUP, 2008).

INDEX